# Flash & Crash Days
## Brazilian Theater in the Postdictatorship Period

David S. George

Garland Publishing, Inc.
A member of the Taylor & Francis Group
New York & London / 2000

Published in 2000 by
Garland Publishing, Inc.
A Member of the Taylor & Francis Group
19 Union Square West
New York, NY 10003



10 9 8 7 6 5 4 3 2 1

**Library of Congress Cataloging-in-Publication Data**

George, David Sanderson.
Flash & crash days : Brazilian theater in the post dictatorship period / David S. George.
p. cm.—(Garland reference library of the humanities ; 2153. Latin American Studies ; 19)
Includes bibliographical references and index.
ISBN 0–8153–3360–9 (alk. paper) — ISBN 0–8153–3839–2 (pbk: alk. paper)
1. Theater — Brazil — History — 20th century. 2. Brazilian drama — 20th century — History and criticism. 3. Women dramatists, Brazilian — 20th century—Biography. I. Title: Flash and Crash. II. Title. III. Garland reference library of the humanities ; vol. 2153. IV. Garland reference library of the humanities. Latin American studies ; vol. 19.
PN2471.G455 199
869.2–dc21 99-044208

Cover photo from "Flash & Crash Days," play by Gerald Thomas, reproduced by permission of Gerald Thomas

Printed on acid-free, 250-year-life paper
Manufactured in the United States of America

*For Edla*

This book was written with a National Endowment for the Humanities Fellowship for College Teachers.

# Contents

# Series Preface

The monographs in Garland's Latin American Studies series deal with significant aspects of literary writing, defined broadly and including general topics, groups of works, or treatments of specific authors and movements. Titles published have been selected on the basis of the originality of scholarship and the coherency of the theoretical underpinnings of the critical discourse. Cognizant of the fact that literary study is an ongoing dialogue between multiple voices, authors in the LAS series have chosen topics and approaches that complement attempts to revise the canon of Latin American literature and that propose new agendas for their analysis. These critical works focus on interdisciplinary approaches to Latin American issues: the bridging of national and linguistic divisions, subaltern studies, feminism, queer theory, popular culture, and minority topics, and many others topics that continue to gain increasing exposure in academic and popular culture.

David William Foster

# Series Preface

# Preface

The research for this book is the end result of support in the form of grants from the National Endowment for the Humanities (NEH) and the University of Illinois/University of Chicago Joint Center for Latin American Studies Visiting Scholars Program. These grants allowed me to write several articles and prepare conference addresses on Brazilian theater in the postdictatorship period in preparation for this study. My previous books, *Teatro e antropofagia* and *Grupo Macunaíma: carnavalização e mito,* as well as the 1992 *Modern Brazilian Stage,* also resulted from NEH grants. I work in a small liberal arts college whose main focus is teaching. I owe my scholarly career, therefore, to the NEH, and I am deeply grateful for the Endowment's continued support.

I have gathered a wide variety of research materials in the course of this study: (a) in Brazil, interviews, videotapes, playtexts, reviews, and attendance at several rehearsals and live productions; (b) at the University of Chicago Regenstein Library, materials related to the political and economic dimensions of this study; (c) at other Chicago-area libraries, particularly Northwestern University and the University of Illinois-Chicago, I have found further works which aided in the development of a variety of methodologies (e.g., postmodernism) utilized here.

# Acknowledgments

I owe a debt of gratitude to a large number of individuals who have provided support and advice in this undertaking:

First and foremost, George Woodyard of the University of Kansas, editor of *The Latin American Theater Review,* has written letters of recommendation to help me secure grants and given me constant encouragement to develop new approaches and themes. *The Latin American Theater Review* and conferences Dr. Woodyard has organized at the University of Kansas have provided a forum for testing many of the ideas contained in this book.

I am also deeply indebted to Sábato Magaldi, who has contributed invaluable information and insights on Brazilian theater in the form of interviews, informal discussions, as well as his own writings. Dr. Magaldi has also opened many doors for me by arranging interviews with writers and directors and securing an invitation to participate in the 1993 Curitiba Festival, which is discussed in Chapter 3. Sábato Magaldi also opened his own archives to me, which allowed me to write about his career. Finally, he wrote recommendations for my successful grant proposals.

Edla van Steen shares the spotlight with George Woodyard and Sábato Magaldi on my stage of gratitude. She generously shared her ideas on women's voices in interviews and informal discussions, provided access to other writers, and invited me to co-author a play with her, the 1997 *À mão armada,* which enabled me to become a player in the post-dictatorship playwriting movement I examine in this book.

Playwright Maria Adelaide Amaral has also made major contributions to this project, in interviews and conversations, in access to her archives, and in collaborating with me on the translation of her play, *Querida mamãe,* which gave me an insider's take on the work rarely afforded by merely reading the play or viewing it staged.

Gerald Thomas has been exceedingly helpful in providing videotapes of his performances and reviews of his work, interviews, e-mail and phone conversations, and invitations to conferences, all of this in spite of my initial negative response to his play performed at the 1993 Curitiba Festival.

Antunes Filho and his company provided videos of performances, invitations to live performances, and copies of reviews.

My Lake Forest College colleagues Richard Fisher and Phillip Simmons have been very helpful, the former with developing my arguments about Gerald Thomas's treatments of Wagner and the latter with conceptualizing postmodernism. Another Lake Forest College professor, Lois Barr, has also offered her encouragement and ideas. My colleague Rick Mallette, Professor of English, aided me by critiquing my NEH proposal. Yet another Lake Forest colleague, Professor Michael Ebner, helped me with the University of Illinois/University of Chicago Joint Center for Latin American Studies grant.

Last but not least, I wish to thank Professors Russell Hamilton of Vanderbilt University, Severino Albuquerque of the University of Wisconsin, and John Berninghausen of Middlebury College for their grant recommendations.

# Introduction

Is the theater in Brazil dead? Did the thriving stage of the 1950s and 1960s wither during the reign of terror in the early 1970s, unleashed in the wake of the 1968 state of siege declared by the generals who had seized power in 1964? Did the return to civilian government in 1985 fail to create conditions for a new theater? A cursory glance at what little U.S. commentary on Brazilian theater has appeared in recent years could well lead one to answer all of the above questions in the affirmative. Scholars—and dilettantes—beyond Brazil's borders appear to have bonded with those individuals and companies that contested and then fell victim to repression in the 1960s and 1970s. So pervasive is this scholarly trend that a vacuum, an empty stage, has been created. There seems to be an unstated assumption that theater in Brazil thrives only under repression and dictatorship. This is an illusory vacuum. If the stage was emptied for a time, it has been repaired and the boards now resound with a multitude of voices.[1]

The rift between theatrical din and scholarly silence raises this question: How and in what forms does theater emerge from the ashes of police-state repression? It is a complex question, which *Flash & Crash Days: Brazilian Theater in the Postdictatorship Period* attempts to address. I begin by affirming my view that the absence of censorship, on

[1] There are, fortunately, exceptions to short-sightedness, scholars in the United States concerned with Brazilian theater who do know the full story; for example, Severino João Albuquerque, Margo Milleret, David William Foster, George Woodyard, B. Campbell Britton, Adam Versayche, and Fred M. Clark.

the one hand, and the removal of the exigencies of protest and ideological purity, on the other, have given rise to a variety of theatrical modes and activity which Brazil has never experienced before. It is true that democratization has silenced some members of the engagé generation, who no longer have a powerful political cause to motivate their art: this is the "crash" referred to in my title. Democratization has checked the dual constraints of persecution by the right-wing military dictatorship and its doppelganger, the so-called "ideological patrol" or left-wing establishment—which included a large number of critics and even artists—that went from opposing military repression to exerting its own forms of repression against those whom it deemed "alienated." Removal of barriers erected by ideologues and demagogues has allowed myriad forms of theater to flourish, experimentation to run unchecked, and all voices the opportunity to be heard in the marketplace of artistic ideas: this is the "flash."

Theater in Brazil receives less attention from foreign critics today because it lacks a powerful external enemy—a dictatorship—as well as the cachet of protest and victimization. At the same time, democratization has clearly left most of the old engagé theater artists (e.g., Augusto Boal and Gianfrancesco Guarnieri) without an active theatrical voice. However, liberated from dictatorial repression and disengaged from the populist dogma of the ideological patrol, a new generation of theater artists may now tap all sources of inspiration (and some members of an older generation have taken up the challenge to develop new forms of theater). Themes once forbidden by censorship or pushed aside by the exigencies of protest against military rule—formerly considered by the ideological patrol as the province of alienated theater—are now privileged: women's perspectives in directing and playwriting; sexual identity, including gender construction and gay perspectives; psychological issues; the individual in society; religion; and formal experimentation. Home-grown comedy, obscured for decades in spite of its deep roots in Brazilian theatrical soil, has made an impressive comeback. Brazil's greatest playwright, the late Nelson Rodrigues, who was censored by successive rightist governments and scorned by the left, has now found a home on the stages of his own land. Foreign classics, especially the plays of Shakespeare, no longer suffer the "imperialist" stigma and are widely staged. Important theater companies, the best example being Grupo Macunaíma, directed by Antunes Filho, have endured. And postmodernist directors have made a major contribution to the current theatrical renewal.

*Flash & Crash Days: Brazilian Theater in the Postdictatorship Period* assesses both broad issues and productions of individual plays.

Chapter 1 examines a fertile and highly controversial theatrical mode of the postdictatorship period, the postmodernist *encenadores,* auteurs in the mold of a Robert Wilson, director-designers, director-playwrights, whose most significant figure is Gerald Thomas. Thomas has directed pieces written or inspired by Beckett, Shakespeare, Wagner, Merimée, Kafka, and Heiner Müller, as well as his own original productions. I focus particularly on two Thomas productions: the 1989 *Mattogrosso* and the 1991 *Flash and Crash Days: Dias de tempestade e fúria,* from which I have taken the title of this study.

Chapter 2 deals with the women, both playwrights and fiction writers, who have become major voices and whose concerns, once scorned by the ideological patrol, have been privileged with democratization. My purpose in including fiction writers is that they were the pioneers in establishing women's voices in Brazilian letters and they set down the themes that would be explored later by dramatists. Several women playwrights are considered. I begin with the pioneers of the New Dramaturgy movement of the early 1970s who made the feminine presence a constant in Brazilian theater. I focus particularly, however, on their postdictatorship successors. First, I consider the extensive playwriting career of Maria Adelaide Amaral, with special emphasis on her 1995 *Querida mamãe* (Dear Mom). I further consider writer Edla van Steen's 1984 novel *Corações mordidos* (entitled *Village of the Ghost Bells* in its English translation) and its links to her 1989 play *O último encontro* (The Last Encounter). *Querida mamãe* and *O último encontro* are both bittersweet dissections of sexual identity and both swept all of Brazil's major playwriting awards.

In Chapter 3 I begin by reviewing the career of Sábato Magaldi, the only drama critic ever elected to the Brazilian Academy of Letters (1995), after which I proceed to the central focus of the chapter, an assessment of a wide variety of current theatrical phenomena, each of which has added an important element to the richness of postdictatorship theater. I begin with a report on the 1993 Curitiba Festival, a national theater festival that provided me a panoramic view of the current theater scene. I further examine some unique phenomena characteristic of the transition between dictatorship and democratization, such as the political opening known as the *abertura*. In this context, I explore briefly a retrospective play about the dictatorship, a short-lived trend: Marcelo Paiva's 1984 award-winning *Feliz ano velho* (*Happy Old Year*), which deals with a family whose father was "disappeared" by the military.

Chapter 3 also considers playwrights whose focus is less political and circumstantial than the previous generation's and whose themes are more universal, including sexual identity, the painful transition from childhood to adulthood, religion, and family life in the provinces. In particular, I explore the rebirth of comedy, an enduring trend in Brazil temporarily eclipsed by the engagé hegemony of the 1960s. I examine three plays in particular, Mauro Rasi's *A cerimônia do adeus* (The Goodbye Ceremony), Miguel Falabella's *A partilha* (The Division), and Flavio de Souza's *Fica comigo esta noite* (Stay with Me Tonight).

Chapter 3 subsequently appraises theater companies, focusing on Antunes Filho, founder and director of Grupo Macunaíma, the most acclaimed company in the history of the Brazilian stage, which has produced a body of work I consider the clearest answer to the now moribund 1960s populist theater. The group's productions, beginning in 1978, have won awards in Brazil and abroad. The work of Grupo Macunaíma has revolutionized its nation's theater by illuminating its path during the transition to democracy.

Brazilian theater came to life in the 1940s and 1950s through the efforts of innovative directors and expanded its horizons in the 1960s with dynamic companies and playwrights. In the late 1960s and in the 1970s and 1980s, it received successive shocks from a ruthless military government and a faltering economy. Television, especially the popularity of prime-time *telenovelas,* kept many former and potential theatergoers home. Predictions of the demise of the Brazilian stage abounded. In the end, however, theater prevailed. It is my hope, then, that the reader will take away from this study a clearer idea of a national theater that has had to overcome myriad obstacles from without and within in order to survive, a theater that has diversified its landscape formally and ideologically, a theater whose richness of voices belies its poverty of resources.

# Flash & Crash Days

CHAPTER 1

# Gerald Thomas and the Postmodernist Theater in Brazil

## I. *MATTOGROSSO* AND THE POSTMODERNIST STAGE

The postmodern wave in Brazilian theater coincides with the postdictatorship period; it is the most controversial theatrical mode of this period. Its creators are the postmodernist *encenadores,* auteurs—in the mold of Robert Wilson—director-playwrights, director-designers, or in some cases, director-designer-authors, whose most significant figure is Gerald Thomas. In his own words, "What I do in theater is put cinema on the stage. I insist on saying this when they call me a director . . . Don't confuse me, I'm not a director. I find that a facile, decorative profession. I'm an author, in the same way a filmmaker is an author. What I author I must stage. Otherwise, who else would do it?" ("Gerald, Thomas, eis a questâo").[1]

There has been a dual evolution in Brazilian theater, in which both the director and the playwright came to the forefront. The evolution of modern Brazilian stagecraft under the command of strong directors, working, usually, in the service of a text, and culminating in the *encenador* generation, began in the 1940s, when Polish war refugee Zbigniev Ziembinski brought to Brazil the theatrical resources of European expressionism. In the 1950s, Italian directors such as Adolfo Celi, associated with São Paulo's Teatro Brasileiro de Comédia, introduced "sophisticated" European stagecraft. In the 1960s, Teatro Oficina's José Celso began to move the attention away from the written play, deconstructing Brecht, Checkov, and Brazilian *modernista* playwright Oswald de Andrade. The prototype of the *encenador,* however, is Antunes Filho, who launched the Grupo Macunaíma in 1978 with his internationally renowned homonymous production of a text by another *modernista,* Mário de Andrade (Antunes Filho and Grupo Macunaíma are discussed in Chapter 3). Celso and Antunes planted the seeds of postmodernism in Brazil. What all of these directors have shared is their integration of international artistic currents into Brazilian theater, each in his own way, thus producing aesthetic cross-fertilization, creating new forms of stagecraft, and initiating the tendencies attributed today to the *encenador:* total control of the theatrical spectacle, careful attention to design, and subordination of the verbal text to audiovisual elements. They all, moreover, have been attacked on nationalist grounds at one time or another; they have not been "Brazilian" enough.

Thomas has aggravated the situation, however, by needling his critics and the theater community. Brazilian theater, he claims, is hopelessly backward, provincial, moribund. Ironically, he owes a considerable debt to his Brazilian predecessors in making such claims. In the 1930s, *modernista* Oswald de Andrade called Brazilian theater "that gangrenous corpse." In the 1960s José Celso, picking up where Oswald de Andrade left off, revived the latter's concept of anthropophagy or cultural cannibalism and outraged theatrical and political conservatives with his production of *O rei da vela* (*The Candle King*), with its potpourri of borrowings from international theatrical sources. Gerald Thomas's indisputable internationalism has lead many to view his work in terms of a resentful *tupiniquim*[2] xenophobia, as does, for example, critic José Carlos Camargo. In his article on the play *Mattogrosso* he rants that, "Brazil, for 'Mr. Thomas,' deserves its mediocre audiences and its stagnant culture, while the arts charge forward in the civilized world. The solution, therefore, is to take 'Mattogrosso' to that world."[3] A further dimension of the controversy is this question: Has the hegemony of the *encenador* had a detrimental effect on national playwriting?

The heyday of the playwright was the 1960s, according to many critics, followed by decline. Dramatists, Nelson Rodrigues excepted, never achieved the status of directors in Brazil. The latter have become steadily more powerful, giving rise to the primacy of the *encenador* in the 1990s. Because playwriting was so tied to immediate events and to protest in the 1960s, its formal and aesthetic side was neglected, it was circumstantial, thus discouraging the development of a dramaturgy later playwrights could build on. In her *Latin American Theater Review* article, Margo Milleret decries the neglect Brazilian playwrights have suffered in a theatrical milieu that privileges the inventive and resourceful director, because the latter's "creative stance makes cooperative relationships between *encenadores* difficult [and] since what the *encenadores* see as creativity would be labeled corruption by the dramatist" (Milleret 1995, 123). The fact is, for better or for worse, directors have been for the most part the pathfinders in Brazil, laying the groundwork for future generations. These pathfinders have only occasionally furthered the cause of Brazilian playwrights; they have always focused on revolutionizing stagecraft.

The late 1980s and the 1990s saw the ascendancy of a new generation of directors, *encenadores* with total control over their productions, including design and occasionally dramaturgy. The most significant names include Bia Lessa, whose best-known works are her literary adaptations: Virginia Wolff's *Orlando,* H.G. Well's *Journey to the Center of the Earth,* and *Cartas portuguesas*. The latter production is discussed in Chapter 3. Other significant figures in the new generation include Gabriel Villela (Calderón's *La vida es sueño* and Nelson Rodrigues's *A falecida,* or *The Dead Woman*); Márcio Vianna, whose highly personal pieces include *Coleção de bonecas* (*Doll Collection*) and *O circo da solidão* (*The Circus of Loneliness*); and Moacyr Góes, best known for his productions of *Nosferatu,* Buchner's *Woyzeck,* and *Macbeth*. Góes's view of the role of the director sums up much of what the *encenadores* are lauded—and loathed—for: "'In my work, the image has been far more important than the word. I'm trying to achieve a balance; that is, to highlight the treatment of the word in order to intensify the clash among the elements of theater.'"[4]

The most active, admired, and execrated figure in this new generation, the artist who has taken the role of the *encenador* to the farthest extreme, is Gerald Thomas, whose theater company—Opera Seca, or Dry Opera—is headquartered in Rio, while its director's main address is in Brooklyn. In the 1970s, Thomas studied theater on his own in London, using the library of the British Museum. He was also active in Amnesty International, working in the Brazilian section and dealing with human rights abuses committed by the dictatorship. He relocated to New York where he began his involvement in the arts through painting and drawing. He became a resident director at La Mama (1979–1985), where he specialized in staging the works of Samuel Beckett. His stay at La Mama culminated in the 1985 "Samuel Beckett Trilogy," in which he worked with three actors who were theatrical pioneers in their own right: George Bartenieff, co-founder of the Theater for the New City; Fred Neumann, founder of the experimental company Mabou Mines; and Julian Beck, co-founder of The Living Theater.

Thomas returned to Rio in 1985, where he has directed pieces written or inspired by Beckett (*4 vezes beckett* and *Endgame*), Shakespeare/ Beckett (*Sturmspiel* or *TempestGame*), Wagner (*The Flying Dutchman*), Merimée (*Carmen com filtro*), Kafka (his "Kafka Trilogy" is comprised of *Uma metamorfose, Um processo,* and *Praga*), Heiner Müller (*Quartett*), as well as his own original productions such as *Electra com Creta, Mattogrosso, Flash & Crash Days, M.O.R.T.E., O império das Meias verdades,* and *Unglauber*. He has also worked a great deal in the United States and Europe, either touring productions he mounted in Brazil or directing European companies, especially opera. Thomas's universal outlook, his refusal to obey the dictates of the previous artistic generation's knee-jerk nationalism, has created a gamut of responses to his work, from scorn to veneration. His willingness to make outrageous statements in public, almost like a character from one of Nelson Rodrigues's plays, have made him the enfant terrible of the Brazilian avant-garde.

How is one to define, classify, explicate Thomas's controversial stagings? One might say that Gerald Thomas is a new Ziembinski, the Polish war refugee who brought to Brazil the new theatrical resources of European expressionism. Thomas may be, at least superficially, a new José Celso, who deconstructed foreign and occasionally Brazilian texts in the service of a leftist nationalist agenda. Though Gerald Thomas shares little of Celso's social vision, he resembles the latter in his bold and innovative stagecraft.[5] Thomas is a member of a generation that benefitted from the innovations of Antunes Filho, who absorbed and "Brazilianized" international aesthetic influences, inserting them within the evolution of the Brazilian stage.

Mariângela Alves de Lima maintains that the work of the *encenadores* contains no traditional categories like character, action, conflict, or dramatic progression. If not for the actors, these productions would be "installations." They aim at the senses; they seek to establish a new sensibility through aesthetic education and appreciation, so they are not mere entertainment. Gerald Thomas goes beyond this tendency by maintaining a dramatic embryo (Alves de Lima, 1992, 17–18).

Gerald Thomas also departs from the other *encenadores* in that he emerged only partly from the Brazilian theatrical context; his inspiration sprang perhaps even more so from European and U.S. theatrical postmodernism. While Gerald Thomas is a member of the new wave of *encenadores,* he received his artistic training in Europe and the United States. The son of Welsh and German-Jewish parents, raised in Rio, Berlin, and New York, his identity is as much international as it is Brazilian. The fact of his working in Brazil is to some extent a happenstance, part of what he calls his *Gesamtglücksfallwerk* ("*teatro do acaso total*" or "theater of total chance"). It is the chaotic chance of postmodernist multireferentiality, not the Brazilian *pósmodernismo,* but the European mode.[6]

Artaud planted the seeds of theatrical postmodernism, with his idea of replacing the "dead" theater of the word and of representation with ritual, sacred theater. While Artaud's contribution was essentially theoretical, Theater of the Absurd took the first concrete steps away from what Artaud viewed as a moribund stage. Ionesco and Beckett expelled the postulates of realism, supplanting them with an expressionist language, breaking the dramatic structure of linear narrative, rejecting the "scientific" psychology of character. Theodore Shank writes that the dramatists of the Absurd invented forms which "embodied their concepts of how it felt to be alive in a world, that, having lost god as a unifying principle explaining existence, was now losing science . . ." (Shank 1990, 240). Beckett and Ionesco maintained the primacy of the text's verbal structure; they remained, in short, modernists. And it is worth recalling that Gerald Thomas began his directorial career staging Beckett's plays, returning frequently to the dramatist's work—even after his immersion into the postmodernist cosmos—because Beckett privileges the language of the unconscious over the language of speech. The function of the word is more rhythmical than informative, more pictorial than linear. Theater for Thomas is painting in movement, and he attempts to communicate with the unconscious of the audience as music and painting do.

In the 1960s and 1970s it appeared that Artaud's vision was coming to life through the work of several directors: Peter Brook, Jerzy Grotowski, Joseph Chaikin, and Julian Beck (who, not coincidentally, acted in Thomas's 1985 La Mama production of Beckett). This period saw a widespread effort to overcome "the superficiality and pretense of realistic acting [to reveal] the genuine subjective responses of the performer. Grotowski put into focus the actual responses of the body and voice by attempting to eliminate the social mask and all other impediments between impulse and reaction" (Shank 1990, 242).

Grotowski and his followers, in the 1968 book of essays and interviews entitled *Towards a Poor Theater,* described the techniques and productions that came out of the Polish Laboratory Theater. Grotowski counterposed so-called "rich" or technologically sophisticated theater, on the one hand, and on the other, poor theater, which depended entirely on actors and multifunctional props, costumes, and sets whose meaning, whose value as signs, changed according to context. Grotowski also proposed, as Artaud had once proclaimed, a return to myth and ritual. The Brazilian company that has developed Grotowski's poor-theater system most extensively is Antunes Filho's Grupo Macunaíma, which from 1978 to the present has utilized the "poor" raw materials of the Third World—cloth, clay, wood, paper—to attain theatrical richness.

Groups from the 1960s—Living Theater, Open Theater, Performance Group, Théâtre du Soleil—attempted to bring to life Artaud's vision by creating ritual forms in such productions as *Dionysus in 69* and Euripides's *The Bacchae*. "In the mixing of actual and fictional elements, theater artists have sometimes employed the technique of putting into focus both the performers and the fictional characters they play" (Shank 1990, 242). *Dionysus in 69* brought audiences into the Dionysian ritual to the point that some spectators entered the action nude—in a production I saw—and, reportedly, may have engaged in sexual acts with the performers.

Groups that I worked with in Minneapolis during the 1970s—the Minnesota Ensemble and Palace theaters, as well as El Teatro Nuevo—reflected the avant-garde practices in New York, Paris, and other cultural capitals. In such plays as *Fresh Meat,* written and directed by James Stowell, the actors transmogrified into animals and stalked each other in the auditorium, pausing to sniff a beard here and there, and at the end of the performance invited the spectators on the stage to participate in rituals. Physical contact between performers and audience has its limitations and risks: actors wield immense power vis-à-vis the audience and it is easy to cross the line from participation to abuse, which is why most theater companies have retreated back into the playing area.[7]

Another scholar expresses the following misgivings about the practices of the time: although they "reflected a time of ritual practice and communal mythic consciousness, the transference of them into a faithless time, even with alterations which addressed the political and spiritual malaise of the present, could not miraculously accomplish the desire to create a new mythic consciousness or a new ritual practice" (McGlynn 1990, 142). In Brazilian theater, however, one could posit that ritual theater does reflect social practice. The master of this mode has been Antunes Filho, whose ritual theater is an authentic reflection of a society, as opposed to the American or French, marked by mythic consciousness and multiple ritual ceremonies, whose origins are African, Indian, and medieval Portuguese. A question I address later is Gerald Thomas's use of ritual: does it parallel Brazilian society or reproduce what McGlynn sees as the questionable ritual theater practices developed in the United States and Europe?

The most decisive influences on Thomas's theater were to come during the 1980s. According to Shank, the new artists who came to the forefront were the opposite of the engagé and communal sixties; they looked inward, creating "concepts that were self-focused and reflexive, expressing their individual feelings about themselves and their art. They devised a great variety of individualistic, nonrealistic forms to express their emotive concepts" (Shank 1990, 249). These individual artists, auteurs who tended to deconstruct texts when they did not create them, include André Serban, Peter Sellars, and Liviu Ciulei. Another group comes not from the theater but from the other arts: Robert Wilson and Tadeusz Kantor (painting, sculpting); Pina Bausch, Martha Clarke, and Meredith Monk (dance). Shank calls them self-referential, "formalist" directors because of their penchant for rigidly organized structures; he refers particularly to Robert Wilson's theatrical chess games (Shank 1990, 252). Several Brazilian critics maintain that Thomas's work owes a considerable debt to postmodern formalist Robert Wilson. Although Thomas has wearied of this comparison—it has become a cliché in Brazil to link him with Wilson—it remains a useful correspondence for non-Brazilian readers unfamiliar with the *encenador*'s work.

This, then, is the international context in which I place the theater of Gerald Thomas: a progression in European and American theater from Artaud, through Beckett and the communal groups of the 1960s and 1970s, to the formalists of the 1980s. There are, however, further theoretical principles which must be clarified. For this purpose I maintain the following: Thomas is Brazil's principal purveyor of international theatrical postmodernism. This observation does not constitute "nationalist" censure, lest the reader think I am about to lapse into judgments about cultural imperialism. What, then, do I mean by "theater of postmodernism"? First, allow me to eliminate a few categories. I am not talking about theatrical texts based on narrative-verbal structures; orderly philosophic and social theories are also out. Gerald Thomas's spectacles are comprised of aesthetic fragments and ahistorical collages in which all the arts are represented. But as he himself frequently tells us, this does not lead to a Wagnerian synthesis of all the arts or *Gesamtkunstwerk* (total work of art) but to what he calls *Gesamtglücksfallwerk* (total work of chance)—an homage, nevertheless, to his Teutonic roots, to Wagner. What this refers to is the art of deconstruction, the essence of the postmodernist project, as opposed to the unity, the synthesis, of modernism.

To clarify this essence, one must understand—and I have attempted to elucidate this in the preceding paragraphs—the evolution of U.S. and

European theater from modernism to postmodernism. As I examine Thomas's stagecraft, I will refer back to that evolution. I will also reiterate the points of contact between Gerald Thomas's art and that of his Brazilian predecessors, in particular José Celso and Antunes Filho.

But let us now examine the proliferation of theoretical formulations on postmodernism and attempt to relate them to the subject at hand. To paraphrase Herbert Blau (1990), the spectator or consumer of artistic products has reason aplenty to feel like the man in Plato's cave, looking out at shadows and reflections and seeing few distinct forms; this is because everything he sees is through the screen of TV; the world is a giant billboard; one no longer perceives nature directly. The postmodern artist tries to peel away a corner of the billboard and take a peek under or beyond. The postmodernist is a recycler of past and present images and forms; there is nothing original left, some might say, so one can only comment on that by recycling images. Gerald Thomas, for example, continually employs a multiple and simultaneous referentiality.

Associate Professor of English Philip Simmons, a colleague of mine at Lake Forest College, posits a series of antitheses between modernism and postmodernism in order to illuminate the latter; his scheme looks something like this:

| | **Modernism** | **Postmodernism** |
|---|---|---|
| GENRE:<br>Separation of Serious and Popular Art: | Pure/Unmixed<br>High Art/<br>Intrinsic Value | Contaminated/Mixed<br>High/Low blurred<br>Exchange Value/ Commodity Function |
| Cultural Position of Artist: | Original/Authentic<br><br>Autonomous<br>Alienation<br>Attack from without | Derivative/Inauthentic<br>Fake/Plagiarized<br>Dependent<br>Complicity<br>Subversion from within |
| Ontology of the Artist and Artwork: | Human Subject<br>Author<br>Artwork | Language/Discourse<br>Author function<br>Text |

Simmons asks a series of questions: Is postmodern, postindustrial, consumer society an incoherent collection of fragments, or does it constitute a total system? How could such a system be described?[8]

Some theorists would answer that postmodernism is more an incoherent and fragmentary collection than a system and that it can be only partially described. The postmodern artist, contrary to the modernist, no longer "creates" original forms but recycles them from the past—inscripted signs from western artistic history—and mixes them with "junk" from the mass media, in a process of multireferentiality. It is the encounter—to take an example from Gerald Thomas's *Mattogrosso*—of Hamlet and Batman. If modernist art was pure, original, and autonomous, postmodernism is contaminated, recycled, and derivative. Modernism maintained the separation of genres, while postmodernism mixes them. The modernist focused on the human subject; the postmodernist is focused on language, or rather, on metalanguage, metatheater. Modernism, reflecting industrial society, questioned that society as a totalizing system. Postmodernism, which emerges from postindustrial society, attempts to deal with the fragments of an incoherent system. The reaction of the modernist was critical; that of the postmodernist is paranoiac. According to two theoreticians, the essential element of postmoderism is panic, the "thrill of catastrophe, [the] deepest and most pathological symptoms of nihilism" (Kroker and Cook 1988, i–ii).

If Kroker and Cook, with their overwrought language, seem to parody themselves,[9] Herbert Blau intentionally points out the ironies of postmodernism: what was covert in Beckett, what the unconscious repressed, has been transformed by MTV into "ocular pornography" approaching obscenity (Blau 1990, 281). The hysterical culture that Kroker and Cook laud becomes in Blau's view simply a hysterically promoted culture of narcissism. The postmodern condition and its relation to art signify the circulation of appearance, images of other images, the artist as image, and the audience as spectacle. It is "as if mediation were natural law and—born again in quotation—the sixties were never repressed" (Blau 1990, 284). The "solipsism and excess" of the sixties, Blau continues, persist but only as style. However, it may be that the obsession with spectacle-as-style threatens to devour the real, if this has not already taken place; Blau cites as an example Christo's "high fashion" packaging of pont-neuf. Aversion to such high fashion has nothing to do with the ancient fear of the deceiving image of appearance; Blau makes this comparison: the Platonic cave becomes a nuclear reactor filled with toxic waste, and therefore representation is obliterated by unchecked reproduction (Blau 1990, 284). And what is reproduced? Quotable sources from mythology, history, and the media, as well as "simulations and the overrehearsed images from a kitsch and archaic repertoire. The argument is that cultural forms and myths are being recycled in order to deconstruct them" (Blau 1990, 287).

Johannes Birringer is another theorist who, like Blau, is a theater insider and questions many of the postulates of postmodernism. He discusses the breakdown of modernist dichotomies such as high and low, subject and object, which "become useless in the face of the phantasmagoric 'global American postmodernist culture.'" At the same time, Birringer distrusts the "cultural logic" which posits the notion of a homogeneous global culture (Birringer 1991, 4). The latter point is especially important when one considers the stagings of Gerald Thomas.

Birringer, however, accords theater a special place outside the special pleading of postmodernist hysterics, because it can concern itself "with the *transformation of visual space* and the difference in attention to the perceptual process produced of scenographies of visual and acoustic images that no longer recreate the appearance of dramatic realism" (Birringer 1991, 31). Theater also is unique in that it "has become eccentric to mainstream culture: it no longer needs to pretend (as Broadway still does) that it must entertain the obvious illusions of the familiar" (Birringer 1991, 32). Adding to the medium's singularity is that although it has "disappeared from the center of postmodern thought, it may be because of the critical impoverishment of its own work at a time when culture itself, having lost historical consciousness and an understanding of art's critical relationship to politics and the community, proceeds to 'theatricalize' all its surfaces" (Birringer 1991, 41).

In spite of the special place he accords the theater, Birringer looks suspiciously on postmodernist invasion of the theatrical space, especially by Robert Wilson, whose "grand opera is only the vain posturing of an irresponsible aesthetic self-consciousness that hides its political innocence behind the mask of ritualistic theater magic" (Birringer 1991, 65). What he aims his barbs at in the end is postmodernism: "Beneath the evasions, Wilson's picture design captures the 'truth' of the radical impoverishment of postmodern culture" (Birringer 1991, 67).

These comments should not lead one to think that Robert Wilson and other postmodernist directors have no defense. On the contrary, admirers are legion. But these objections are useful in that they foreshadow the critical assault Gerald Thomas and the *encenador* generation will endure in Brazil.

Among the staunchest defenders of postmodernism in theater is Fred McGlynn: "The task of postmodern theater is to . . . continue to pursue the illusive foundation of an unfounded appearance. Rather than stand in opposition of life, theater is the most accurate mirror of life; the unfounded apparency of the actor caught within the dispersion of the text and the playing space mirrors the unfounded apparency of the social self caught within the dispersion of culture and social space" (McGlynn 1990, 152). It is this unfounded apparency that Gerald Thomas questions. In this regard, McGlynn quotes Daniel Mesguich, who explains that the postmodernists are not political innocents as Berringer would have them: " 'To interrogate the paternal function and what externalizes it, to interrogate the meanings of a text and their history, to interrogate meanings, to interrogate the body with the text, and the text with the body, to interrogate interrogation: there can be no more profoundly political gesture today' " (McGynn 1990, 149).[10]

Mesguich, via McGlynn, also provides the postmodernist rationale for multireferentiality, one of Gerald Thomas's trademarks:

> the text is not simply the "dead word" of the absent author, Shakespeare, composed in the seventeenth century and now condemned only to an endless, slavish repetition in the theater of representation. For him the *mise en scène* is not only the fixed text of the absent author, but also the long history of its innumerable productions and all of the previous and still proliferating commentary that has been devoted to plumbing its depths and showing its relevance to the innumerable occasions of its production. It has interacted with Freud, Lacan, and the entire cultural history of the West which has transpired since its original inscription. Mesguich attempts to open up the text to the indefinite layering of its inscriptions in our culture, including his own production. . . . (McGlynn 1990, 148)

Multireferentiality, lack of "respect" for the icons of classical drama, and intertexuality, according to McGlynn, are all tied together in postmodernism:

> Mesguich sees theater, with its play between the text and production, between history and presentation, as the essential interrogative act of the artist today. Rather than being enslaved by the dead word of master authors, the theater is the very space where the critical play of cultural interrogation takes place. It is where the play of representations and simulation which is postmodern culture can be called into question. It is the place where "intertextual play" is possible. (McGlynn 1990, 150)

McGlynn presents the historical evaluation of these issues in a single paragraph:

> Artaud recognized the decadence of a theater which had forgotten the unfounded nature of its appearance. . . . Both the sacred and the secular groups we have discussed sought to resolve the problem by abjuring the "mere" *apparency* of theater for the presumed *reality* of either a sacred or secular community which they could not succeed in founding. Beckett recognized the problem to which Artaud pointed, but also seemed to recognize the impossibility of a resolution. So he created a theater out of the anguish of that impossibility, introducing the first stage of that crisis of consciousness of meaning and the means to meaning which has become postmodern theater. Mesguich and Blau have sought to pursue the problem, recognizing that the occurrence of theater within any time always involves "the division of a body by a text and the division of a text by a body," which creates that *play* of difference which is the space of the play of theater. Theater, thus understood, mirrors postmodern culture caught within the freeplay of its unfounded apparency. (McGlynn 1990, 153)

Postmodernism, thus framed, resurrects "dead" theater: "If, as Blau argues, theater at its best has always been suspicious of its own apparency, it may not be 'dead'; rather it may be the ideal site for the postmodern era to rethink the density of its inscriptions and the ambiguity of its margins amidst the clamor of our time" (McGlynn 1990, 154). Shank, himself, in spite of his reservations about such postmodernist auteurs as Robert Wilson, points to the historical raison d'être of their productions when he writes: "For a century now audiences have accepted the conventional realistic theater as an appropriate expression of our culture, even as an objective depiction of reality. However, anyone who thinks about it knows that realism is no more an objective representation than any other style; each involves abstraction" (Shank 1990, 271).

How, then, do theories of postmodernism, particularly those developed in the United States and Europe, help us understand and critique the theater of Gerald Thomas? Two fundamental aspects of his stagings are deconstruction and multireferentiality, the chaotic and ahistorical play of inscripted cultural signs. Haroldo de Campos, critic and co-founder of the concrete poetry movement, in his review of *Carmen com filtro 2,* writes that Thomas's Carmen does not possess "the gypsy's eyes nor the skin browned by the Andalusian sun as in Gautier's version (or Merimée/Bizet's). She is an expressionist Carmen . . . as if Edvard Munch had reimagined the willful *sevillana* in a Gothic black-and-white snippet of a Murnau film" (Campos 1990, E9). This is, according to Campos, a Carmen deconstructed, who does not conform to her myth.

I explicate below two of Thomas's stagings, and as I do so I will discuss the expressionist elements Campos alludes to, as well as the deconstruction of cultural myths, and I will weave in and relate the postmodernist theoretical constructs described above. I begin with Thomas's 1989 production entitled *Mattogrosso,* which received attention not only in Brazil but in the New York press, partly due to the *encenador*'s collaboration with Philip Glass. In addition to illustrating the problems of postmodernism in Brazil, the reaction of the foreign press sheds considerable light on cross-cultural misunderstanding.

The 1989 *Mattogrosso*[11] is comprised of aesthetic fragments and scattered references: a postmodernist collage, mixing high and low: Batman, Donald Duck, and Mickey Mouse, now aged and decadent, meet Darwin, Shakespeare, and Wagner. This is the postmodernist freeplay of cultural interrogation, of representation and simulation, the indefinite layering of inscripted signs. In the *encenador*'s own words: "'I tell the story of a Nibelungenlied, a life immersed in myths. These heroes are fragments of a curse. They are hallucinations . . . in relation to a civilization that has been shattering the myths that created it. Batman and the others are aspects of a civilization that juxtaposes, that superimposes the strong over the weak, in an imprecise and escapist manner.'"[12] Arthur Dapieve writes that, "Thomas gambles on images. And on images evoked by other images. And so forth, ad infinitum. *Mattogrosso* is, therefore, spacious enough to house *Der Ring des Nibelungen* . . . Greek myths reworked by Scandinavian countries; Shakespeare; the sunken Titanic; Batman, Donald Duck, and Mickey Mouse. And *mytholungen* were created in the bargain . . ." (Dapieve 1989). The *mytholungen* refer to Thomas's mythology—roots, sedimentation, indefinite layering of inscriptions—of western art. Thomas believes that he is putting the history of western art on stage in a process of "disencyclopediazation" of signs.

Macksen Luiz, though not always sympathetic to Thomas's aims, points to the process by which the *encenador* layers cultural inscriptions: "Stagecraft represents to Gerald Thomas a memory bank filled with scattered impressions. . . . It doesn't matter what he says, scenes are spotlights which illuminate or darken random references to a vague fable about modernity. The spectator's gaze is drawn to images that move through an assimilated culture like a planetary video clip, underscored by a formal precision that mechanizes movement in order to decode concealed meanings . . ." (Luiz 1989, "Samba"). Worth citing here is Blau's critique of "simulations and the overrehearsed images from a kitsch and archaic repertoire. The argument is that cultural forms and myths are being recycled in order to deconstruct them" (Blau 1990, 287). And that is precisely the intent of Thomas's intertextual or collage approach: his multireferentiality mixing European "high" culture and contemporary mass media—with a counterpoint of Afro-Brazilian motifs—amounts to a deconstruction of modernism, which is, after all, one of the essential aims of postmodern artists. Is postmodern deconstruction a derivative act—as Shank and Birringer insist—or can it be original?

Marco Veloso, regarding the process of multireferentiality and layering of inscriptions, writes that "creation is the point of departure and not the contrary" (Veloso 1995, "Crítica"). This turns the formula on its head: that is, multireferentiality, rather than a mere recycling of artistic forms, becomes in Thomas's theater a creation, perhaps a re-creation, or as he describes it a mythological formulation: "'When I direct an actor, I'm trying to create a mythological composition of all the creatures who comprise the theater. How can you separate Hamlet from Medea? How can you separate Estragon from Hamlet? How can you separate Kafka's Titurel from Wagner's Titurel in *Parsifal*? How can you separate history from itself?'"[13] Thomas is referring to the roots of Western art, a process in which the artist examines centuries of inscriptions, of cultural sedimentation built layer upon layer.

The avant-garde has always represented a return to roots. Wagner and other revolutionaries of the romantic school looked back to the middle ages; the early cubists and surrealists were inspired by the "primitive" art of Africa and Latin America; the magic realists of Latin America immersed themselves in Amerindian mythology. And so it is with postmodernist avant-garde artists, who turn their gaze to the beginnings of modernism, such as silent films, especially of the expressionist school, and even to such progenitors of modernism as Wagner. But Gerald Thomas and other postmodernists dig deeply into centuries of artistic roots, which are Mesguich's indefinite layering of inscriptions:

> The work of the *encenador,* according to Thomas, is that of an archeologist who, late in this century, recycles images detached from his historical time and lodged in the performing space. Staging technique is similar to the process of memory. It is a search for stored images which, through an analogical mechanism, are recreated on stage, setting up parallel meanings. The scenic insertion of visual situations

> is the point of confluence of a torrent of perceptions from western culture, materialized in emblematic moments. (Fernandes 1992, "Espectador," 72)

An example of this process is the emblem of the Titanic in *Mattogrosso,* described below in terms of its association with Wagner, Fellini, and García Márquez. The search for roots also leads to postmodernism's apocalyptic vision, to a consciousness of the decay of western civilization.

A particle of this decay, and part and parcel of postmodernist style, is the breakdown of genres; Thomas does not call *Mattogrosso* a play, but an opera. Because there is no singing, only Philip Glass's musical score, it is a "dry" opera (he calls his troupe, the reader will recall, Companhia da Ópera Seca). The main operatic influences—as in so much of Thomas's work—are Wagnerian: *Der Ring des Nibelungen* and *The Flying Dutchman*. The actors in *Mattogrosso* refrain from speaking as well. Thus, we end up with a paradigmatic postmodernist conundrum: a play in which actors do not speak, an opera in which performers do not sing, a ballet in which they do not dance. The performers, moreover, are nearly overwhelmed by Daniela Thomas's apotheosized design, which often occurs, as well, in the productions of formalist directors such as Richard Foreman and Robert Wilson. Traditional theatrical genres, at any rate, are blurred nearly beyond recognition in *Mattogrosso*.

In the program, Gerald Thomas provides a plot synopsis, not a description of linear action but a text of signs inscribed in his metatheatrical conception. He describes the "Matto" of the title, who ties together all the disparate images scattered about the stage, as a fictitious nineteenth-century German explorer, Friedrich Ernst Matto. While the character has Nietzsche's first name, "Matto" is a deliberate misspelling of the western Brazilian state "Mato Grosso," known for its Pantanal, a vast wetlands area, one of the world's largest ecological preserves threatened by development. Matto is an anti-Darwinist—Thomas defines him as a Schopenhauserian Darwin, Darwin's shadow—whose motto is "survival of the defeatist," an allusion to once victorious western civilization, the "fittest", now in decline in the late twentieth century. This decline, it should now be clear, is another of postmoderism's central themes. "Mr. Thomas said Darwin's theory of the survival of the fittest gave man an intellectual excuse for crashing unimpeded through the Amazon" (Brooke 1989). Matto shares none of the heroism of the archetypal nineteenth-century European explorer; he is gaunt and ragged. In other words, the real story, or plot, or libretto, such as it is, does not concern his explorations and voyages, it is a deconstruction of all western voyages of exploration and conquest. The postapocalyptic set design communicates the widely held view—and totters precariously on the edge of cliché—according to which the Western voyages of discovery have lead ultimately to environmental destruction, particularly in the tropical latitudes. *Mattogrosso,* in short, attacks positivism and its offshoot social Darwinism, as does much of modern Latin American art. Critic Marco Veloso writes: "The spirit of disillusionment points less to philosophical negativism than to a reaction against the ideology of progress" (Veloso 1989, "Sintetiza," 7). Gerald Thomas clearly reinforces this view when he states: "'I am denouncing the false, absurd positivism perpetuated by science and the arts, the philosophical discourses which preach progressivism.'"[14]

On his voyage through the tropics, Thomas proclaims in the program notes' text of signs, Matto whistled Lohengren and "discovered that the true genius of the species was Wagner." The primary cultural sign or "mythological" source—as he likes to call it—of much of Thomas's art is Wagner. The text of signs refers as well to Hegelian theses, surrealism, and Marco Polo. Matto had visions of Virgil, "right on the border of Hamlet's sanity." These signs, this mythology, or archaeology, refer to cultural layers, to the idea that all cultural signs have embedded in them remnants of previous signs. Hegel's dialectic of absolute reality precedes surrealism's—and Thomas's avant-garde—ontology of total chaos. Virgil's—that is, Eneas's—fictitious epic voyage of the hero precedes Marco Polo's historical voyage. They both constitute archetypes in the mythology of Ernst Matto's voyage, which, because it is unheroic and uncertain, deconstructs them. The epic voyage of the hero thus loses the grandeur of its quest, the certainty of its mission, the linearity of its action, its elevated literary tone, its masculine-military code, the hero's acclamation upon his return to civilization after traveling through the lands of the "barbarians" (Matto's perambulations through the rain forest), and its unequivocal optimism. The supremely confident and victorious epic hero has become a "defeatist." Such epic deconstruction also has its own antecedents, its mythology in Brazil. One could mention, for example, Mário de Andrade's *Macunaíma* or João Guimarães Rosa's *Grande Sertão, Veredas*. But they are verbal texts, and *Mattogrosso*'s real text is not the program notes of verbal signs but Thomas's audiovisual metatheater.[15]

*Mattogrosso* also deconstructs dramatic linear structure, the notion of sequential acts, by presenting three thematic segments entitled "The Canyon," "The Light," and "Matto Grosso." Marco Veloso writes that the three segments refer successively to "pre-revolutionary time," "non-time," and "present-day epoch" (Veloso 1989, "Sintetiza"). Each segment is comprised of a series of tableaux, which may include movement or be made up of static pictures. The production begins in silence. The lights come up slowly to reveal the set, a layering of inscripted signs, cultural and historical references in postmodernist style. Transparent scrims separate the stage from the audience and divide the performing area into multiple spaces.

The most prominent feature on stage is a partially sunken model of the Titanic made from mosquito netting, adding to the effect of transparency and impermanence. As one would expect, there are other signs present here, such as Fellini's film *E la nave va,* which also featured an intentionally artificial craft, reminiscent of a stage set. The ghostly ship refers explicitly to *The Flying Dutchman,* not only to Wagner's work itself but to Thomas's own previous staging of the opera; moreover, it alludes, in the director's scheme of mythology of signs, to the legends on which Wagner's opera is based, the phantom vessel doomed to sail eternally—off the Cape of Good Hope, or in the North Sea—a vision boding disaster. The Portuguese title of Wagner's opera is *O navio fantasma,* or "the ghost ship," which brings to mind García Márquez's use of the symbol of the ship for the decay of western civilization in the tropics: Hilacsilag, the nineteenth-century passenger liner that runs aground in his story "Last Voyage of the Ghost Ship," as well as the landlocked Spanish galleon in *One Hundred Years of Solitude*. Thomas himself says that the vessel in his stage set represents the shipwreck of western civilization: " 'To preserve the treasures of the [Titanic] and defend it from plundering by humans, God creates the forests and the waters. Ecological disaster then befalls the earth, and the water evaporates from the river and its bed dries up. The vegetation and the land-locked Titanic are revealed. Consequently, ailing nature commits euthanasia, leaving the Titanic abandoned to its destiny, to be raped by human beings.' "[16] The guarding of the treasure and the ship itself are also Wagnerian references: *The Flying Dutchman* and *Götterdämmerung* of the "Ring" tetralogy.

A multitude of postapocalyptic images—here one imagines the hysterical delight of Kroker and Cook—fill the stage at various times: petrified human forms; rocks strewn about an eternal nightscape, with moon and clouds overhead; sandpits or boxes which sometimes represent graves holding naked corpses, many of which are mutilated;[17] skeletons;

hanging animal carcasses; a dinghy sticking halfway out of sand, at one point "rowed" by an actor; fiery cauldrons (Dante? Bosch?); the Berlin Wall;[18] a table on a raised platform with a group of modern scientists studying a globe to puzzle out—according to Gonçalves Filho (1989, "Caetano," E3)—the causes for the demise of planet earth. The "opera" ends with a sandstorm in the desert; the entire stage is lit to reveal rocks, a slightly swaying barren tree—a minimalist suggestion of deforestation—the burned out nave of a church. The set designer, Daniela Thomas, Gerald's former wife, also appears to work within a postmodernist modus operandi: " 'Today everyone recycles, no one creates.' "[19]

Multilayered set and lights, music, stylized movement, voiceovers, these are the essential elements of Thomas's dry opera. There is little dialogue; Thomas replaces the "dead" theater of the word with audiovisual spectacle. The actors rarely speak on stage in the productions Thomas himself authors, and *Mattogrosso* is no exception. Voiceovers provide "text": the audience often hears recordings of Thomas's own voice—the postmodernist artist as his own subject—or actors lipsynching recorded dialogue. The production begins with an electronic voice: "I would like to be another person, another person." Flora Süssekind writes:

> The opera *Mattogrosso* begins with a recorded and electronically distorted voice attempting to attach itself to a body visible on stage but at the same time underscoring in that utterance ("Another. Another person") its alterity and inescapable distance. The voice serves in this instance as an a priori objectification, in the opposition between sound and image, as a muffled tension, which appears to accompany further tension—depicted at several points—between rows of bodies, cadavers and paupers, and the people who pass among them with difficulty during the course of the performance. (Süssekind 1992, 44)

It is a dying voice, slowing down and becoming fainter, like Hal in *2001*.[20] The voice seems linked to action on stage, and yet the artificiality of the situation is purposefully accentuated. One might liken this to a Brechtian distancing effect, albeit a postmodern one, because what Thomas is pointing toward is not political alienation or Marxist dialectics but—to return to Philip Simmon's categories—the inauthentic, derivative position of the postmodern artist in the postindustrial age. The image of the disembodied voice, of the actor tenuously connected to the voice of the electronic other, continues throughout the production; another example is the metatheatrical pronouncement, "Unintelligible . . .

Unintelligible . . . Dramatic convention only exists if we believe in it." Some critics take a disparaging view of Thomas's use of verbal language: ". . . the word is no longer a vehicle of communication but a sign of confusion" (Gonçalves Filho 1989, "Nibelungos," F1).

Thomas replaces the "dead" theater of the word, but does he fulfill Artaud's vision of a sacred, ritual theater? An example in *Mattogrosso* is a scene in which a man smashes a table after which a waiter and diner fall on the table. The scene is repeated three times; that is, there are three levels, beginning downstage, going upstage, in which set and action are echoed: (1) a diner is slumped over a table and standing next to him is a waiter; another man examines the table and then, stumbling, he searches through a pile of rubble where he finds a baseball bat; he smashes the table, which collapses; the diner falls on the table, the waiter falls on the diner; the table-smasher runs around in agony and disappears into darkness; (2) lights come up on the next level, where the table-smasher is frozen in geometric position, his back to the audience, ghost-like; a new table-smasher, table, waiter, and diner appear; the new smasher stops to observe his "ghost" from level 1, repeats the previous action, and becomes the new "ghost," now holding up a cross; (3) after the third repetition is completed, a bishop enters and discovers the bodies of the waiter and the diner, which marks the end of the segment. At various times during these repetitions the actors are frozen and arranged in an inert geometry in contrast to the mobile geometry of the repetitious smashing-collapsing. It would be questionable, however, to place this activity in the realm of Artaud's sacred ritual.

Mircea Eliade has theorized elaborately on the nature of sacred ritual. Ritual acts imitate mythical paradigms established by gods in the time of Creation. Ritual repetitions of the original Creation suspend linear time and recreate the cyclical time of the mythical paradigm. Rituals, therefore, constitute regeneration, an eternal return to "pure" time, leading to a new Creation. Human life is constantly destroyed and regenerated in a grand cycle of eternal return. Destruction is necessary for the beginning of new cycles, death and sacrifice are imperative for the regeneration of humanity. In what way does the destruction of the table-smashing scene, repeated three times, constitute a "ritual"? The answer is that what the audience witnesses is an anti-ritual, a ritual parody, underscored by the cross and the appearance of the bishop. The stylized movements and freezes are characteristic of the task-acting postmodernist auteurs such as Pina Bausch are known for. Theodore Shank cites an example of repetitive task-acting: "In *Café Müller,* by Pina Bausch's

Tanztheater Wuppertal, a woman is hugged by a man; when he releases his grasp, she slips to the floor. She picks herself up to be hugged again, and again slips to the floor, over and over again" (Shank 1990, 254). The gods have fled from the postapocalyptic universe of *Mattogrosso,* and all we are left with, apparently, are burlesque mythical re-creations. If there is mythology in the production, it relates to the myths of western artistic icons such as Wagner. I asked above if Gerald Thomas's performances parallel Brazilian society or reproduce sterile ritual theater practices developed in the United States and Europe. The answer, I believe, is that they fall somewhere in between because Thomas's theater, like Antunes Filho's, borrows from a Brazilian cultural matrix closely bound up with ritual. The curtain call in *Mattogrosso,* for example, features the *encenador* himself walking on stage playing a large samba drum—*bumbo* or *surdo*—representing Brazil's African culture, a culture in which Thomas participates. Besides playing Afro-Brazilian percussion, he has collaborated with a Rio Samba school and uses the *surdo* to time blocking in rehearsals. One might say, then, that even Thomas's rehearsals have something of the character of Afro-Brazilian rituals.

Ritual entails repetition, and the repetitive motifs of the *Mattogrosso*'s early scenes are expanded upon as the play continues. Black-robed penitents crawl agonizingly across rocks in a barren desert, downstage from the bishop who appears at the end of the table-smashing episode. The references here are multiple in postmodernist fashion: the penitents most surely correspond to the Valkyries from Wagner's *Die Walküre* in the "Ring" cycle; they may be Catholic penitents, on the one hand, or Indian and/or African slaves on the other; they may also constitute a visual reference to the women in Federico García Lorca's *La Casa de Bernarda Alba.*[21] Their stylized movements are imitated by a figure in oriental dress. Workers, perhaps slave laborers, pick up stones—gold?—and pass between the penitents and bishop's group. Later, the penitents, or Valkyries, descend into an orchestra pit filled with fire—represented by a lighting source located beneath the main set—and stage smoke; they are attacked by musicians from the orchestra and by Gerald Thomas himself; this is followed by a lighting effect that suggests simultaneously rain in the desert, acid rain, and an apocalyptic rain of fire. These images hark back to the European colonization of Brazil and subjugation of its native peoples. They are also images out of a Bosch painting. At the same time, they refer to a future postindustrial apocalypse.

Ritual images of death and mutilation abound, often underscored with a liturgical motif composed by Philip Glass. A figure is seated in a chair—electric chair? throne?—while another kneels before the first and stabs the seated figure. A woman walks over graves carrying a staff. From behind a coffin another woman emerges.[22] Near the graves a bishop speaks,[23] while behind him two penitents hold another figure whose head hangs backward as if sacrificed or dragged to execution; behind them a man rows a boat half submerged in sand; during this scene we also see hanging carcasses, probably a visual reference to Francis Bacon's painting "Head Surrounded by Sides of Beef." Like Bacon, Thomas may be trying to startle the spectator into a perception of brutality and violence, but with so much activity on the stage it is difficult to maintain the focus of a single painting. Thomas's 1992 *Flash & Crash Days,* on the other hand, highlights the themes of cruelty and violence and brings them to the center of focus.

The parallels to Robert Wilson are clear in this production, although as I have noted Thomas himself has wearied of being compared to Wilson. Theodore Shank, in his discussion of "formalist" directors, writes:

> Robert Wilson's five-hour opera *Einstein on the Beach* (1976) is an example of a formalist work with a mathematical structure. The opera has nine scenes, and there are three dominant visual images: (1) a train and a building, (2) a courtroom and a bed, and (3) a field with a spaceship. Each of the images appears in every third scene so that each is used three times. Not only do images recur on a mathematical schedule, but the postmodern choreography of Andrew de Groat and Lucinda Childs and the music of minimalist composer Philip Glass were also precisely constructed on numerical systems. (Shank 1990, 252)

The collaboration of Philip Glass—the "mathematical" minimalist composer—and Gerald Thomas has led to similar results. Most of Shank's comments could apply to *Mattogrosso.* While perhaps not as rigidly mathematical as *Einstein,* some images and motifs do "recur on a mathematical schedule."

What is Glass's contribution to the production? The score is minimalist, full of repetition, with snatches of liturgical music, Strauss, and particularly Wagner. Musical fragments parallel the multireferentiality of the postmodernist production design. Glass's music is suggestive and contemplative, an interface between audience and the stage. In Glass's own words: "'It's a collage of images . . . My music gives it a musical window to look through.'"[24] Among the critics who take a positive view of the Thomas/Glass collaboration is Nelson Motta (1989): "Philip Glass's music is simply exceptional and is executed with a talent and precision unusual in our local orchestras." On the other hand, detractors maintain that the play and the music are at odds with each other, that the latter is gratuitous, merely background: "Glass's score runs parallel to the dramatic action—the scenes one witnesses on stage are stronger than the reiterative sounds that emerge from the orchestra pit—establishing merely a musical background for the actors' silence" (Luiz 1989, "Samba"). According to Reynaldo Roels, Jr. of the newspaper *Jornal do Brasil*: "'Halfway through it was clear that the music and the scenes were conceived independently, and the link between the two was entirely gratuitous.'"[25] Gerald Thomas and Philip Glass have collaborated on other productions besides *Mattogrosso: Uma metamorfose, Um processo,* and *Carmem com filtro 2*. Glass has this to say about his collaborator:

> [Gerald] has a good understanding not only of theater, but of painting, of literature, of music, especially music. He has one of the best ears of any theater person I know. But more importantly, he has a good grasp of the visual arts. He has a background in drawing. So this is really what makes him special. He is also very international. He has seen work from all over the world. When he was a young man he was very much taken by Peter Brook. Later he saw all the pieces of the Living Theater, Mabou Mines. He knows the field. In my opinion, the future lies in this integration of staging, design, of movement, of music, of literature. The big piece we did was *Mattogrosso* which was like an opera. But that was really made from pieces we'd already done. Many people came. I suppose some didn't like it, some did. His staging and [Daniela's] design and the music united really well. From an artistic point of view it was very successful. ("Gerald Thomas, eis a questâo")

Although some critics assert that the music and the play are unrelated, in the postmodernist context this kind of dissonance may be considered part of the aesthetic whole, and Wagnerian motifs deserve special attention within this aesthetic whole.

Gerald Thomas has stated repeatedly that he owes a special artistic debt to Wagner; his *Gesamtglücksfallwerk* (total work of chance) is a postmodern homage to the Wagnerian synthesis of all the arts, or *Gesamtkunstwerk;* the Wagnerian synthesis becomes fragmentation, collage, and deconstruction. "The expression originated from a cross between the Wagnerian 'total work of art,' synthesis of all the arts, and German philosopher Friedrich Nietzsche's expression 'every occurrence is chance.' Thomas's 'art of total chance' can be defined as a nonverbal aesthetic discipline" (Veloso 1989, "Sintetiza"). But *Gesamtglücksfallwerk* is really more of a postmodern pastiche of signs. Its multireferentiality is an anti-synthesis; there is no closure, denouement, resolution, epiphany, catharsis. Neither is *Gesamtglücksfallwerk* directly related to any artistic school such as Artaud, expressionism, or surrealism; rather, these become in Thomas's postmodern pastiche that which Mesguich defines as layered inscriptions, intertextual fragments to be deconstructed in a process of "cultural interrogation." And yet the Wagnerian sign remains central, it is much more than a fragment, and Gerald Thomas's identification with Richard Wagner is a work of total design.

I offer an anecdote here: in his wide-ranging conversation with the camera in the TV Cultura documentary (see Works Cited), Gerald Thomas describes Wagner as a source of strength; when he is stuck in one of the nightmarish traffic jams for which large Brazilian cities are infamous, he plays a Wagner tape and is rescued from the ordeal. Thomas does not say this, but his remark might lead one to imagine Brunhilde, surrounded by fire, being rescued by Siegfried. The fundamental question is this: Why is a high priest of postmodernism so drawn to the high priest of late romanticism/early modernism? In a nutshell, both were artistic revolutionaries, both transformed and blurred their respective artistic genres, both generated heated controversy. To begin with, Wagner's artistic program had the iconoclastic and avant-garde qualities of Thomas's postmodernism. They are both deconstructionists, and what Wagner deconstructed was the grand opera of high romanticism. Romantic opera had become formulaic, and Wagner exploded the rigid framework with such measures as eliminating the overture—for the most part—as well as the distinction between singing and speaking. Indeed, Wagner claimed to dislike opera; his interest was in what he called "musical drama," and his ideal was Beethoven's Ninth Symphony with its synthesis of music and poetry. I have already discussed the ways in which Thomas and other postmodernist have blurred genres, the *encenador* particularly dismissing the notion that he is a "theater director." Wagner was for his time sui generis; Thomas occupies a similar position in the realm of the Brazilian stage. Wagner, in spite of his legacy of rigidity, evolved constantly, never satisfied with what he had already created. Thomas, though he may "mathematically" construct some scenes, is equally restive in his search for new forms. Critic Marcos Santarrita, in his review of Thomas's *Flying Dutchman,* suggests a similar comparison: "Everything is possible. It may be that [with] Gerald Thomas

Richard Wagner his found a worthy interpreter: megalomaniac and revolutionary in his own time, author of somber works which irritated sensitive ears accustomed to the sweet warblings of romanticism" (Santarrita 1987, B1).

Two aspects of Wagner's position in his time especially remind one of Gerald Thomas a century later: (a) creations characterized by hallucinatory intensity and aesthetic extremism and (b) an outlandish public persona. Both have experienced notable successes and failures. When Wagner originally staged *Tristan and Isolde,* with its overheated yet cerebral romanticism, he believed it would be a crowd pleaser, but it bombed (it has of course become a staple of the now staid and protected Wagnerian precinct). When he tried to write a comic opera, the bloated five-hour *Meistersingers of Neurenburg,* it suffered a similar fate. Thomas, too, has suffered his falls from grace; for example, his production entitled *O império das Meias verdades,* on which I comment in Chapter 3. Thomas himself admits to failure with a 1995 production entitled *Don Juan,* a text by Otavio Frias Filho, based on the myriad versions of the Don Juan myth. The piece was praised by at least one critic. Filmmaker Arnaldo Jabor[26] writes that, "Gerald's dream has acquired a profound and sinister light [which] creates a chain of metaphors as difficult to endure as the idea of death without afterlife. In this way, the production becomes a metaphor of our futility in the face of sexual utopia" (Jabor 1995, C15). Audiences, including Thomas's supporters, were shocked or at least discomfited by the "perverse" production, which featured Don Juan as an impotent gynecologist.

Thomas's labors in the theater are also infused with Wagner's works and motifs. He has staged Wagnerian operas, in Brazil and in Europe. His 1987 staging of *The Flying Dutchman* (*O navio fantasma*) set off a firestorm of critical protest, particularly for its allegedly gratuitous and anecdotal allusions to other works of art: "[In his] staging of Wagner's opera *The Flying Dutchman* . . . the director referred self-indulgently . . . to twentieth-century paintings and sculptures" (Brandão 1992, 32). Mário Henrique Simonsen, former minister of finance during the military dictatorship, wrote a diatribe in the news magazine *Veja,* scorning the production as "an anthem of confusion." Simonsen was particularly upset by Thomas's postmodernist proliferation of cultural references, the placing on stage of "incongruous elements" such as models of Duchamp's bicycle wheel and Rodin's "The Thinker," as well as a set design that included the Berlin Wall, all of which "obscure and muddle the plot." None of this is original, Simonsen alleges, it is "psychedelic" and constitutes a lack of inspiration, not art but *besteirol* or mindless farce (Simonsen 1987, 113–114). Subsequently, Simonsen threatened to sue Thomas because the latter called him a "thief." Thomas later amended his statement to " 'thief of ideas,' " but then added that Simonsen had colluded with the " 'fascist generals' " in " 'sinking the nation's economy' " and that the threatened lawsuit showed that the former minister was well versed in repression ("Simonsen quer processar Thomas 1987").

While Simonsen's views were seconded by one group of critics, other commentators viewed the production much more positively. For example, Marília Martins saw the controversy itself as a positive opening of the closed, elite world of opera in Brazil. She invoked Oswald de Andrade's anthropophagy—a cultural theory I discuss below—to defend Thomas's *Dutchman*: ". . . the anthropophagic staging of this opera constitutes a sort of anti-museum which negates obsolescence" (Martins 1987, 41).

Wagner is a frequent visitor to Thomas's stages. The landlocked Titanic, with its hoard of treasure, refers in part to the tempest-tossed ship in *The Flying Dutchman* (a reference not only to Wagner but to Thomas's own staging of the opera). *Mattogrosso* is related to the first and last parts of the tetralogy *Der Ring des Nibelungen: Das Rheingold* and *Götterdämmerung*. The last part, *Götterdämmerung,* the twilight or "extinction" of the gods, has special significance for Thomas's production, which deals with the twilight of western expansionism, with the extinction of modernist myths. The hero Siegfried—from medieval Germanic legend—slays the gold-hoarding dragon and awakens the Amazon *Walküre* Brunhilde from her enchanted sleep. It is important to remember that Wagner not only borrowed Norse myths but recreated them, just as Gerald Thomas has in turn transformed Wagner's mythological themes. The hero is now the protagonist Matto, a down-and-out Siegfried, a "defeatist" who awakens a bevy of keening *Walküre*. But these Valkyries do not conduct fallen heroes to Valhalla; rather they descend into a fiery underworld (the orchestra pit). Siegfried's followers are dwarves known as Nibelungs, which Gerald Thomas transmutes into mytholungs—postmodern inscriptions and deconstructions of sedimented layers of western art—who dance the samba at the close of the production. I discuss later in more detail the Wagnerian elements in Thomas's *Flash & Crash Days*.[27]

Finally, one should keep in mind that Wagner spearheaded the undoing of a long-lived movement that maintained a near hegemony over the arts: romanticism. At the same time, his work marks the beginning of another protracted period in the history of western art: modernism. Thomas's work corresponds to another moment in this cyclical process of death and rebirth: the postmodernist crusade to extinguish hegemonic modernism.

A precursor to this crusade materialized almost immediately following the birth of Brazilian *modernismo*. I mentioned above two names in this regard, Oswald de Andrade and José Celso. Oswald, one of *modernismo*'s patriarchs and its principal theorist, wrote a 1928 tract he titled *Manifesto antropófago*. The ideas embraced by the manifesto did not bear directly on the arts until Brazil was well into its *pós-modernista* period. José Celso, whom Gerald Thomas recognizes as his precursor, staged a play in 1967 by Oswald de Andrade entitled *O rei da vela* (*The Candle King*). He informed the production with the principles of anthropophagy, or cultural cannibalism, in a process I have previously termed the "Tupy potpourri": "unfettered utilization of a myriad of sources, whatever their origin, without respect for the integrity of those sources" (George 1992, *Stage,* 77). Those sources included the early European avant-garde (e.g., *Ubu Roi* and futurist decor), Brecht, classic western literature (e.g., *Macbeth* and the story of Heliose and Abelard), a revolving stage modeled after a Berliner Ensemble production, Italo-Brazilian opera, American pop culture (e.g., comic books, Groucho Marx, Shirley Temple), exotic Tropicalist kitsch created by foreigners but consumed by Brazilians (e.g., a Busby Berkeley number featuring Carmen Miranda), Brazilian circus and carnival and vaudeville (*revista*) motifs, the comedy of manners (*comédia de costumes*), the work of film director Glauber Rocha, visual references to Brazilian political figures, and musical recordings ranging from the western classical repertoire to American jazz to Brazilian pieces in many styles. The list could go on. The sheer quantity of cultural references and puns rivals those in *Mattogrosso*. But the purpose of Celso's multireferentiality, although a harbinger of postmodernist style, was quite different from anything Gerald Thomas had in mind. The 1967 production of *O rei da rela* presented its potpourri of recycled—to use a postmodernist term—images to a specific ideological end: the decolonization of Brazilian culture and concomitant emancipation from "imperialist" subjugation. José Celso and his collaborators also used their art as a means to rail against the military dictatorship. Their subjects, in other words, were external and political. Gerald Thomas's subject, and that of postmodernists in general, is the artist himself.

In spite of the outpouring of ideas—aesthetic, environmental, ontological—in Gerald Thomas's work, he does not produce a theater of ideas in any uniform or programmatic sense. In spite of all the references to and parody of theory—e.g., Darwin in *Mattogrosso*—there is no fixed theoretical foundation in his theater. Of the new "visual" directors, Thomas is perhaps the most subjective, his work most closely linked to his own personality and idiosyncracies, not to mention his vast knowledge of artistic culture. He spills out on stage gigabytes from a databank of his own unconscious images and conscious cultural obsessions. The ultimate meaning of *Mattogrosso* may thus pertain to Gerald Thomas himself, to his own psyche. It is also certain, whatever judgment one makes, that the multiple and simultaneous references *Mattogrosso* presents—temporal, spatial, literary—project the inner world of the *encenador*. At the same time, his work refers to and parodies itself, with continual references to previous productions in terms of sets, lights, and characters.

> Unconstrained by the ties that would bind it to immediate reality, Thomas's theater, encased in its self-as-context, seems insulated from contemporary representation. The *encenador*'s logos, a sort of theatrical navel, reflects a basic premise: on the eve of the twenty-first century, there is no "dialogos" on stage, no expression of a communal discussion of ways to achieve results. Drama has been replaced by the fragmentary explosion of theatrics, all referring, in the last analysis, to the creator's own agenda. (Fernandes 1992, 72)

What Shank has written about Richard Foreman could apply as well to Gerald Thomas: the creation of "productions that reflect his concern with his own consciousness and the structure of his thought. [Foreman] pointed out that we have a natural inclination to make things cohere, to find connections, to make order out of chaos. He thinks it is important to poke holes in this order, to disrupt, to avoid going with an emotional flow or providing a single meaning" (Shank 1990, 256). Shank reaches similar conclusions about performance artists: "the content was the artist's own cognitive and perceptual processes . . ." (Shank 1990, 254), as well as another theatrical figure whose work is self-referential, Lee Breuer of Mabou Mines. Shank writes: "The performance is an objectification of Breuer's mental process as he tries to create—his insecurities, his attempts to discover his relationship to objects and events in the world and to the work he is creating . . . " (Shank 1990, 258). Yet an auteur whose productions take the form of personal confessions is Tadeusz Kantor, whose personal experience is turned into theatrical fiction. Shank notes:

> However, lest we become so absorbed in the images that we lose the connection to the actual person, Kantor himself is continually present on stage as a reminder that we are experiencing his subjective world. Sometimes, as in *The Dead Class* (1975), he is visible just outside the acting area conducting the performance; and sometimes, as in *I Shall Never Return* (1987), he is within the action but still outside the aesthetic frame and therefore not absorbed into the illusion." (Shank 1990, 259)

Gerald Thomas, as we have seen, may appear in the midst of a play, at the end, and in voiceovers. A final question to keep in mind is this: self-referentiality does not necessarily mean that the creator is always taking himself seriously. On the contrary, his interjection in a scene may be a way of poking fun at himself and his public persona. This is certainly true of Thomas's theater, which walks a fine line between seriousness and self-parody, a point that many detractors as well as supporters miss. An excellent example of Thomas's self-referentiality and concomitant self-parody is his production entitled *Flash & Crash Days*.

## II. *FLASH & CRASH DAYS*: NELSON RODRIGUES WITHOUT WORDS

*Flash & Crash Days—Tempestade e Fúria* bears Gerald Thomas's trademark postmodernist multireferentiality manifest in *Mattogrosso*. One of the most intriguing references is to the work of Brazilian playwright Nelson Rodrigues. Myriad cinematic images are recycled in the production, and Wagner is once again a central musical and dramatic inscription.

*Flash & Crash,* as I will henceforth call it, was created and directed by Gerald Thomas—he also designed the lighting—with set and costumes by Daniela Thomas. The production opened on 8 December 1991, in Rio's Centro Cultural, administered by the Banco do Brasil, which commissioned the project. *Flash & Crash* carries the droll subtitle, "a play about a Mother and a Daughter and a heart!" The two nameless protagonists, whom I will refer to simply as Mother and Daughter, are played by a mother–daughter tandem of actresses: Fernanda Montenegro, the grande dame of the Brazilian stage, and Fernanda Torres, a distinguished actress in her own right. Fernanda Montenegro, who began her career in the 1940s, has starred in countless films, stage productions, and telenovelas. Fernanda Torres has performed in several films and won a Best Actress award at the 1988 Cannes festival.

As one might expect, Thomas puts this tandem to good use, and therefore acting here is far more important than in *Mattogrosso;* indeed, it is the centerpiece of *Flash & Crash,* in spite of its spectacular visual effects. The performance style is not Stanislavskian, it does not create an illusion of reality, but it is in many ways reminiscent of expressionism, particularly expressionist films of the silent era. That is, the actors' movements, facial expressions, and intonations mirror inner states, some of which are accessible to the audience, some of which can only be guessed at—or analyzed using the tools of psychoanalysis—but which nonetheless strike a powerful chord. Like expressionism, the actors' histrionics verge on melodrama. Expressionist acting, as I discuss later, is also characteristic of Nelson Rodrigues's theater. The gestural acting has a great deal to do with opera, particularly Wagnerian opera, as one would expect from Gerald Thomas: "Gestures . . . are orchestrated to conform to a rigid operatic score" (Luiz 1991, "Estilhaços," B1). Acting is very physical and occasionally very comic, and in this way integrates the commedia dell'arte tradition. The characters' archetypal status, their costumes, Daughter's makeup, and their endless skirmishes are reminiscent of that archaic farcical mode. Other traditional forms of slapstick come to mind as well, such as the Punch and Judy show, albeit a Punch and Judy in the manner of grand guignol. One might also think of grotesque comic theater pieces such as Federico García Lorca's *El retablillo de don Cristóbal,* in which the protagonist commits mass murder when he discovers the infidelities of Doña Rosita, his betrothed.

The music for the play is entirely recorded, and provides an almost continuous backdrop of emotion and presence, very much like a movie soundtrack.[28] The music tends to be loud, insistent, and dissonant, with a preponderance of violins, as if the bathtub scene in Hitchcock's *Psycho* had lasted for nearly the entire movie (the association is not arbitrary, given the horror film signs inscripted in *Flash & Crash*). Compositions include segments by Wagner, Philip Glass, and Thomas himself. Thomas's trademark voiceovers, often distorted electronically, reverberate throughout the play. The actors' voices are also heard, sometimes live, other times recorded.

Daniela Thomas's set design initially displays the New York skyline—the *modernist* cityscape par excellence—with a lighted window in the Empire State Building. As if a camera had zoomed through the lighted window, the scenes that follow take place in a room with tall doors, windows, and transparent walls. The set also includes a volcano placed upstage, a constant menacing presence, variously symbolizing eruptions of violent emotion, blood, and repressed sexual craving. The volcano suggests unconscious impulses which may explode at any moment. The smoke that spews from it continually drifts across the stage. Its form, which is both protuberant and recessive, suggests at once female and male sexual organs. The lava running down the side of the volcano is one shade in a palette of reds: costume pieces range from scarlet to crimson and heavily gelled lights frequently bathe the stage in red. It is, obviously, the color of blood, and *Flash & Crash* is as blood-soaked as any horror flick. Other effects include circles of light projected on the stage which periodically isolate the characters. Daniela Thomas says this about her set and costume design: "'My work is a recycling of the world. . . .'"[29] The idea of recycling images places the designer squarely within the postmodernist current.

As the lights come up on the set, Thomas's voiceover, from beyond the tomb, explains that he had been trapped in a building, the deserted city beset by warnings of a volcanic eruption. The narrator had been observing a woman living in the Empire State Building; she is known to have scrawled a notice on a wall, an homage to those who have lost their lives in political trials and wars. Below the notice is the drawing of an eye (which will appear at the end of the play). The voice proclaims that, suddenly, he was no longer himself present there: he had been transformed into the woman. Flora Süssekind writes that this voiceover structures the whole play, that it is the monologic self which invades the other characters and their dialogue. It is the invisible subject of the play (Süsskind 1992, 44). "The device of Thomas's own recorded voiceover, which guides and underscores the production, reveals to the audience this authorship: it is the narration of a contemporary epic which filters the myths of artistic creation in order to transform them into a private odyssey" (Fernandes 1992, 72). This "private odyssey" is the inner voyage, the self-as-subject, self-referentiality of the postmodernist artist.

Contrary to what several critics have written about Thomas's productions, design is not the centerpiece of *Flash & Crash;* rather, it provides an ever-shifting and oneiric environment for the psychic and mythic interplay of the main characters. While the monologic voiceover repeats "I . . . I . . ." the first character appears on stage; it is Mother, played by Fernanda Montenegro. She wears a medieval costume in purple and brownish tones, with a high conical hat, an apron, and a dress covered by a red plastic cloak. She is Brunhilde, as I explain below, from Wagner's "Ring" tetralogy. An arrow pierces her throat and sticks out the back of her neck. She retreats out of a lighted entranceway toward the volcano, staggering about in agony, as Gerald Thomas's characters often do. This choreography of anguish is the movement of nightmares, the dance macabre of helplessness and impending doom.

In at least one performance, Ms. Montenegro parodies the scene. She sighs and makes a rather obscene masculine gesture of exasperation—"*Que saco*!" would be the verbal equivalent in Portuguese, or "balls!"—the audience laughs, she throws up her arms in parody of melodramatic gesture, and collapses, once again provoking laughter. If this moment was planned, as I suspect, then once again we see Thomas poking fun at his own work.

Mother crawls to a dummy with an arrow in its heart. Motifs are foreshadowed, repeated, mirrored, echoed throughout the production, in this case the arrow and especially the heart. Mother rises and moves with arms outstretched, lightning crashes—the "Flash & Crash" of the title—and she falls to the stage. Two sinister "archangels" appear dressed in jumpsuits (at other times they wear business suits), miners' helmets, with wings strapped to their backs. They climb onstage carrying flashlights, examine Mother, and pick her up. During the course of the play they will serve as helpmates for Mother and Daughter in their endless and deadly clashes (perhaps one should say "crashes"). The archangels are archetypes, but ironically not of transcendence; instead they hold the women down, dragging them over and over again back into their murderous combat.

Mother has attempted to abort Daughter with the help of the angels.[30] Daughter, her face twisted in agony, slowly crosses the stage carrying a bucket, a symbol of filial subservience. Her costume, also medieval, is red. She kneels, puts her face in the bucket, and vomits; Mother has tried to poison her. A look of horror, then sadness, crosses her face, her mouth opens, she silently mouths words, her expression changes to pathetic. This rapid metamorphosis of emotions is a constant in the play; it corresponds to the fluctuation of dreams and the mood swings of childhood.

In subsequent scenes Mother and Daughter torment each other between acts of incest. The two angels approach in the darkness behind Daughter, their flashlights illuminate her, their oneiric movements simultaneous and in slow motion; she looks back in terror. Lightning crashes and Mother appears in a fright wig like the bride of Frankenstein: horror movies constitute one of the main allusions in the play's postmodernist multireferentiality. Daughter tries to escape Mother but the angels grab her and hold her down, spread her legs, and place her hand on her sex.

Daughter makes incoherent childlike sounds while she masturbates and mumbles, "I don't know what my name is, I don't have one," which is repeated later by a slow, low-pitched electronic voice. Her namelessness gives her archetypal status, perhaps in the Jungian sense as I suggest later. Daughter reaches orgasm and Mother sucks avidly on a lollipop.[31] Daughter lies in a fetal position. Mother hides behind the volcano and screams at the angel, "agua, aguaaa," while Daughter performs a ballet, dancing around Mother and taunting her with a goblet of water. While on point she begins a paroxysm of agony, grabs her neck, and collapses. Mother crawls to Daughter, who grabs her by the throat and chokes her, smiling. She gets on top of Mother, slaps her, spreads her legs, grabs her own and Mother's breasts, and simulates sex with her. Both protagonists, in their continual convulsions, deaths, and resurrections, remind one of the typical horror movie monster that refuses to die. This monster flick, with its tongue-in-cheek (no pun intended here) sadomasochistic overtones, hints at the "Rocky Horror Picture Show."

The angels enter with birthday cakes, which they place on the stage. But this will be no child's birthday party: the music stops, the audience hears a recorded heartbeat. The angels, in one of the most startling moments in *Flash & Crash,* rip Mother's heart from her breast. The angels throw the heart to Daughter. Her bloody hands arise from behind the volcano, then her face, the heart in her mouth. She is completely covered with blood. She eats the heart and spits out pieces of flesh and blood, she looks at the others, smiles, continues eating and impishly offers to share it with them. Her expression changes to distress. She creeps toward Mother, falls in her lap, tries to embrace her, and the angels pull her off. Without warning, Mother yanks off Daughter's head. Daughter writhes, Mother and the angels play catch with the head, the violins stop, the audience titters. Blackout. The birthday cake scene ending in mutilation brings to mind myriad references: countless films and stories have based their horror on childhood innocence contrasted with or transformed into demonic abomination, from Grimms' fairy tales to B movies such as *The Exorcist, The Bad Seed, Village of the Damned, Children of the Corn*—the list could go on. I discuss later specific associations with the removal and devouring of the heart and the beheading.

Daughter, her head back in place, returns to the stage. Gerald Thomas's electronic voice, lipsynched by Daughter, states: "Goodness, ma'am, how poorly you slept last night." The humorous reference—"it was all a dream"—resonates beyond this moment when one realizes that the nightmare will go on throughout the performance. Flora Süssekind's analysis of the monologic voice is also pertinent here: "Identical voiceovers (Gerald Thomas's) interfere with the voices of other figures (the two women) visible on stage, in *Flash & Crash Days*. This fact seems to constitute a further indication that both represent the replication of a single voice-subject" (Süssekind 1992, 46).

Mother and Daughter begin a demented card game which provides comic relief—from the recurring nightmares—and which produces eruptions of laughter in audiences. Daughter sits next to Mother and they play with exaggerated gestures, attempting to cheat one another, fiendishly trying to see each other's hands. Mother puts a foot in Daughter's face to keep her from peeking, they snicker mockingly at each other while throwing down cards, Daughter sobs angrily at Mother, who cackles, Daughter gives Mother a sinister smile and she chortles, and so forth. This card game is as mad as the tea party in *Alice in Wonderland;* it is also highly reminiscent of commedia dell'arte, with its hyperbolic and grotesque gestures and droll one-upmanship.

A romantic ballad plays: it is Billie Holiday singing "Solitude." Sinister music slowly drowns out the ballad. To explain this scene, Flora Süssekind writes that electronic sounds serve to render the self-referential subject invisible, making possible, "for example, the simultaneous reception of various sounds, such as the quiet voice of Billie Holiday . . ." (Süssekind 1992, 45).

An angel approaches Mother with a goblet, his face peeking out from under a cloak, another false head above him. The two-headed angel then carries in a dummy with an arrow in its heart. Daughter returns and, like an adolescent, smokes a cigarette and puts on makeup. Mother pantomimes Daughter smoking, she looks in a mirror and sees Daughter's face, Mother and Daughter stare at each other, they slowly come together and mirror each other's gestures, hands up to face, touching lips, hands down to hips.

Mother, that is, Fernanda Montenegro, speaks in her own voice:

> No, it's not that I haven't found everything, it's not that I haven't faced everything, recognized it, attached importance, it's not that I haven't recognized everything up till now, I have recognized everything up till now, it's not that I haven't come up with some lovely creations, for example, it's not that I haven't found beauty, I'm a human being after all, in new scientific and technological discoveries, in new mathematical theorems, in new manifestations of life and death, here or somewhere else, I think. Thank you.

This, again, is the monologic voice speaking through Mother. It is a pause in the action in which the monologic self refers to what has transpired on the stage to this point ("I've found everything up to now recognizable") and searches for values ("the new discoveries"). But the voice is halting, unsure; the postmodernist is not about to give anything away. Usually, however, the sounds the actors make do not conform to naturalistic speech patterns:

> It should not be surprising, then, that a major portion of the voiceovers alternate strangely, that a certain multilinguistic mode at times takes hold of the dialogue; that other types of noises produced by the body (tongue clicking, heavy breathing, sobbing), or voice play (such as Fernanda Montenegro's mimicking of Woody Woodpecker's cartoon laughter . . . in *The Flash & Crash Days*) frequently replace conventional speech and well-enunciated voices. (Süssekind 1992, 46)

Mother turns over the dummy, gasps, finds a note, reads, "to go or not to go, that is now the quest . . .", collapses, and dies. Daughter appears suddenly with an arrow through her neck, transferred from the dummy, she sits down in a chair, falls to the stage, kneels, tries to light the candles on the birthday cake, attempts to revive Mother, the angels open a door revealing a painting of a giant eye, Daughter leaps off the stage, climbs back up, staggers toward the eye, the angels reappear as blind men, with dark glasses and canes, an angel smashes the eye with his cane, Daughter enters the space where the eye was placed, the angels close the door behind her. A heart is pulled up by a rope, an angel pulls another heart from his jacket, Daughter screams behind the door, the angels approach Mother and place a heart in her breast, she resuscitates, rises, they place the conical hat on her head, triumphal music plays, the blind angels lead Mother across the stage, Mother pulls the angels downstage and pushes them off, wipes her hands, pulls out cards, staggers toward Daughter who is trapped behind a scrim, throws cards into the air. Daughter behind the scrim pantomimes Mother's movements, music fades, and lights dim. There is a curtain call to a standing ovation. Gerald Thomas comes onstage to thunderous applause. He summons Daniela Thomas and they both bow.

The reader can imagine the perplexity of some critics and audience members: nonsense to the *n*th degree, visual splendor in the service of emptiness, the author staging his own incomprehensible and irrelevant psychological problems. Some examples:

> Surely director Gerald Thomas could have found some more subtle image to represent a daughter's hostility toward her mother than to have the younger woman strangle the older one; then stab her, rip out her heart and later eat it. . . . Except to proclaim that some mothers and daughters don't get along, it's unclear what "The Flash & Crash Days" is about, other than poses, stage smoke and strangeness . . . in this aggressively obscure piece. (Jacobson 1992)[32]

According to an unsigned review in the magazine *Veja* (1991, "Ginástica," 105), the spectator has to "endure a ruthlessly incomprehensible spectacle. There's not a thing to make sense out of. . . ." Brazil's most distinguished critic, Brazilian Academy of Letters member Sábato Magaldi, who has had the highest praise for many of Thomas's previous productions, writes that, "Gerald Thomas's most recent and personal production left me unsatisfied, in an area where the creator should not be careless; that is, literary concerns should be the foundation of any artistic endeavor: *The Flash & Crash Days,* in spite of the *encenador*'s undeniable talent, sinks into the realm of subliterature" (Magaldi 1992, "Onde está o teatro," 8).

Not all critics scorned the production: "It is a simpler, tighter, more comprehensible play. To say that it is comprehensible may be an exaggeration. One cannot understand everything. But at least one can follow the action on stage—in the same way we follow a dance program with our eyes, or listen to a musical composition" (Coelho 1991, E12).

What Coelho is referring to here are the aesthetic features of the production, the "old" and the "new" forms in the title of his piece—"the struggle between the old and the new"—relate to the struggle to push forward the limits of theater. To "understand" *Flash & Crash,* one must begin with an examination of stagecraft: set design, lights, and sound effects. In regard to the latter, Flora Süssekind discusses Thomas's frequent use of voiceovers in different vocal registers, as well as clocks ticking and heartbeats, "constituting a true amplification—through sound—of the performing space . . ." (Süssekind 1992, 44). Like a jazz musician, or a samba musician, which he is, Thomas does not attempt to create a harmonious and totally integrated work of art.[33] Rather, he plays the elements off each other in audiovisual syncopation, his vocal intromissions create dissonance, they push against the stage action as much as move it forward. They establish a dialogue with what the audience sees on the stage, or perhaps one could express it in terms of a postmodernist monologic intention, so that once again the subject of the production becomes the artist himself.

Gerald Thomas says this about what he is trying to communicate:

> My plays are my own personal problem, and my problem above and beyond that personal problem is to turn both into metaphors that audiences in general can grasp, through fantasy, through a code of seduction. Because nightmarish images aren't always that seductive. [It is] a Machiavellian process by which you turn something terrible into something visually beautiful, into a dream, a fantasy, in which the audience can be included. . . . ("Gerald Thomas, eis a questâo")

*Flash & Crash Days,* then, is clearly intended as a nightmare. The dream, as the director's comment indicates, is designed to include the audience, which gives it a collective form. It may, therefore, be useful to examine the dream structure with the psychoanalyst's tools. Jungian analysis, in particular, provides guidelines that apply to dreams, as well as to artistic expression and mythology.

Carl Jung posited the existence of a collective unconscious that generates a set of symbolic images known as archetypes, which take human form in dreams and represent aspects of the dreamer's personality or psyche. Jung defined many of the archetypes as gender-specific, the "anima," for example, representing supposedly female qualities and the "animus" male characteristics. Although his theories have been attacked in recent years for alleged gender stereotyping, it is important to remember that what he was aiming at was a balance of the male and the female in each individual. The man, he believed, must counterbalance his masculine traits with the feminine, and the woman must reconcile her femaleness with the male in her. Most important, the end result of this male–female reconciliation—Jung called this process "individuation"—is the mature individual in contact with all aspects of his or her psyche, including both the conscious and unconscious realms.

The narrator at the beginning of *Flash & Crash* has stated that he saw himself transformed into a woman (the Mother character). The anima symbol, in Jung's system, is the man's inner woman, and in dreams represents the dreamer's mother, but not necessarily his "real" mother; rather, it is the internal mother, who emerges from the depths of the collective unconscious and enters the individual dreamer's psyche. So who is Mother in *Flash & Crash Days*? The *encenador*'s mother? The Daughter's? The answer is both. She is the author's anima mother, but for Daughter she represents another archetype, the "shadow," which appears as the same sex of the dreamer and symbolizes aspects of the psyche which have not been integrated, which are repressed and surface only in dreams (or in artistic expression). The mother's murderous impulses, particularly, are a shadow projection of Daughter's own repressed desires. Who, then, is Daughter? For the dreamer she represents another anima figure, a different stage, as it were, of the female component of his unconscious. And she is herself a dreamer, and what she dreams is the dance macabre with her own homicidal passions. The angels are her male animus figures, who alternately rescue and destroy her. Their wings represent the search for transcendence, for growth, but their maleness pins her to the earth. The anima, however, is the central archetype in the play.

The anima, according to Jung, is manifested at different levels and in varying stages of development. It is the mother to the infant, but not necessarily the nurturer; it may embody the forces impeding development, maintaining the individual in an eternal infantile state. Daughter is such an anima: puerile, impetuous, all id—to borrow here from Freud—with no superego. Daughter is turned inward away from the world, as evidenced by her fetal positions and especially by her onanism. And when she projects sexuality outward it is only Mother she sees, the infant's immediate source of gratification. The infantile anima tries to grow into adolescence, as when Daughter attempts to smoke a cigarette and put on makeup. The anima, according to Jung, may be a menacing, even murderous figure. Daughter eats Mother's heart, greedily devouring her love and yet annihilating the obstacle to her growth. She delights in smearing herself with the blood, as an infant may play with mud or feces. Daughter cannibalizes her enemy to gain her power.[34] The removal of the heart, which is then devoured, reminds one as well of Aztec sacrifice of captured enemy warriors.

The mother anima may be at times a death demon; Mother is annihilated and she annihilates, piercing with the arrow, pulling off Daughter's head, and so forth. Mother and Daughter are manifestations of the same anima; they repeat each other's actions, they are mirror images. As the play closes, Daughter, dream-like behind a scrim, pantomimes Mother's movements. In the end they have merged, each a dream image of the other.

What also lends archetypal stature to the duo is their namelessness; they are merely Mother and Daughter. Indeed, the latter mumbles at one point that she has no name. Nor do the actors personalize them in the Stanislavskian tradition. Gerald Thomas states:

> I imagine that my theater must be very hard for actors with linear, Stanislavskian training. Because I struggle with each scene. I'm not concerned about stories that start at the beginning and conclude at the

> end, that have an Aristotelian middle. Every moment must contain a truth, which counts only for the actor, which can be contrary to the truth that I am relating in the production. Now, how the actor will fill that in with a metaphor, realistically, matters little to me. Each one makes up his own little story and it's his job to make it come alive on stage. ("Gerald Thomas, eis a questâo")

Another Jungian archetype present in *Flash & Crash Days* is the mandala, a circular symbol in dreams representing the "self," the central core of the psyche, the dreamer's inner refuge. In mythology, the mandala appears in many pictorial forms: the round table of Camelot, the sacred hoop of Amerindian civilization, the Buddhist symbol of the universe, and so forth. Gerald Thomas projects the mandala of his dream through lighting, particularly in the circular patterns that frequently cover the stage and that isolate characters, as if they had withdrawn into the refuge of their psyche's innermost self.

Not everyone would agree with psychoanalytic interpretations of *Flash & Crash*. Marcelo Coelho writes that, "Thomas's intentions are not psychological-Freudian. . . ." Rather, the critic believes, more than a conflict between mother and daughter, "we have a conflict between the old and the new. Between the avant-garde and tradition . . ." (Coelho 1991, E12). I agree with the latter part of Coelho's observation; it is a metatheatrical work about art and its evolving nature. But because the piece operates on so many levels, one cannot cancel out the psychological dimension. And at least one participant perceives a Jungian archetypal element in the production: "A reader of the psychologist Jung, Fernanda sees in the plays 'a pulsation of archaic entities' " (Garcia Lima 1992).

The dream of the *encenador* is expressed through the oneiric quality of his stagecraft: the liberal use of scrims and smoke which blur actors and objects; electronic distortion of voices and music; the non-naturalistic movement and choreography; constant metamorphosis—the arrow transferred from the dummy to Daughter; the disembodied voice which shapes the action and its circular logic; timelessness or breakdown of linear time—medieval costumes/flashlights/modernist cityscape; and most of all the realms of the unconscious in which dreams are played out.

> Gerald Thomas frequently generates temporal variance by means of a marked tension between the verb tenses utilized and a mutual interference between past and present and, in general, between narration in the

> past and emphasis on the present time of the staging. This is what one observes in *The Flash & Crash Days,* where the plot is presented in the past (and, therefore, one is aware that what is narrated by the self-declared dead man's recorded voice has already taken place), and yet the conflicts between the narrator's two female replicants are so immediate that they visually take the place of his speech and take the shape of a continuous and indefinite present, in an increasingly silent scene, an endless card game (somewhat reminiscent, because of the costumes, to the chess game in Ingmar Bergman's *The Seventh Seal*)—a present that takes control. (Süssekind 1992, 47)

In the context of Brazilian theater, Süssekind's analysis of the unseen narrator—who shapes the onstage action—and of the breakdown of the linear structure of time, clearly bring to mind the works of dramatist Nelson Rodrigues, who also made liberal use of such narrators and abolished linear time. One may say, therefore, that *Flash & Crash* is Nelson Rodrigues without words.

Both make use of expressionist acting styles and distortion to produce shock. The voiceovers which Rodrigues introduced to the Brazilian stage in *Vestido de noiva* (*Wedding Gown*) and *Toda nudez será castigada* (*All Nakedness Will Be Punished*) are used extravagantly by Thomas; Rodrigues's *Nakedness* begins with and its structure is informed by the protagonist Geni's voice from beyond the tomb, while *Flash & Crash* is informed by a similar voice. The cinematic techniques and the oneiric atmosphere which were Rodrigues innovations are second nature to Thomas. They have both practiced, in short, a pure theater, a total theater,[35] without the spatial and temporal constraints of realism, a theater unconcerned with verisimilitude and which appeals to imagination and fantasy.

All of these dream-like effects bring to mind in particular Nelson Rodrigues's plays *Wedding Gown* and *Family Album* (*Álbum de família*), which shattered the facade of rationalism—and theatrical naturalism—and laid bare the secret realm of unconscious desire. His plays probed the forbidden and the perverse, turned sexual repression on its head, and exposed the incestuous family coil, with its often brutal, even murderous consequences. Nelson Rodrigues was a Brazilian expressionist, a Strindberg or an O'Neill. His plays are filled with acute passions and grotesque hyperbole, bordering on the melodramatic, on the one hand, and turning the unconscious inside out, on the other. Nelson Rodrigues does all of this using both a complex verbal structure and cinematic stage directions.

Gerald Thomas, in *Flash & Crash,* presents the same themes and produces similar effects in his own unique visual style. Once again, the modernist and the postmodernist converge: Rodrigues's trademark, murderous and incestuous family ties, are pushed to the limit and exploded in Thomas's production; both Rodrigues and Thomas parody the Brazilian genre known as *comédia de costumes,* or comedy of manners, based usually on the trials and tribulations of family relationships; characters in Rodrigues's plays speak from the deepest recesses of the unconscious, while Thomas's characters act directly out of those recesses when Daughter devours Mother's heart and the latter beheads the former. Nelson Rodrigues and the *encenador* are concerned with a fundamental problem of guilt and repression; in Thomas's words: "My theater is done entirely in secret as if some great repressor were to appear there and order the lights turned on and catch everyone red-handed. My theater is a theater of guilt, as if some kind of guilt surrounded the actors' performance" ("Gerald Thomas, eis a questâo"). But neither Thomas nor Rodrigues have anything to do with what Robert Brustein defines as theater of guilt, whose characters "preserve their own innocence through being victimized by others" and whose themes are inspirational and morally elevated (Brustein 1995, 15). Although the issue here is American playwriting, it applies as well to Brazil, which has witnessed its own sacrifice of art on the stage of noble causes. The converse of theater of guilt, according to Brustein, is "to penetrate the puzzles of the human heart: to honor complexity, appreciate mystery, expose secrets, invade dreams" (Brustein 1995, 15). And that is precisely what Gerald Thomas and Nelson Rodrigues attempt.

Both Nelson Rodrigues and Gerald Thomas have generated heated controversy, both have had remarkable successes and dismal failures. Does Gerald Thomas pay homage to Rodrigues or does he deconstruct the latter's work? Both perhaps, but if there is deconstruction it is affectionate, and relates not to theme or style but to the structure of the verbal text. However visual and cinematic Rodrigues's plays may be, he himself was a successful journalist and his texts reflect his journalistic experience. Gerald Thomas, on the other hand, rails against the notion of a theatrical verbal text: "Why does theater have to be verbal? Who came up with the idiotic notion that theater is text? Newspapers are text. Theater is everything" ("Gerald Thomas, eis a questâo"). Nelson Rodrigues would have agreed that theater is everything; he would not have accepted the view, however, that theater is not fundamentally verbal text.

Nelson Rodrigues brought into his plays material he had gathered as a crime reporter. Gerald Thomas also uses external reality as a subtext for *Flash & Crash Days*. The obvious psychological level of the mother/daughter relationship, the "psychic combat of eroticism and violence" (Mitchell 1992), the rites of birth/death/renewal, and the daughter's attempt to break the mother's hold and forge her own identity are derived in part from the relationship of the real-life mother–daughter actress team. As Robert Myers (1992) reports in his *New York Times* piece, the play is a "domestic drama that draws on the real-life mother–daughter relationship of Miss Montenegro and Fernanda Torres." He quotes Fernanda fille's take on the relationship as a source: " 'But my mother is also a monster to me . . . and Gerald understood that and used it. The play between being a monster and a real person is what the work is about.' " The word "monster" in English, however, does not convey all of the meanings of *monstro* in Portuguese, which in the full form Ms. Torres alludes to, *monstro sagrado,* refers to the diva, to the mythical status of her mother as an actress. But she also points to the mother–daughter aspect of their relationship: "Miss Torres . . . refers to the play as a kind of Oedipal boxing match (with the archangels as face-patting corner men)." The mother, Fernanda Montenegro, also quoted in Myers's article, confirms her daughter's observation about the dual nature (mother–daughter/legendary actress–aspiring actress) of the rivalry: "Miss Montenegro, who has never performed before in the United States, said: 'This isn't just any mother and any daughter. People outside Brazil could even ignore that, but we know it, and so for us it's also a domestic game.' "

However significant Thomas's sources in "real life," his theater derives in the main from art itself. The Wagnerian element, present in so much of Thomas's work, is as much a point of departure as the mother–daughter relationship and, indeed, as the *encenador*'s own internal psychic sources. *Flash & Crash* is based loosely on the final part of Wagner's "Ring" tetralogy, *Götterdämmerung,* or "The Twilight of the Gods." Wagner is present in the recorded music, with orchestral selections also from the "Ring" cycle, particularly in the final climactic moments. Mother's role, as initially conceived, is manifest in the title Thomas originally contemplated for the production: *A imolação de Brunhilde*. As Wagner's Brunhilde is surrounded by the ring of fire that would immolate her, so too, is Mother surrounded by the sinister forces that would destroy her: the fiery volcano, the daughter's murderous designs. There is no Siegfried to rescue Mother, however, only the sinister archangels, who are both tormentors and rescuers.[36] The transcendent hero figure undergoes deconstruction in postmodernist manner, becoming ambiguous, corrupted. The clash between the two Fernandas, however, maintains a Wagnerian mythic quality as a battle of the gods (or goddesses, as it were). But these are not the gods of Valhalla, and given Gerald Thomas's penchant for multilevel aesthetic puns we may be witnessing a battle between mythical goddesses of the acting world in a kind of Wagnerian telenovela. Myth involves ritual, in this case, because the murderous rites are repeated over and over yet at the end both Mother and Daughter have survived, their battle destined to continue eternally. Antonio Gonçalves Filho interprets the production as a Wagnerian parody, assigning roles to the characters in a way that differs somewhat from my analysis: Brunhilde is Daughter, who masturbates instead of redeeming gods and men. Mother is a cross between Wotan (Zeus) and his wife Fricka (Gonçalves Filho 1992, "Satiriza," E3). Again, in their role as divinities, one is reminded that the two Fernandas are also "goddesses" of stage and screen.

Mythical elements in the production, including Wagner's Nordic sources, are more than scattered references; they inform the very structure of the play. The same could be said of many of Nelson Rodrigues's works. Indeed, Sábato Magaldi, in his four-volume edition of Rodrigues's plays, subtitles volume two as *Peças míticas*. Myths take place outside of time, *in illo tempore,* and so, too, does *Flash & Crash* suspend linear time. The interminable altercations between the two protagonists mirror the clash of titans, the warring of the gods in universal origin myths, whether Greco-Roman, Norse, Amerindian, or Afro-Brazilian. The two archangels reinforce the mythological space inhabited by the protagonists in Thomas's production. The supernatural dimension of myth extends to fairy tales and legends, which proliferate, directly or indirectly, in *Flash & Crash*. In fairy tales the protagonist must overcome almost impossible obstacles, trials and tribulations, to fulfill a quest. Daughter's obstacles are supplied by Mother. Daughter must even overcome mutilation and death. Her quest? To grow and develop by freeing herself from the dragon, her enemy—Mother—and by destroying her. Does she succeed? Her quest remains unresolved by the end of the production, for *Flash & Crash* is meta-myth, meta-fairy tale, meta-legend, a layering of signs.

Brazilian legends based mostly on Amerindian sources constitute the initial layer of signs (children growing up in Brazil, including Gerald Thomas, are immersed in these legends). Following are a few examples of legends involving female characters who possess many of the traits of Mother and Daughter and which Mário de Andrade also utilizes in his seminal *modernista* work, *Macunaíma.* The Iara, or *mãe d'agua* ("mother of the water"), is a kind of siren who lures the hero Macunaíma into a pool, where she mutilates him. The evil serpent Maria Caninana, from a tale known as "Cobra Norato," poison's the breast of Macunaíma's lover Ci and kills their child. The Icamiabas, or Amazons, are warrior women who aid Macunaíma on his quest. There is the Caipora, or Caapora, a monster of the forest, which in some forms of the legend takes female form as Ceiuci, a gluttonous old woman who pursues and attempts to devour Macunaíma. Another traditional figure in Brazilian legend is the *mula-sem-cabeça* (headless mule); it is the fate of young women of bad conduct is to become *mulas-sem-cabeça.* A theme that runs through all these legends, and by extension informs both *Macunaíma* and *Flash & Crash,* is mutilation. Mother at times takes on the form of Ceiuci in her ruthless pursuit of Daughter, like the evil serpent Maria Caninana she poisons her child, disobedient Daughter becomes a *mula-sem-cabeça* after her beheading, the two protagonists are Iaras luring each other to destruction, and both are Icamiabas, warrior women in a continual state of battle.

Other legendary sources inscribed in the production are much more familiar to non-Brazilian readers. Mother and Daughter are tricksters who fall prey to each other and themselves; they are shape changers; they are banshees; Daughter takes on at times a sylph-like persona. Western myths and fairy tales are easily accessible here: in addition to the Nordics myths such as Brunhilde and Siegfried recreated by Wagner, one thinks of Snow White and the cruel queen who attempts to murder her, Cinderella and the wicked stepmother. The latter two stories, which have been recycled by Disney, are especially pertinent here because Gerald Thomas, like other postmodern artists, is fond of mixing pop references into his cultural melange.

Popular cinematic influences represent yet another postmodernist recycling of signs in the production. There are multiple references to horror movies. Mother in her fright wig is the bride of Frankenstein; the blood-smeared Daughter is a vampire; at other times she is the young daughter possessed by the devil in *The Exorcist;* the extreme gore and the sinister figures from the beyond are reminiscent of the work of Clive Barker; the "Nightmare on Elm Street" series, with its continual dream-state metamorphosis, may have been an inspiration; there is a parodic allusion to the spate of slasher films spewed out by Hollywood in recent years (Fernanda Torres herself compares her role to that of Jason in the "Friday the 13th" series); Murnau's 1922 expressionist *Nosferatu*—as well as Herzog's more recent version starring Klaus Kinski—and the 1919 *Cabinet of Dr. Caligari* may have contributed to the visual and acting styles.[37] The grisly humor may owe a debt to the old comic book—and more recently HBO TV–series—"Tales from the Crypt" (Fernanda Montenegro has characterized the production as a grotesque cartoon). The soundtrack and heavy reliance on music are, as I observed earlier, cinematic, as are the voiceovers, the special effects, and the overall privileging of the visual over the verbal. Jumpcutting—through lighting effects and actors' transitions—characterizes the action, in contrast to the theatrical tradition of linear, naturalistic plot design and movement. Scrims, gels, and smoke serve the equivalent functions of camera lens filters.

There are further dimensions of postmodernist multireferentiality in *Flash & Crash,* though that is less obviously an end in itself, contrary to *Mattogrosso:* Myers (1992) puts a spin on the Wagnerian element when he writes that Mother is "dressed like Brünnhilde . . . with an expression straight out of Fritz Lang's cinematic treatment of Wagner's Ring Cycle." Emily Mitchell (1992) states, "Mom is a towering figure straight out of Greek tragedy," probably in reference to Medea, who slays her own children. The scene in which the severed head is tossed about calls to mind myriad beheadings throughout the history of dramatic literature (e.g., *Macbeth, Salome*). Critics have suggested other sources of inspiration: "Stylistically, Mr. Thomas's play suggests a Samuel Beckett clown show washed with Latin American surrealism" (Holden 1992, C15). Although the attribution of "Latin American surrealism" may be facile, a reflexive American response to any artistic phenomenon arriving from south of the border, the Beckett association is on the mark. Beckett is one of Thomas's enduring sources of inspiration, and *Flash & Crash* owes much to *Waiting for Godot,* with its endless, circular, unresolved interplay between the two protagonists. Another Theater of the Absurd association one might make here is with Ionesco, especially his one-act *The Lesson,* in which a professor ritually rapes and murders a student.

To conclude, *Flash & Crash Days* occupies a peculiar position in the annals of the Brazilian stage. It is an esoteric avant-garde exercise, filled with references to many areas of the arts—not always easily ferreted out—a difficult and challenging work of art panned by many critics, who, one would think, would enjoy intellectual and aesthetic playfulness and punning, the way they might enjoy reading Nabokov, another lover of embedded references, or enjoy examining a painting by de Kooning. The plot thickens, the irony deepens, when one considers that

*Flash & Crash* was a huge box-office hit in Brazil, tremendously popular with spectators, who numbered, according to several reports, over 100,000. Not all supported the production, but many were seduced by the powerful images, the black comedy, and the duet macabre performed grandly by mother/Mother and daughter/Daughter. To repeat that art is often one step ahead of the critics is a cliché, but sometimes audiences are, too.

Detractors and supporters of Gerald Thomas are legion in Brazil, considering the abundant attention he has received since he began his theatrical experiments there in 1985. While some critics have seen him as a visionary, others have been lambasting him for a decade. Tânia Brandão criticizes Thomas and other *encenadores* for their extreme individualism and their hegemonic and authoritarian presence. "Because, no matter how much one talks about ensemble, about the artistry of the actor, collaboration of the set designer, contribution of the dramaturge, or about stage direction as collective creation, the axis of and key to the conception of the staging is in the hands of the director, in the case of the most recent tendencies" (Brandão 1992, 30). From this perspective, Gerald Thomas, Bia Lessa, Moacyr Góes, Márcio Vianna, et al are, in spite of their association with theater companies, lone wolves. "The companies that surround them are unstable. Organization similar to the old companies and groups no longer exists; basically, what we now have are 'firms' which lend feasibility to the director's productions, with the group as a mere adjunct" (Brandão 1992, 30).

Brandão further complains that the *encenador* system is harmful to the health of the acting profession: "The bloated figure of the director amounts to the obliteration of the actor." Often, she alleges, they are reduced to puppets. The blocking, the repetition, turn them into robots. Masks and heavy use of makeup deform the actor. In some cases, design, formalism, and abstraction predominate over everything else. "The actor is 'used,' but like a tool; obviously this fact determines the overvaluing of presence and physical expression, in detriment to what was customarily called 'theater of the word' and in the absence of the traditional precepts of acting" (Brandão 1992, 30). She believes that in general "the actors appear on stage as automatons, reduced to the design materials that envelop them" (Brandão 1992, 32). Other critics share her view of the role of the actor in the *encenador* system: "In this system, the actor, like the other objects on stage, is not an interpreter but a sign. He is limited to what he presents, he does not intervene nor does he propose anything that would allow one to identify him with real human beings and, by extension, with the spectator's own experience" (Alves de Lima 1992, 17). Otavio Frias Filho, in his article "O Fim do Teatro," goes even further in his denunciation of the disfigured art of the thespian: "Actors are only permitted to speak on the condition the issues are not articulated: characters parade across the stage, a deaf-mute, lisping, hoarse, mentally defective legion, their mouths taped shut . . . their shouts inaudible beneath the rumble of some machine; in sum, shadows to be seen or sensed, more than heard" (Frias Filho 1992, 56). It is no small irony that Frias Filho became a Thomas collaborator in 1995 when the *encenador* staged his text entitled *Don Juan*. Antunes Filho, director of Grupo Macunaíma, disparages not only the conception of the *encenadores* but their very capacity to direct actors: " 'I see them more as designers than as directors. Anyone who works with lights and visual effects should stick to set or light design . . . In the theater you're only a director if you direct actors, if you have the courage to get to the bottom of the actor's craft. All I see today on stage are effects and much ado about nothing.' "[38]

Johannes Birringer levels the same charges when he surveys the work of postmodernist directors in the United States: "Within this landscape, dramatic characters and emotions are irrelevant." From Robert Wilson's stagings, "the actors have disappeared too." Human figures "are solely defined by their geometric position in the landscape and their stylized, often Oriental movements . . . We become aware of some abstract gestural language that we do not understand, foreign alphabets that are as irreducible as the weight and gravity of the objects that lie on stage" (Birringer 1992, 64).

Otavio Frias Filho also indicates that there are two sides to this issue, at least in the case of Gerald Thomas: "I've heard contradictory reports; [Thomas] delegates a lot of power to the actors, scenes are developed by the actor." On other hand, Frias explains that he has heard reports according to which Thomas prefers that the actor not feel or think, that he be an empty puppet, the *encenador* being concerned only with that which is gestural and external. "I can't say with certainty" ("Gerald Thomas, eis a questâo").

Thomas's actors, in the TV Cultura documentary, strongly reinforce the first part of Frias's observations. They defend Thomas fiercely, maintaining that he does create theater for actors. Beth Coelho, one of Brazil's most accomplished young actresses, played the lead role of Joseph K. in Thomas's Kafka-inspired production entitled *Um processo:*

> I think Gerald's a terrific *encenador*. I've yet to meet anyone who could compare with him. I find him passionate about what he does.

> He's able to produce fabulous, oneiric images on the stage. Usually only film manages to do what he does on the stage. In my case, we were lucky in that our sensibilities were in tune; we always clicked; it's been a very positive experience. ("Gerald Thomas, eis a questâo")

Fernanda Torres discusses his collaborative approach with the actors: "If the scene he's planning isn't worked out in rehearsals it's cut. Everything is resolved by doing." The *encenador,* she maintains, brings embryonic ideas to rehearsal and creates on the basis of what the actors develop. It is a puzzle which Thomas puts together on basis of actors' work. The idea that his actors are a mere appendage of the design concept is absurd, she insists. He writes with his actors in mind. Gerald Thomas's work is entirely based on actors, according to Torres, "as opposed to what many think." Fernanda Montenegro talks about how she was trained in great dramaturgy, but how beneficial it is to be able to work in both currents, to understand when gestural language can replace a "mountain of words." Luiz Damasceno, who played one of the archangels in *Flash & Crash* and who has worked with Thomas for several years, states: "Here things are created by all of us. He writes for his actors. He knows who he's working with. This can only by done in a group." Actress Vera Zimerman says that it is "great to work with him. Everything goes. You let it all hang out, and he shapes it as he goes along." Actor Ludolval Campos, who played the other archangel, explains that often Gerald Thomas's ideas do not work initially and it is the contribution of the actors that eventually makes a scene function. Actress Milena Milena: "What Gerald does is let you express yourself. And this business of changing the show every day. It feels like real life." Actor Domingos Varela: "He's interested in everyone's view. That's the most worthwhile and gratifying thing."

Thomas himself affirms basically the same themes expressed by his actors: "I make a point of maintaining a company. Because I write for certain actors. I know who they are. I know how they react. I know what kind of associations they'll come up with. Luiz Damasceno is a master of commedia dell'arte. I know the way he can deconstruct a scene in three seconds." At another point in the documentary he describes his method of directing actors: "My tendency is to conduct actors musically. I indicate pauses with my hand, my eyebrows. . . ." The documentary illustrates this technique as Beth Coelho prepares Hamlet's "to be or not to be" soliloquy for a Shakespeare reading. She supplies the emotions; Thomas, like an orchestra conductor, directs her with hand gestures, wordlessly, guiding her timing and pitch. It is a very impressive display of a director perfectly in tune with his actor. Finally, Thomas, who often has only the worst to say about the quality of Brazil's theater, has nothing but praise for its actors: "Brazilian actors are the best in the world. Wonderful actors. Their power of fantasy is absolute. They throw themselves totally into everything, they're fearless. And most important, they haven't been ruined by academic training."[39]

The evidence, I believe, belies the critics. Gerald Thomas's actors are not puppets, they are not automatons, they are not robots. They are essential contributors to what he puts on stage and they bring the full force of their craft and imagination to his productions. A final point on this matter: fifty years ago, when Ziembinski introduced expressionism to the Brazilian stage, some critics levelled charges about his direction of actors from the Os Comediantes group which sound surprisingly similar to those made against Gerald Thomas:

> We have frequently heard the criticism . . . that the actors directed by Ziembinski are not natural. [But] if they wanted to copy life, reproducing it exactly as we observe it every day, we could then correctly denounce their anti-naturalism as a flaw. . . . But it so happens that the "Comediantes" are aiming toward something else. On the basis of one of modern theater's most characteristic ideas, that theater is theater and not life, it is inevitable that the actors directed by Ziembinski would create an anti-naturalistic theater, which would theatricalize and not merely reproduce events by deforming—or interpreting—them artistically. To accuse them of being anti-natural is tantamount to criticizing a ballerina for dancing on point. . . . (Almeida Prado 1956, *Apresentação,* 157)

Another criticism of Thomas and the *encenador* phenomenon relates to the issue of the verbal text and playwriting. Margo Milleret states:

> While they can be credited with bringing vitality to the theater and attracting new audiences, they have not offered support to their cohorts, choosing instead to adapt European classics or resuscitate Brazilian masters. Unlike traditional directors who work within the framework of dramatic texts turning the written word into a living story, the *encenadores* become the major creative force, shaping the performance to their will irrespective of the written or implied demands of the text. (Milleret 1995, 123)

The loss of status of the dramatic text in many of Thomas's productions, the death of the word, are a source of much concern for such critics as Tânia Brandão: "It should be noted that these directors, almost unanimously, do not value dramaturgy, they do not stage great texts and some do not even put on plays, they do not consider the text important or they even use conventional texts to search for themes that are alien or distant from them" (Brandâo 1992, 31).

This is another old polemic that has reappeared with regularity over the last six decades. Ziembinski was often accused of taking unwarranted liberties with the dramatic text:

> No one in Brazil had ever seen a director dissect a text the way the visionary Pole did. Under Ziembinski's direction, production values gained equal footing with the text, and on occasion they would submerge the text, a characteristic—viewed unfavorably by many—of experimental theaters in the 1960s and 1970s. His interference in the script and the innovative and idiosyncratic nature of his stagings produced resounding successes and dismal failures. (George 1992, *Stage,* 12)

It should also be recalled that Thomas, even when he is working in his deconstructive mode, has mounted so-called "verbal texts" in their entirety, particularly Beckett. As poet Haroldo de Campos, in his review of *Endgame,* elucidates: "Gerald Thomas, the deconstructor, the kill-joy of texts, pays . . . a consciously faithful tribute to Samuel Beckett's excruciating text" (Campos 1987, "Urinol").

The attempts by the *encenadores* to create their own "texts" has also stirred controversy: "Since Gerald Thomas's productions, for the most part, do not make use of playtexts, but of director's scripts, it seems clear that his work also points to the 'death of the word,' because his scripts are generally thin, irrelevant as dramaturgy, and lack even secondary importance in the dynamics of the staging" (Brandão 1992, 32).

Sábato Magaldi has written the most even-handed critique of Thomas's work and the text controversy:

> When he directs *Quatro Vezes Beckett* and Heiner Müller's *Quartett,* texts by true playwrights, Gerald Thomas stretches his talent as a stage magician, supported by the unfailingly lovely set designs by Daniela Thomas. The Kafka Trilogy is uneven: *O processo,* which is in itself a more dramatic book, is successfully adapted by the *encenador; A*

> *metamorfose,* in which the narrative does not lend itself as well to dramatic conflict, does not achieve the same effectiveness onstage; and *Praga,* an original creation, inspired by Kafka's world, seems like a pale epilogue for a grand spectacle. (Magaldi 1992, "Onde está o teatro," 8-9)

Many critics—including those who have been disparaging—defend Thomas. Mariângela Alves de Lima, as I noted earlier, differentiates Thomas from the other *encenadores* because he maintains a dramatic embryo in his work, "in reference to an exemplary form of theater's dialogic tradition. Electra and Carmen, as myths, are two examples. By means of those citations Thomas's theater delineates cultural references and disassembles them through emphasis and repetition" (Alves de Lima 1992, 18). She refers here to what I have defined as postmodernist multireferentiality and deconstruction. "The irreality of the actors and the images is not self-sufficient because it relies on imaginary constructions that precede the stage productions" (Alves de Lima, 18). This latter point corresponds to what Thomas has called the *mytholungen,* the indefinite layering of western art inscribed in his productions.

Another Thomas advocate is Renato Cohen:

> Some paradigms of paratheatrical production (freedom from narrative, stage production based on *mise-en-scène,* literalism in the use of space and signifiers, use of a text of images) point to production models that provide a keener response for contemporary understanding of phenomena. Incorporating technology, fragmented and subliminal narratives, rational and irrational cognition (use of both cerebral hemispheres), are approaches typical of Robert Wilson, Richard Foreman, seen as well in the stagings of Gerald Thomas.*[F]urthermore,* recovering primordial forms of knowledge, presenting complex signifiers, rather than direct perception . . . recovering the sacred in the relation of the artist to the phenomenon, the universe of paratheatricality suggests a holistic, revitalized stage . . . functioning as a path diverging from institutionalized theater, the last refuge of experimentation free from the corrupt apparatus of the market. (Cohen 1992, 84)

Severino Albuquerque, a Brazilian theater scholar who teaches in the United States, writes that Gerald Thomas provided "the most valuable individual contribution to the revitalization of mise-en-scène in Brazilian theater in the decade of the eighties" (Albuquerque 1992,

"Teatro," 23). Alberto Guzik, drama critic for São Paulo's *Jornal da tarde,* has always taken a keen interest in Thomas's work: "I consider Gerald's work always a work in progress. It's never work that you go to see and in a few months it'll be the same thing. He's an artist who never stops evolving" ("Gerald Thomas, eis a questâo"). The late Yan Michalski wrote in 1986 that he welcomed the return of experimentation and renovation brought to the Rio stage by Gerald Thomas, "the restless artist who obstinately searches for a theatrical path, based on abstract aesthetic stimuli, which would be capable of . . . transmitting to the spectator emotions comparable to those which great musical compositions and the visual arts traditionally supply." Finally, it is my practice in my writings on Brazilian theater to give the last word to the most highly respected and impartial figure in the field, Sábato Magaldi: "[The] current phase in which the *encenador* takes precedence . . . is the consequence of a legitimate theoretical stance, based on the recognition of theater's artistic autonomy, which is not merely a branch of literature" (Magaldi 1992, "Onde está o teatro," 7).

All the controversy Gerald Thomas has stirred up demonstrates that the avant-garde, from modernism to postmodernism, continues to *épater les bourgeois,* at least those members still thin-skinned when it comes to fine art tainted by pop art. "Reviews in Brazilian newspapers today confirmed that Mr. Thomas and Mr. Glass may have achieved the venerable goal of the avant-garde: frightening the bourgeoisie" (Brooke 1989). The *Times* writer, however, does not stop there. I stated above that the reaction of the foreign press sheds considerable light on cross-cultural misunderstanding. The issue of the generation of controversy by Thomas's productions has given the New York press a pretext to indulge in a bit of condescension towards Brazil. The *New York Times,* in Brooke's and other articles, has exaggerated the negative reaction to Gerald Thomas's productions. Other such comments by Brooke include the following: "after the opening night applause died away on Monday, many in the audience seemed unaware that the opera's theme was environmental destruction." According to Brooke, Thomas's production had a "lone defender" among the critics, Marco Veloso.

But it would be more accurate to say that critics were divided, that there were many defenders. The fact is, many supporters of the Brazilian *encenador* see him as a purveyor of fine art, a creator of "countless moments of audio-visual beauty, in which several of the fine arts mix and blend, centuries of painting, light and shadow, surrealism, the Flemish school, dance and movement, music . . ." (Motta 1989). In a somewhat misleading article, “In Brazil, It’s Lonely in the Avant-Garde,” Alan Riding (1988) writes of Thomas that “the fury of some of his critics has helped draw the world of drama into the public spotlight for the first time in almost two decades.” Riding stretches the truth. Thomas’s controversial status and his significant contributions are undeniable, but “the world of drama” never disappeared from the spotlight in Brazil, in spite of military repression, which Riding correctly singles out as a culprit. Teatro Oficina, especially, held theater in the spotlight until 1971; several other companies kept the candle burning in the dark years of the 1970s, particularly Teatro Ipanema, Asdrúbal Trouxe Seu Trombone, and O Pessoal do Víctor; from the late 1970s to the present, Grupo Macunaíma, under the direction of Antunes Filho, has received as much attention nationally as internationally, and has drawn theater into the spotlight in a similar fashion to Gerald Thomas’s productions. Riding goes further: Thomas’s “attacks on recent Brazilian theater had earned him an army of enemies waiting to block the incursion of an experimental director into the cultural mainstream.” Brazil has had many experimental directors attacking the theatrical status quo; Thomas has not been blocked at all but has received financial support from the cultural and financial mainstream. Indeed, it is this support that has, as much as anything, incurred the wrath—and jealousy—of others. Without qualifying the nature of the controversy surrounding Gerald Thomas, without placing it in context—and by selecting a narrow range of critical reactions in the Brazilian press—the *Times* articles suggest an attempt—apparently unconscious—to reinforce the stereotype of a backward and unenlightened Brazil. Such a recondite sphere as the Brazilian “world of drama” breaks into the mainstream U.S. press only when a westernized savior appears to stir up the natives, to bring light into the darkness. Gerald Thomas is no savior; what he does represent is one significant dimension of a broad effort to resurrect theater in Brazil during the postdictatorship period. Thomas’s specific contribution has been to add postmodernist style to a rich theatrical stew, to advance Brazilian stagecraft as Ziembinski, José Celso, and Antunes Filho have done before him. Thomas, along with Antunes Filho, has aided Brazilian theater immeasurably by opening its doors to international influences, and the converse, by bringing Brazilian theater into the international arena.

This, in the end, is the antidote for narrow cultural nationalism, “ethnocentric anarchy, tribal divisions, Balkanized enclaves” (Brustein 1995, 25). Gerald Thomas, for all his recycling of signs and deconstruction of western artistic icons, attempts to rescue those icons rather than to denigrate them. He seeks to blend them with Brazilian art, and in doing so is practicing not the tribalism that all too often masquerades in the United States as cultural diversity, but genuine multiculturism in which "the work of one civilization [is] invariable enriched after borrowing from another" (Brustein 1995, 20). By this means José Celso, Antunes Filho, Gerald Thomas, and other *encenadores* have strengthened the Brazilian stage immeasurably, enhancing its resources, and creating a foundation on which future theater artists can build. For what is at stake here is not merely the quality of the theatrical arts, but their very existence.

## NOTES

[1] This and all other translations from Portuguese in Chapter 1 are mine.

[2] *Tupiniquim* is an often pejorative adjective Brazilians apply to themselves when they emphasize their provincialism or jingoism.

[3] It is easy to see that Brazilian theater needs an infusion from international sources, but it also needs theater that maintains national traditions, from Antunes Filho, who projects those traditions on the world stage and therefore makes the national international, as the magic realists have done in fiction, to "domestic" comedies such as Mauro Rasi's *A cerimônia do adeus*—explored in Chapter 3—which keeps alive the *comédia de costumes* or comedy of manners tradition. Any of these phenomena in isolation presents a picture of incompleteness; together they make up the richness of the Brazilian stage.

[4] Quoted by Brandão 1992, 32, from the *Jornal do Brasil,* 30 May 1991.

[5] On 3 December 1993, Gerald sent me a fax containing an article, entitled "O maior espetáculo da terra," which he published subsequently in São Paulo. He praises effusively José Celso's production entitled *Ham-let,* speaks movingly of Celso's return to full form, and criticizes those who had given up on him. Celso, he writes, "only became passé because he was umbilically tied to a social moment, to an ideological movement that was smothered by and evaporated under the hegemony of cynicism and the commercialization of the underground."

[6] Brazil's *pósmodernismo* refers to post-1945 artistic production, after the 1922 *modernista* movement had run its course.

[7] In the mid-1980s I attended a Chicago performance of two Tom Stoppard pieces, in which the actors performed such audience participation activities as forcing spectators to show identification and poking them with nightsticks. When, during a post-performance discussion period, I objected to what I perceived as abuse of power, my assessment was treated as conservatism. It was, in fact, based on my own experience as a performer.

[8] I have drawn Professor Simmons's definitions from talks he has given on the Lake Forest College campus and on discussions he and I have had on the subject of postmodernism.

[9] Birringer (1991) writes scornfully of Kroker and Cook: "What is also at stake is the extent to which we allow a genuine critique of contemporary culture to thrive on ideological constitutions of the postmodern that move back and forth between apocalyptic, cynical and affirmative diagnoses. Such a critique may implode into purely rhetorical games with cynical affirmations of the kind we meet in . . . *Excremental Culture and Hyper-Aesthetics*" (20).

[10] The original quote is from Mesguich 1977, 119.

[11] *Mattogrosso* was created and directed by Gerald Thomas, with sets by Daniela Thomas, and music by Philip Glass. Supported by the Mesbla corporation—which according to newspaper reports invested nearly $200,000 in the production—it opened in the Municipal Theater on 21 October 1989, in association with the 20th São Paulo Biennial Art Festival. A live orchestra accompanied the São Paulo production; it performed in Rio to recorded music.

[12] Quoted in Fonseca and Jorge 1989.

[13] Quoted in Fernandes, 73, from Ricardo Voltolini, "Desafiando Kafka," in *Jornal da Tarde,* 8 April 1988.

[14] Quoted in Fonseca and Jorge 1989.

[15] One cannot fail to mention that in 1978 Antunes Filho adapted Mário de Andrade's work to the stage and in the process created his own metatheatrical anti-epic. It was one of the most highly regarded productions in the history of the Brazilian stage. Perhaps it, too, might be construed as a chapter in Thomas's "mythology."

[16] Quoted in Fonseca and Jorge 1989.

[17] Mutilation, as the reader will see in my description of *Flash & Crash Days,* is a constant in Thomas's productions. Mesguish's commentary comes to mind here: " 'When the actor of a text enters the scene we have the monstrous division of a text by a body as well as that of a body by a text' " ("Book," 113, quoted in McGlynn 1990, 147).

[18] The Berlin Wall also appears in Thomas's production of *Flying Dutchman,* one of his many stints directing opera: postmodernist multireferentiality includes self-referentiality, reinforcing the view that the true subject of postmodernist performance is the performer—director, designer—himself.

[19] Quoted in Cândido Galvão 1992, 59.

[20] Science fiction films constitute further inscripted signs; in addition to *2001,* other critics see references to the postapocalyptic *Blade Runner*.

[21] This reference, whether Thomas intended it or not, is credible. Bernarda, after the death of her husband, confines her daughters in the closed, oppressive space of their house and forces upon them the sterile rituals of religion and empty, repetitive tasks. One might say that Bernarda Alba has imposed a "defeatist" philosophy on her family.

[22] The woman holds a cigarette and is dressed in fifties style, with a pillbox hat and matching purse and ensemble. She and another figure perform a piece of task-acting as they hand umbrellas to the table-smasher and the oriental character; their movements, again, are synchronized; the bishop moves in between them and blesses the table-smasher and the oriental; they kneel before him and he gives them an apple—this Adam and Eve motif appears in a later production, Thomas's 1993 *Império das Meias-Verdades;* the umbrellas are handed back to the woman in the pillbox hat.

[23] The bishop lipsynches a recorded, electronic voice. The text consists of verbal fragments: "movimento social," "imbecis," "humanísitico," "filosófico, "metafórico," "corpo," "esta ópera," and so forth.

[24] Quoted in Brooke 1989.

[25] Quoted in Brooke 1989.

[26] Jabor is best known for having filmed works by Nelson Rodrigues, which may help to explain his affinity for Thomas's production. I explain below the affinities between the latter and Rodrigues.

[27] I owe a special debt of gratitude to my colleague Richard Fisher for his invaluable insights into Wagner and his relationship to postmodernism. Dr. Fisher is an Associate Professor of German and Chair of the Foreign Language Department at Lake Forest College.

[28] "Movie music isn't merely a convention; it's a habit. Just as nature abhors a vacuum, so the cinema abhors silence, and when there aren't people talking we seem to need music to maintain a human voice, a hum, a rhythm. This may even be the main purpose of the film score: not to tell us what to feel but to reassure us that someone is there, that this vision we've been forced to take over doesn't have to be our responsibility—someone else is looking after it for us" (Griffiths 1995, 87).

[29] Quoted in Cândido Galvão 1992, 59.

[30] Abortionists in Luso culture were once known as "tecedeiras de anjos," or weavers of angels.

[31] The mother in José Celso's production of *O rei da vela* also sucks on a phallic lollipop.

[32] Jacobson reviewed the production when it played in the series called Serious Fun, in New York's Lincoln Center, 1992. After its New York run, *Flash & Crash* went on a European tour.

[33] Thomas participated as a percussionist with Rio's Rocinha Samba School in the 1992 Carnival.

[34] This scene is also a reference to the cannibalism or anthropophagy that informed the staging of *O rei da vela* by José Celso, Gerald Thomas's admired predecessor.

[35] Here again one is reminded of such expressionists of the theater as Max Reinhardt, Erwin Piscator, and Vsevolod Meyerhold, whose approach to design and directing produced a total, unified picture. Polish émigré Zbigniev Ziembinski was very much influenced by their work when he began directing in Brazil in the 1940s. It is no coincidence that his greatest triumph was his production of Nelson Rodrigues's *Vestido de Noiva*.

[36] Antonio Gonçalves Filho maintains that the angels are references to Wim Wenders's cinema.

[37] Bergman's neo-expressionism in such films as *Persona,* in which two personalities merge, as well as *Autumn Sonata,* about a love–hate relationship between mother and her daughter, both actresses, may be another piece of the multireferentiality in *Flash & Crash*.

[38] Quoted in Labaki 1992, 24.

[39] My own experience directing theater students at the University of São Paulo's Escola de Comunicações e Artes corroborates Gerald Thomas's view of Brazilian actors.

CHAPTER 2

# Women Writers and the Quest for Identity

## From Fiction into Playwriting

Women have long been recognized for their contributions to the Brazilian stage as actors; the list of legendary names is extensive.[1] They have played such landmark roles as Alaíde, protagonist of Nelson Rodrigues's 1943 *Vestido de noiva* (*Bridal Gown*), which put theater in step with the *modernista* movement. But as writers, women came late to the Brazilian stage. Their way was paved by poets and especially by fiction writers. And much of women's focus, whether writing fiction or drama, has been the quest for identity.

Latin American literature in general and Brazilian literature in particular include a legacy of quest. Brazilian narrative begins with the epistolary "texts of information," reports from explorers sent to the Portuguese sovereign and filled with hyperbolic depictions of the nascent colony with the intention of luring Portuguese noblemen to set sail on a quest for a mythical utopia. The New World did not turn out to be the El Dorado described in the texts of information, and for the colonized, the Amerindians, and those brought in chains, the Africans slaves, it was an anti-quest, an endless torment. Colonial Brazilian literature, therefore, is born with a quest that fails as it begins.

There are many strains of quest literature in postcolonial Brazil. Jorge Amado's early neorealist novels deal with the quest of destitute *retirantes,* or migrant workers, from Brazil's poorest region, the Northeast, who embark on a search for wealth ending in a struggle for survival. In their quest they join the rush to the centers of export booms, such as the *cacau* region in Bahia state, where they end up as serfs on newly created plantations or prostitutes in the boom towns. Other novels deal with the *retirantes'* quest in the form of migration from the countryside to the growing urban centers, examples being Graciliano Ramos's now classic *Vidas secas* (*Barren Lives*) and the 1977 *A hora da estrela* (*Hour of the Star*), by Clarice Lispector. More recently there is a quest narrative in which the promised land myth is de-urbanized, such as Edla van Steen's *Corações mordidos* (*Village of the Ghost Bells*). I examine the two latter works in detail later.

The quest paradigm is framed by the epic and patriarchal discourse of the Portuguese colonizers. Modern literature is replete with epic quests of bold—and violent—men who tame the rain forest and carve out vast agricultural estates, construct roads, and erect cities. Yet other works parody the epic quest narrative and its colonial underpinnings. Mário de Andrade's 1928 *Macunaíma carnivalizes*—to use Bakhtin's term—epic patriarchal quest with an Indian hero whose modus operandi is flight from danger and whose quest takes him from the rain forest to the great urban metropolis, which he tries to tame with guile and with tribal magic arts. The one epic bellicose figure in *Macunaíma* is the warrior-woman Ci. In epic patriarchal narrative per se, woman's quest leads her to kitchen and bed, even when she is immensely resourceful and appealing, such as Gabriela from Jorge Amado's eponymous novel.

There has developed slowly over the course of this century a body of quest literature written by women, whose main concern has been the search for identity. The pioneers in Brazil, writing in the first half of this century, attempted to overturn romantic images of the feminine. Later writers intensified the quest for identity by looking inward. The two most prominent figures from the contemporary period are Lygia Fagundes Telles and Clarice Lispector. In her two-volume book of interviews with Brazilian writers, *Viver e escrever,* Edla van Steen asks Lygia Fagundes Telles about her experiences as a woman writer. Her response is:

> It is well to remember that the hardships women in our society had to endure in order to seek fulfillment in this career were much greater than today, for obvious reasons: there was a frightening degree of vitriolic suspicion directed at those who were so bold as to challenge the status quo. And the sarcasm was all the greater if the challenge came from a pretty woman, since there was also a bias against beauty, a greater trust in ugly women . . . Our early writers were the brave ones, women damned for tearing off their corsets and standing, bosom thrust out, on the front line. Everything is so much simpler now, the suspicion has slowly faded. Even the old irony has flagged. Nevertheless, a cer-

> tain critic emphasized the narcissism of Brazilian women writers, overly concerned with the 'self.' With their own navels. But he failed to go back to our historical roots and discover the reason for that monologic, intimist tendency. . . . Closed in behind locked doors, not even a crack left open through which she might express herself. But now she's finding herself, like a child who, before becoming interested in things around her, discovers her own body . . . Woman discovering herself: what other world would she show if not her own? (van Steen 1981, 92)[2]

Clarice Lispector has achieved a kind of cult status beyond Brazil's borders for her profound and often anguished meditations on the inner lives of her female characters. *A hora da estrela,* her last work, departs from her previous fiction in that the meditations are those of a male narrator, while the female protagonist is viewed externally. Published in 1977, and adapted to the cinema in the 1980s, *Hora* represents a case of failed quest, in both social and spiritual terms. Lispector's narrative takes up the migration/utopia myth and focuses it through complex narrative filters. The work presents an anti-utopian vision of urban space and can be placed in the tradition of narratives dealing with migration between the Northeast and the urban center. *Hour of the Star* counterpoises locales at the beginning and end of the protagonist Macabéa's quest: the Northeastern Alagoas she has left behind and Rio de Janeiro, the "urban monster," where she has come to fulfill not only a socioeconomic quest but implicitly to gain a new sense of self. Carol P. Christ, in her book *Deep Diving and Surfacing: Women Writers on Spiritual Quest,* describes a fictional character's quest which "begins in nothingness" (Christ 1980, 55). Macabéa's quest, ironically, begins and ends in nothingness; it is not oriented by what Christ calls "the energies of life, death, and regeneration" (Christ 1980, 10). Macabéa comes from the "primitive" Northeast, yet carries with her to Rio no ritual patterns by which to live; her rite of initiation in the impersonal urban space is bereft of the sacred. In writing about Lispector's *A paixão segundo G.H.* (*The Passion According to G.H.*), Daphne Patai states, "the pattern of an initiation rite is followed principally in the first two stages: separation and the initiation proper, which involves an ordeal" (Patai 1983, 81). Macabéa's quest takes on the outward form of ritual passage and initiation: she is separated from her homeland, experiences ordeal in Rio, but socioeconomic barriers and urban chaos obviate integration into a new society. Failed quest becomes failed ritual passage. Sense of place becomes alienation from the urban object of quest and nostalgia for the Alagoas left behind. There is only a circular ritual leading nowhere, to an impersonal death on a Rio street. If there are no epic dimensions to her quest, no conquering of physical space, is there a spiritual quest? Yes; the irony is that it belongs not to Macabéa but to Rodrigo S.M. Relato, the male voice who narrates her trajectory. Nelly Novaes Coelho observes the "growing bias on the part of first-person male narrators, a tendency which . . . reveals clearly that the quest concerns the human being, no longer something specifically 'feminine' or 'masculine'" (Novaes Coelho 1977, 38).

Could there be something more going on in *A hora da estrela* beyond what Novaes Coelho's remarks would suggest? I would posit that Clarice Lispector's use of the male narrator carnivalizes patriarchal literary discourse: the passive woman on a failed quest is fodder for the narrator's "spiritual" quest; he reproduces the tradition of the Northeastern novel which denies for the characters of the poorer classes self-reflexivity and interior life. One need only recall that in Graciliano Ramos's classic novel *Vidas secas* (*Barren Lives*) the most "human" character is the dog Baléia. Like *Macunaíma, Hour of the Star* is a mock quest, both in epic and spiritual terms. Marta Peixoto states the following: "Starting with her earliest fiction, Lispector turns an acute gaze to the exercise of personal power, to the push and pull of the strong and the weak and particularly to the dynamics of victimization. Mostly but not always the victims are female . . . Through these trials the victims conduct their quest for meaning with the narrator's discreet mediation" (Peixoto 1987, 84).

Yet something more subversive is going on in Lispector's novelette: a parody of the ways in which the privileged class feeds off the dominated class. Macabéa suffers so that the narrator may wander about in his own metaphysical musings. The narrator dwells on Macabéa's ugliness, on her bodily odors, on her total lack of charm and social graces, turning her into a kind of anti-Gabriela. When he is through with her, he crushes her like a bug under the wheels of an automobile. In Christ's words: "Inability to find an image of self makes women especially vulnerable to . . . 'the emptiness, formlessness, and chaos at the center of human consciousness'" (Christ 1980, 56).[3] This is the experience of *A hora da estrela*'s protagonist. The cruel irony of the names the narrator ascribes to her sums all of this up: Macabéa refers symbolically to biblical revolt—she is unreligious and passive—and her nickname, "Maca" or "Stretcher," suggests the sickliness of a hospital patient.

To conclude, *A hora da estrela* casts doubt on the possibility of fulfilling utopian, spiritual, and identity quests, given the social milieu of modern Brazil. In Clarice Lispector's short novel, Judith Christ's triad—life, death, regeneration—is incomplete. The work raises disturbing questions about the nature and objectives of the quest motif and the efficacy of the utopian myth. Macabéa travels from Alagoas in the north to Rio in the south, but this is a travesty of an epic voyage, and the spiritual quest is the male narrator's, not hers. Is the quest impossible? Perhaps not, but it is clear that the novel suggests the necessity of changing social conditions to complete the quest.

The last decades have seen a proliferation of women's writing in Brazil. The tendencies, styles, and themes they represent are too numerous to analyze here. In addition to several authors already cited, among today's most distinguished fiction writers one could mention Ana Maria Martins, Judith Grossman, Julieta de Godoy Ladeira, Marcia Denser, Nélida Piñon, and Lya Luft. One should add to the list those women who double as playwrights and fiction writers, especially Maria Adelaide Amaral and Edla van Steen (both are discussed in this chapter). Not all critics see the work of these women as independent, on an equal footing with men's fiction. Professor Judith Bisset, in her MMLA paper "A Space in the Wilderness" (1993), maintains that, "the Brazilian woman belongs to a world in which social structures limit her as a woman and as a writer." Bisset analyzes Nélida Piñon's novel *A república dos sonhos* (*The Republic of Dreams*), according to a model developed by cultural anthropologists Shirley and Edwin Ardener, which describes women as a muted group who occupy a space partially within the dominant male sphere and partly without. This latter space is the "wild zone," where women speak outside the realm of male consciousness, although there is no such thing as writing totally outside the dominant male structure. A corollary is that woman's silence is a form of social protection. Transgression of this code of silence can lead to ostracism and punishment. Professor Bisset applies the model to homologize Piñon's *The Republic of Dreams,* that is, to analyze the family dynamics and gender relations of the generations of a storytelling family at the center of the novel.

At the same time, Brazilian women writers themselves have, more individually than collectively, their own view of the issues examined above, so let them, rather than we, the critics, have the last word. When asked in a recent interview what it means to be a woman writer, Ana Maria Martins responded:

> I want to make it clear that in my opinion literature has no sex. There's good literature and bad literature. It's obvious that a woman—whether

> a writer, a painter, or a professional in some other area—acts and feels like a woman, and in the act of creating she does not shed her feminine condition . . . On the other hand, there are woman writers who create texts the reader cannot identify as masculine or feminine. . . . Regarding the woman writer's space and working conditions, I believe the difficulties are the same as those of any woman who moves in professional circles. That is, too many responsibilities—the result of unfair division of labor within the home—the struggle to prove she is just as capable or more so, the struggle against vestiges of deep-seated and often disguised prejudice. (Martins 1990, 60)

And finally, Edla van Steen, in her introduction to her anthology of women's stories, asks:

> Why an anthology made up exclusively of women's stories? The idea seems at first glance to have little justification, especially since I believe that working artists have no sex: they are artists, period. However, women, both quantitatively and qualitatively, are occupying an ever more distinguished place in our literature. This anthology intends, therefore, to display, to signal the richness of their production. (van Steen 1981, 5)

Have women dramatists achieved the same "richness of production"? Do they continue to focus on the quest for identity? Are they as reluctant as fiction writers to embrace what in the United States might be considered a more clearly feminist stance? These are some of the questions that I address next.

Playwriting, even for men, began late in Brazil. Nelson Rodrigues made a promising start in the 1940s, other dramatists such as Jorge Andrade and Dias Gomes hit their stride in the 1950s, and in the 1960s Brazilian dramaturgy mushroomed with the engagé plays of such writers as Gianfrancesco Guarnieri, Oduvaldo Vianna Filho, and Plínio Marcos. Women playwrights became the equals of their male counterparts in the momentous year of 1969.

In her book *Um teatro da mulher* (1992), Elza Cunha de Vincenzo explains that the 1950s and 60s saw the slow emergence of women playwrights in Brazil. In 1954 distinguished novelist Rachel de Queiroz wrote *Lampião,* about a famous bandit from her native region in the Northeast of Brazil, and in 1960 she produced *Beata Maria do Egito* (*Saint Mary of Egypt*). Sábato Magaldi believed she had a genuine gift for playwriting—all she needed was more experience in stagecraft—and encouraged her to continue. However, as he wrote in 1962, "unsuccessful in her two forays into the theater, without the welcoming embrace of critics or audiences, Rachel de Queiroz insists she will never again write for the stage" (Magaldi, *Panorama,* 248). She kept her promise and never wrote another play. In 1959 Edy Lima produced the first notable play written by a woman. Her *Farsa da esposa perfeita* (*Farce of the Perfect Wife*) had a successful run with São Paulo's Teatro de Arena, one of Brazil's prominent companies in the 1950s and 1960s. That would, however, be her only triumph.

The two pioneers in the 1960s were Hilda Hilst and Renata Pallotini. Hilst, who has had a long and distinguished career as a poet and fiction writer, wrote eight plays, all between 1967 and 1969. She won an important playwriting award, the Anchieta Prize, for her *O verdugo* (*The Executioner*). She also discontinued her playwriting career, preferring other forms of creative writing. Renata Pallotini was Brazil's first woman playwright to establish a lengthy career, now in its fifth decade. Her first play, *A lâmpada* (*The Lamp*) was written in 1958 and staged in 1960. In 1968 she won the Anchieta Prize for *O escorpião de Numância* (*The Scorpion of Numancia*), inspired by Cervantes's tragedy *The Siege of Numancia.* Like many dramatists writing during the military dictatorship, she used a historical subject as a metaphor for oppression and resistance. Later playwriting prizes included the prestigious Molière. She subsequently wrote two plays based on João Guimarães Rosa's short stories, a strategy later used to spectacular effect by Antunes Filho and his Grupo Macunaíma with their 1985 *Matraga.* She directed some of her work in Escola de Arte Dramática—later combined with the University of São Paulo's Escola de Comunicações e Artes—where she continues to teach. In addition to her playwriting and teaching activities, she has served as the president of the São Paulo State Theater Commission, authored short stories and children's literature, and published an academic treatise on playwriting entitled *Introdução à dramaturgia.*

The year 1969, as I stated earlier, was a milestone for women's theater, when three plays by three women suddenly burst on the scene: Consuelo de Castro's *À flor da pele* (*Thin-Skinned*), Isabel Câmara's *As moças* (*The Girls*), and most important—in the nearly unanimous view of scholars—Leilah Assunção's *Fala baixo senão eu grito* (*Speak Softly or I'll Scream*). Part of a movement called Nova Dramaturgia (New Dramaturgy), their feminine condition was not at first singled out. If anything, it was ignored, even scorned, especially by the ideological patrol.[4]

Cunha de Vincenzo links women's playwriting in the 1960s to the rebirth of feminism on the world and on the Brazilian stage, as well as to a specific moment in the political and social life of Brazil: the AI5, the acronym for the Institutional Act Number Five (December 1968), the military declaration of state of siege and the beginning of an eight-year reign of terror. The new plays, however, have a personal, confessional vision of urban life; absent are the Marxist-oriented, Brechtian sociopolitical theories of Augusto Boal and theater companies such as Teatro de Arena and Teatro Oficina.[5] "They positioned themselves, then, against the system, in whatever form, whether the bourgeois or the leftist establishment, both standing for submission of the individual to society" (Almeida Prado 1988, *O teatro brasileiro moderno,* 104). This opposition to the ideological patrol and raising the banner of individualism led to the branding of these plays and subsequent works by women as "alienated theater." Either that or many leftist critics simply ignored them. The ideological patrol, in other words, stigmatized women's theater at the very moment it was about to blossom. Audiences, nevertheless, responded favorably and a few critics realized that something novel was taking place. Most prominent among the latter was Sábato Magaldi, who realized that the ideological formulas of the 1960s were wearing out.

In spite of the charges of alienation, Cunha de Vincenzo asserts that the Nova Dramaturgia did provide a political response to the moment by calling into question the living conditions of individuals in society. The emphasis on individuality, anathema to the purveyors of engagé theater, had the positive effect of focusing on each person's uniqueness, as well as illustrating the military's successful destruction of the idea of collective struggle. This theater, Cunha de Vincenzo believes, constituted a political denunciation as suitable as Arena's or Oficina's had been a few years earlier. While those companies focused on the struggles of collective heroes and the proletariat, the Nova Dramaturgia focused on the middle class, exposing its dark side. Nelson Rodrigues had been doing the same thing since the 1940s, but these playwrights were speaking to a new generation.

While this theater's fierce satire was aggressive, following the lead of Teatro Oficina,[6] its pathos and humor also asked for the middle-class audience's complicity, as it looked at itself in the mirror. "It is, as Anatol Rosenfeld called it, 'porcupine' theater" (Cunha de Vincenzo 1992, 7). Audience members, one might say, did not find it easy to extract its quills.

The Nova Dramaturgia also carved out a new aesthetic path. Nelson Rodrigues and Oswald de Andrade excepted, playwriting in Brazil up to that point obeyed either the traditional rules for well-wrought drama (e.g., linear plot, verisimilitude, round characters), or more recently, followed the dictates of Brechtian estrangement (or Boal's reworking of Brecht). Leilah Assunção and company violated

> dramatic rules and strict psychological verisimilitude, bringing into reality the grain of madness as necessary to daily living as the work of art. These authors, in short, demanded for themselves the same autonomy they were willing to give to their characters. Life and art should together escape from servitude to excessive rationalism. (Almeida Prado 1988, *O teatro brasileiro moderno,* 105)

Beginning with the Nova Dramaturgia, women's presence will be a constant in Brazilian theater, in terms of playwriting and as a specific feminine position vis-à-vis issues fundamental to Brazilian life. Women's social consciousness and sensibility are now clearly revealed: failure of relationships, deterioration of the social fabric, Brazil's political climate. When asked in interviews about feminism, the Nova Dramaturgia women authors respond as do fiction writers; in most cases they refuse to define themselves as feminists: "what one perceives is the difficulty, the resistance on the part of most women dramatists" to separate opposition to the dictatorship from "a specifically feminine agenda in terms of sexuality, male–female relationships" and in terms of working conditions (Cunha de Vincenzo 1992, 16). The author of *Um teatro da mulher* places these women in the feminist current in the sense that even in the absence of feminist organizations—which would begin to emerge in the 1970s and 1980s—they were influenced by the changes in thinking about women's issues that took flight after Simone de Beauvoir's 1949 *The Second Sex.* Sixties- and early seventies-style feminism in Brazil was to some degree subsumed in the struggle against the dictatorship. The plays of the Nova Dramaturgia blended together women's issues and the problems associated with police-state repression. Women's themes were part of a broad spectrum of social concerns (Cunha de Vincenzo 1992, 16).

Women's playwriting in Brazil exhibited a "doubly political character[,] a political infusion common to all phases of the New Dramaturgy, but it is concomitantly infused with the sense of another politics: contemporary feminism." Women's themes were part of a broad spectrum of social concerns which "crisscross and form such an intricate web that it is not easy . . . to distinguish them, especially since the two levels of discussion mirror each other: the struggle against oppression and its consequences." The AI5 set off a general crisis of identity, because the projects begun in the 1960s were cut off and a single set of values was imposed. The question of woman's unique identity, her attempt to overcome second-class citizenship, her status as "other," as second sex, her "feminine" image imposed from the outside, the power implicit in male–female relationships, continue after the period of intense repression has ended (Cunha de Vincenzo 1992, 18). At the same time, it is important to reiterate, women writers themselves frequently deny adherence to feminist ideology even in the decade after the end of the dictatorship, as the reader will see later in interviews with Edla van Steen and Maria Adelaide Amaral.

I discussed above the quest for identity in women's fiction. Cunha de Vincenzo posits a parallel quest in women's playwriting. She defines the problems implicit or explicit in women's playwriting in Brazil as the affirmation of feminine sexuality, sexual roles defined by division of labor, power and submission, inferiority and superiority. Women's texts prior to 1969 often showed the negative aspects of the feminine condition: violence against women in daily life and competition and rivalry among women. The characters were often oblivious; the playwrights themselves were frequently unaware of "invisible circumstances and obstacles, invisible because they are concealed by socioeconomic institutions" (Cunha de Vincenzo 1992, 19). But with the Nova Dramaturgia, "these questions are expressed directly by women in liberated, aggressive, and surprisingly raw language [and] scrutinized without sentimentality or uncertainty in front of the audience and in the open and public space that is the theater" (Cunha de Vincenzo 1992, 19–20).

The most acclaimed of the Nova Dramaturgia plays was Leilah Assunção's 1969 *Fala baixo senão eu grito*. The play won several prizes, including the coveted Molière, and has seen myriad performances in Brazil and abroad. The play suffered at the hands of the censors, not only the usual cuts in the text but a closing in the middle of its initial run in Rio. Even though it did not openly challenge the military regime, its confrontational language and warping of the traditional images and roles imposed on women were jarring to the defenders of established order.

The protagonist is Mariazinha, a sarcastic name that alludes, on the one hand, to the concept of *marianismo,* devotion to the Virgin Mary and by extension to patriarchal society's virginity fetish. On the other hand, the cutesy-pie diminutive of the name Maria speaks to the protagonist's insignificance and infantile mind set. She is a *solteirona,* an "old maid," who is not, in fact, so old. She lives in a fantasy world of women's magazines and soap operas. She holds imaginary conversations with her prince charming. But then her boardinghouse room is invaded by a nameless *Homem* (*Man*), who taunts her and breaks down her world of illusions. He destroys her chintzy furniture, speaks disparagingly of her loneliness, and tries to goad her into using profanity. She insists at first that her life is full and active but eventually gives in, counterattacks with her own verbal assault, and even joins him in the demolition of her wardrobe. By the end of the play, however, she is ready to begin another day, acting as if nothing had happened; in fact, it is not clear to the reader/spectator that anything has. The author does not rigidly separate "fiction and reality, keeping the audience in the dark whether or not a man, perhaps a burglar, breaking into the room of a repressed single woman is a fact or a fantasy liberating her from her repressive tendencies—or both" (Almeida Prado 1992, *O teatro brasileiro moderno,* 105). That is, the whole episode may be yet another fantasy in Mariazinha's illusory world. "The unnamed man who one fine night enters Mariazinha's modest boarding house room . . . is a projection of the less repressed component of the lonely woman's personality. That the stranger's bursting into Mariazinha's meager world reflects her own desire for change is stressed by the fact that the door has been left unlocked . . ." (Albuquerque 1991, *Violent Acts,* 238). This projection, in Jungian analysis, refers to the animus, the so-called aggressive male archetype in the woman's psyche which appears as a man in dreams and fantasies. What is most important about *Fala baixo* is language itself: "The problem of language forbidden to woman . . . is contained in the play's odd title, which expresses the fear oppressing her, forcing her to hide from outside eyes her doubts and anxieties, especially those that pertain to her sex life—in which bourgeois morality has placed all of its 'honor' " (Cunha de Vincenzo 1992, 95). Critic Sábato Magaldi provides, as he usually does, the definitive statement on the play's legacy, when he writes that "it renders the most intense picture of the feminine condition in Brazilian playwriting, in a faithful portrait that goes beyond the middle class to mirror the condition of almost all women."[7] With *Fala baixo senão eu grito,* the playwright sent the theatrical search for women's identity on an entirely new path.

Leilah Assunção went on to continued success, although nothing ever equaled the notoriety gained by her first play. *Fala baixo* forms a trilogy with her 1970 *Jorginho, o machão* (*Boy George, the Macho Man*), "a merciless satire of the masculine myth," and with her 1975

*Roda cor-de-roda*—the title is a pun on the word for "rose-colored"—which "inverts the social roles of the dominating husband and the submissive wife, transforming her into the subject and making him the object in their domestic relationship" (Magaldi 1993, "Teatro Social," 51). She wrote more overtly political material such as her play *Sobrevividos* (*Survivors*) for the *Feira brasileira de opinião,* discussed later. In the piece, a kind of Brazilian *Big Chill,* a group of formerly committed theater artists meet to discuss the filming of a TV commercial. She wrote two musicals, the 1975 *Kuka de Kamaiorá* and the 1983 *O segredo da alma de ouro* (*The Secret of the Golden Soul*). The latter play, directed by Jorge Tacla, was a debacle in terms of audience and critical reaction.[8] The 1981 *Seda pura e alfinetadas* (*Pure Silk and Pin-Pricks*) was written for fashion designer Clodovil; it was a box-office success but the critics dismissed it. Her most recent plays are the 1984 *Boca molhada de paixão calada* (*Moist Lips Sealed by Passion*), the 1986 *Lua nua* (*Naked Moon*), and the 1992 *Quem matou a baronesa?* (*Who Killed the Baroness?*). The latter play was staged by director José Possi Neto with actress Marília Pera.

Leilah Assunção and the other women of the Nova Dramaturgia, as well as their predecessors Hilda Hilst and Renata Pallotini, were the pathfinders. By consensus the most important post–Nova Dramaturgia woman playwright—according to many critics the most significant contemporary playwright irrespective of gender—is Maria Adelaide Amaral. Her name appeared suddenly in the spotlight in 1978 for three plays, before any of them had been staged. Two of them, written before 1978 but staged later, were *A resistência* (*The Resistance*) and *Cemitério sem cruzes* (*Cemetery without Crosses*). The former play had won an important prize and the latter was to be part of a theater festival which was banned. "Living through the last year of the AI5, writers were aware they were closely watched, or in the best-case scenario 'forgotten' by the duly constituted public agencies, when their work was considered troublesome due to the oft-times inscrutable logic of Censorship. . . . No one had much faith in the political opening" (Cunha de Vincenzo 1992, 188).

Maria Adelaide Amaral's first two pieces, her third piece, *Bodas de papel,* along with the 1981 *Ossos d'ofício* (*Professional Bones*), form a tetralogy of post-economic miracle plays. Her first play staged was the 1978 *Bodas de papel: filhos do milagre econômico* (*Two-Year [Paper] Wedding Anniversary: Children of the Economic Miracle*),[9] which "ruthlessly demolishes the small world of a new professional category: executives who become 'winners' by selling their souls in exchange for short-term benefit" (Magaldi 1993, "Teatro social," 55).[10]

The play's title and external reference were very opportune. In spite of resistance to the state of siege, some middle-class sectors supported the dictatorship because it temporarily tamed inflation and increased the gross national product, a success story touted internationally as the economic "miracle" of the developing world. The miracle, however, soon foundered and left in its wake hyperinflation, currency free-fall, massive foreign debt, and shrinkage of the gross domestic product (GDP). The military had built its economic ship from deficit spending, coupled with printing of money and liberal borrowing of the petrodollars that swelled the coffers of foreign banks. Economic growth was measured by a rise in the GDP and wasteful showcase projects such as nuclear reactors and the Trans-Amazonic Highway, which in the end only added to the billions of dollars of debris that littered Brazil's economic shores. The "miracle" led to corruption on a mammoth scale and to the enrichment of a small group of people, government bureaucrats (known as *marajás,* or "maharajahs") and executives who often collaborated with the generals. The closing of the "miracle" was the most direct cause of the *abertura* or opening: the military had lost not only its ideological but its economic bearings.

The *abertura* provided Maria Adelaide Amaral an opportunity to attack the generals indirectly by launching a strike against their "children." The two-year anniversary of the title refers both to the social gathering that provides the setting of the play and to the short-lived "miracle" and the ephemeral success of its "winners" as well. The protagonists of *Bodas,* celebrating their wedding anniversary, are an executive in a multinational corporation and his second wife and former secretary. The festivities end up with the celebrants at each other's throats: the air is filled with accusations, insults, painful truths, and humiliation. All the ordinary rules of social courtesy are suspended. The women are secondary and decorative for the men, although the men accuse the women of being the cause of their problems. The women are mostly ignored but cause irritation when they try to get involved in "serious" male conversation about business; they are dismissed as "stupid" and "fat." As Cunha de Vincenzo explains, it is a world in which there is no room for ethics, friendship, or love, and relationships among the women reflects the men's. Only one value reigns supreme: financial worth, which equals human worth. "In this universe, the woman has no material worth whatsoever; she is merely a consumer" (Cunha de Vincenzo 1992, 193).

The play was received positively by the critics, winning for Maria Adelaide Amaral the Molière Prize for best author, the first of four. It wasn't a box-office hit during its first run in São Paulo, but Amaral stated in our interview that it was a critical success. Later, its 1981 staging in

Rio, in the wake of the success of the author's play *A resistência,* did attract large audiences. Although most critics received *Bodas* positively, some censured its "nonrevolutionary" linear plot structure and its naturalism. That short-sighted view failed to take into account the play's trenchant and timely insights into the historical moment. And, as the playwright herself has stated: "'My theater has no pretense to revolutionize Brazilian dramaturgy formally, and it doesn't bother me that some people say I'm doing outmoded theater. My main concern is to portray my reality; I'm trying to do what Arthur Miller once stated: "the dramatist writes with his ears." And that's what I do.'"[11] The truth is, the desire for more experimental forms has been realized in Brazil, especially in the theater of Antunes Filho and Gerald Thomas. But the well-wrought play has also maintained its position, demonstrated most clearly by the continued success of Maria Adelaide Amaral's work.

The dramatist's next play was both a critical success and a box-office hit. *A resistência,* written in 1975 and staged in 1979, won the SNT (Serviço Nacional de Teatro) Prize in 1977. Because Brazil was still in a precarious stage of political opening in 1977, there was no public recognition of the award, nor could the play be published or staged: "Although *Resistência,* for example, may not have been censored exactly, one can discern that it is the new veiled censorship, which everyone is wary of and to which Amaral refers when she mentions the delay in awarding prizes and in fulfillment of the commitments which the SNT had assumed with regard to the prize-winning authors" (Cunha de Vincenzo 1992, 188).

The play deals with a group of characters who work for a newspaper, journalists and copy editors. It is an eventful day at the office; the firm is downsizing, the ax is about to fall, but on whom? This leads to an increasing panic; personal revelations and psyches are laid bare. While the bosses are deciding the fate of the staff members, the latter try to organize a "resistance" against layoffs. Amaral explained in our interview that the characters are part of the generation that survived the dictatorship: some became hippies, some joined guerrilla movements, some were coopted. The characters in the play, therefore, argue about their various positions vis-à-vis the dictatorship. The author describes the play's trajectory in this way:

> *A resistência* was quite successfully staged in Rio. The play had been looked at by several people but no one seemed interested. But then it took off. It was the great success of the 1979 Rio season, along with

> Vianinha's *Rasga coração*. It was all the rage. It was beach chatter. In the year amnesty was declared. (Amaral, personal interview)[12]

*A resistência* might have had problems in 1978, but by 1979 things were more relaxed. For the first time the issues brought up by the play were being discussed openly; the characters were very familiar to the audience. According to Amaral, everyone who initially rejected the play claimed that no one would seriously consider a work set in a newspaper office and dealing with the generation of 64 (the generation of the dictatorship). The author heard that view of the play so often she started believing it herself. To her surprise, audiences identified with the characters, and many spectators went back to see the play again and again (Amaral, personal interview).

The third in the dramatist's post-*milagre* tetralogy is the 1977 *Cemitério sem cruzes,* published in 1978. Whereas the other three plays focus on the white-collar professions, *Cemitério* deals with construction workers. Maria Adelaide explained in our interview that actress–theater impresario Ruth Escobar asked her to write it for the 1977 *Feira brasileira de opinião* (*Brazilian Opinion Fair*), the intended sequel to the 1968 *Primeira feira da opinião paulista* (*First São Paulo Opinion Fair*).[13] The Brazilian fair comprises pieces by several notable writers.[14] In her *apresentação,* Escobar sets out the ideological design of the fair: "This collection is called 'urgent' theater because it proposes a theater of action, a theater of change, a revolutionary theater [to overcome] division of class and of labor, both intellectual and manual, division between high culture and popular art" (Escobar 1978, 7). Blocked by the censors, as was the 1968 fair, the 1977 sequel was never staged. However, the *abertura* had advanced far enough to allow its publication in 1978. Why was it not staged after that? The post-*abertura* and postdictatorship period marked the end of theatrical populism. The only *feira* piece that has survived is Maria Adelaide Amaral's *Cemitério sem cruzes.*

*Cemitério,* which the author defines as a dramatized news story (Amaral, personal interview), is a deftly rendered slice of life. Told in one act, the plot deals with a group of construction workers from the northeast, Brazil's poorest region, which provides a steady stream of often illiterate workers for industries in the large cities, workers who are exploited economically and worse, as the play wrenchingly demonstrates. *Cemitério* takes the reader/spectator immediately into the tragic circumstances of this lumpen proletariat and sustains its dramatic tension until the last line of dialogue. What the piece demonstrates, as clearly as an outraged human interest news story, is that the workers arrive in a São Paulo train station, are picked up by labor contractors (members of their own class), promised proper documentation and benefits, and put to work in dangerous construction projects where they are exposed to serious injury and death, in which latter case they are buried near the construction site in unmarked graves (a cemetery without crosses). They are kept in virtual bondage by start-up loans they do not request and goods sold at inflated prices. The sick and injured receive no medical attention and the widows of those killed in construction accidents collect no compensation (the widows, in fact, may never learn of their husbands' deaths). The disabled and the dead are replaced immediately by the unending river of *nordestinos* (northeasterners), who may also end up in cemeteries without crosses. The play's brief scenes cut among three settings, a train station, a bar, and a construction-site bunkhouse. There are five characters in the play: Zé-Gato, the corrupt labor contractor who betrays his own class; Antonio, the newly arrived *nordestino* recruit; Fidélio, a veteran of the construction site; Valdisar, the furious, grieving worker whose brother has died in a fall from the scaffolding the week before and who seeks restitution; Pedro, who, unable to afford boots, has stepped on a nail and contracted an unnamed infection (probably tetanus) and whose death is announced in the last line of the play by the newcomer Antonio.

*Cemitério sem cruzes* survived its initial ban and the cancellation of the *Feira brasileira de opinião*. Maria Adelaide reports (personal interview) that it is now a staple of pro-union *teatro da periferia,* theater staged in the working-class neighborhoods that ring São Paulo (as they do all of Latin America's large cities). Another interesting facet of the play is that it is one of the few women's plays in Brazil to deal with a group other than the middle class. It is a testament to the author's ability to draw vivid characters who come into clear relief with only a few lines of dialogue, stepping out of her own milieu and creating a terse yet moving portrait of working-class conditions in Brazil.[15] *Cemitério* skirts the edge of melodrama yet never succumbs to it, a hallmark of Amaral's writing. A sharply focused human interest story, it has none of the populist ideology of a Boal or a Guarnieri piece. It is ironic, then, that a piece about the working class, written by an unreconstructed, anti-ideological writer, has survived where the plays of populist writers have not, and has remained a staple of the ideology-driven *teatro de periferia* movement. The play's durability, I would conclude, has as much to do with its artistry as with its social documentation.

The play could be further compared with Clarice Lispector's *A hora da estrela* in that it deals with the failed quest for a better life—and therefore a new identity—of poor northeasterners in the urban south. As in the case of Lispector's novelette, the northeasterners are "squashed like bugs." There are obvious differences between the works; missing from the play is the ironic distance between narrator and characters. Maria Adelaide Amaral did not begin to explore the issue of women's quest for identity until later.

The fourth play in Maria Adelaide Amaral's tetralogy is her 1981 *Ossos d'ofício,* unpublished, about men and women losing jobs and ending up on the junk heap (the *Death of a Salesman* theme). It deals with a society which uses up and discards people, an issue relevant to the downsizing of the 1990s. Amaral shifts her class focus, this time to low-level, white-collar workers,

> who face almost always deadly social forces—the forces, that is, of technological progress—which steadily transform workers into the human and social refuse Arthur Miller talks about; but the accusation in this case is much more damaging. The characters live not only off the "bones" of the profession which they once held . . . they are themselves the "bones" left over from their days as once-active employees in a major bank. (Cunha de Vincenzo 1992, 200)

In our interview, Amaral gave the play this succinct, if somewhat skeptical, summation:

> I spent four years working in a bank. And I wanted to talk about the accommodation of people who, as a result of pre-1964 labor laws, could not be fired after ten years on the job. Many years later, these people were placed in a kind of dead file. I wanted to write a comedy and not a tragedy about this, even though it's a terrible situation. Now, I was well aware that the play was no masterpiece. A group from the Santo André district [of São Paulo] decided to stage it and it had a modest run. But it was nothing to write home about in terms of box office and reviews. It's not a piece I disavow but it really didn't add much to my career as a writer. Let's just say that it's the weakest thing I've ever written. (Amaral, personal interview)

These early plays dealt only indirectly with the issue of women's identity, although the passive executives' wives of *Bodas de papel* do provide a caustic commentary on the issue, within the microcosmic universe of the "children of the economic miracle." Beginning in 1983, however, the author propels her playwriting on the quest for female identity. Amaral's next play was her 1983 *Chiquinha Gonzaga,* also unpublished, for which she won her second Molière Prize. The 1983 São Paulo theater season had presented for the most part a discouraging panorama, with few high points. The severe post-*milagre* economic crisis, which would later earn the 1980s the appellation of "the lost decade," appeared to have tainted all aspects of national life. Theater was no exception. Coupled with economic troubles was the fact that the energies unleashed in the late 1970s with the *abertura* appeared to have dissipated. Although Brazilian public life was democratizing and censorship was on the wane, the military had still not given up power in spite of mass mobilizations such as the *diretas já* movement, in which hundreds of thousands of people marched in the major cities clamoring for the direct election of a civilian president. What was particularly disturbing, but not surprising, was the common response to the crisis: escapism. The São Paulo stage was inundated with inconsequential and poorly executed musicals, such as Leilah Assunção's *O segredo da alma de ouro* and *Band-Age* (by Zé Rodrix, a composer of TV commercial jingles), not to mention the Broadway musicals *Chorus Line* (referred to in a derisive pun as *choros* or "crying" line) and *Oh Calcutta!*. As part of the advertising campaign for *Calcutta* the producers touted its high-tech innovations, such as a computer-driven revolving stage. According to rumors circulating at the time, the stage was actually propelled by group of *nordestino* workers from a cramped space beneath the boards.

A notable exception to the spate of hollow musicals was Maria Adelaide Amaral's *Chiquinha Gonzaga.*[16] Indeed, it might have been the Brazilian answer to the musical comedy if theater artists and the public had insisted on the continuation and growth of the form (they did not).[17] The play, directed by Osmar Cruz, was commissioned by the state labor agency for its own theater, the Teatro Popular do SESI. The performance was intended primarily as a cultural event provided free to state industrial workers.

According to the author, "the play was commissioned, an extremely expensive production. I wanted to create a broad portrait of the period because when I did the research for the play I rediscovered Brazil, the nineteenth century, the history of Brazilian popular culture, especially Rio culture of the time. And the business about a totally forgotten career. No one knows who that woman was" (Amaral, personal interview).

Chiquinha Gonzaga, whose most productive phase ended in the 1920s, was an extraordinary woman, an early feminist, a pioneering composer of popular music, especially for the theater. The play dealing with her life, therefore, was a means to rescue from oblivion Chiquinha Gonzaga and her universe.

> There's very little biographical material about her. I managed to reach her through the memoirs of her contemporaries. In that search I uncovered a completely new and fascinating world. So I felt I had to share all of it, to seize the opportunity to make people aware. That's why I gave it an epic dimension, not in the pretentious sense of the word but in the sense of using forms from nineteenth-century musical theater. I think she would have approved. (Amaral, personal interview)

Elza Cunha de Vincenzo writes that the play narrates episodes in the life of Chiquinha—who lived to age 90—linked by narration, chorus, and musical numbers. The historical panorama is prominent: it begins at end of the reign of the second emperor, Dom Pedro II, who was deposed in 1889. The protagonist was an abolitionist and republican, the two political movements that converged to bring an end to the Empire and initiate the First Republic, which would last until 1930. *Chiquinha Gonzaga* closes in the early decades of this century. The play includes a potpourri of popular types—with a mixture of historical and fictitious characters—dances, and songs from Rio. It presents a blend of the theatrical modes of the time, such as vaudevillian and dance hall forms known as *burleta* and *revista,* for which Chiquinha wrote music. There are scenes from Chiquinha's private life: arranged marriage and separation, her family's disapproval of her career in popular music and theater, the prejudice against women she suffers, the support she finally gains from people in the theater and the press, a second marriage of her own choosing (but also failed), attempts at rapprochement with her family (including the children she left behind), growing success in musical theater, a third marriage with a younger man (whom she introduces to friends as her son), travel to Europe, technological changes (film, radio, phonograph), and SBAT (Sociedade Brasileira de Autores Teatrais, which she helped found). "And it ends in a crowd scene in the street, with the success of 'Ó abre alas,' the name of one of her most famous compositions, which probably led to her acclaim as one of the most important Brazilian composers of popular music" (Cunha de Vincenzo 1992, 210–212).

When I attended *Chiquinha Gonzaga* in 1983, I felt it was one of the most spectacular productions I had witnessed; in terms of its scope I compared it in my own mind to *Nicholas Nickelby,* which I had seen in New York the previous year. *Chiquinha* included 124 characters played by 32 actors. I was immediately struck by the fact that the musical was based on the life of one of the few women in the pantheon of Brazilian popular music and a seminal figure in the history of Brazilian feminism. It was at that time the only Brazilian play I had seen that focused on a strong and independent woman. So different from the spate of musicals inundating the Brazilian stage, the ideas behind the play, I believed at the time, could have provided the foundation for a native musical theater: Brazil's musical roots, historical tableaux, and epic sweep. Amaral's musical was held together by a fascinating libretto in whose main character the audience became totally involved, a character whose story was told in a succession of short, well-paced scenes that included dramatic dialogue, song and dance, healthy doses of humor, and much spectacle. If the cast members did not always measure up to the Broadway ideal of musical-comedy craft, their energy was unflagging and contagious. In technical terms, the most absorbing feature of the staging was the set and use of space. Osmar Cruz made optimal use of the Teatro Popular do SESI stage, a deep semi-thrust, by basing his design on fixed and moveable platforms, curtains and scrims, and an excellent lighting plot. The setting changed quickly, from the Rua dos Ouvidores (Rio's answer to Tin Pan Alley), to shipboard, to a palatial ballroom, to a train station, to the room containing the piano where Chiquinha Gonzaga composed her sambas.

The play was a box-office and critical success, but we are left with several questions. Why did Maria Adelaide Amaral choose not to continue in the musical theater vein? Why, indeed, did other theater artists fail to provide continuity? The author herself provides a succinct answer: "Today for you to mount a play with five actors is already an absurdity" (personal interview). Economics, even now after the post-"miracle" crisis and the lost decade have ended, have been a determining factor in the development of the postdictatorship theater. Playwrights have great difficulty staging their plays when a large cast is required; indeed, most plays written by contemporary Brazilian playwrights are staged only when they are limited to two or three characters. All of the playwrights I have interviewed, such as Naum Alves de Souza, Edla van Steen, and Maria Adelaide Amaral herself, have several manuscripts gathering dust because producers shy away from having to hire more than a few actors. A further issue is the musical theater form itself. In spite of Brazil's rich musical traditions, in spite of successful forays into the musical—Teatro de Arena's *bossarenas* plays, Chico Buarque's *Gota D'agua* and *Ópera do malandro*—there are no deep roots. There is nothing like the Broadway tradition, the British music hall, no operetta—and little opera—no Spanish *zarzuela*. As important as economics and lack of tradition is the fact that Brazilian actors receive limited training. The few schools that train theater artists, such as the University of São Paulo's School of Communications and Arts, where I taught in 1984, have courses in acting, directing, and playwriting, but actors receive no formal instruction in music and dance. The typical American "triple threat" is a rare bird in Brazil and only appears fortuitously. Finally, the musical tends to be scorned as a serious art form. There are, today, only two kinds of stage production with large casts: the ever-popular comedy of manners and the postmodernist extravaganzas of the *encenadores* like Antunes Filho, Gerald Thomas, and Bia Lessa.

Maria Adelaide Amaral's next play, the 1984 *De braços abertos*—which could be translated as *With Open Arms* or *With Empty Arms*—secured her reputation as a playwright and advanced her focus on the quest for women's identity. The play is based in part on a novel she was writing at the time and subsequently published under the title *Luísa (quase uma história de amor)*, or *Luísa (almost a love story)*. In our interview the author explained that the play was in a sense commissioned. While she was working on *Luísa,* Cécil Thiré, who had directed *Bodas de papel,* suggested to her that "if it ain't broke don't fix it," and asked her if her novel couldn't be adapted to the stage. After she had shelved the project temporarily, actress Irene Revache, who was turning forty, informed her that she'd like to be able to talk about women her age, about failed love affairs, about the notion that often even couples who love each other deeply find living together painful and end up separating. As the actress spoke, Amaral realized that what she was talking about was the theme of the novel she had been writing and which she had put away. She started seeing what Ravache was talking about theatrically, imagining it on the stage. The actress read the rough draft of the novel and found that it spoke precisely to her concerns. The play, adapted from the unpublished work of fiction, was then written in twenty days.

*De braços abertos* is a play about two characters, Luísa and Sérgio, who meet five years after their love affair has ended. Their relationship and subsequent search for individual identity are portrayed both in their conversation, which takes place in the time frame of the present, and in flashbacks. The author calls the play an "amorous power game" (Amaral, personal interview). The two characters discuss old friends and the newspaper office where they were once colleagues, their failed relationship, and they make wary appraisals of one another. Luísa clearly has the upper hand; she is mature, while he behaves childishly. She has recovered from the experience, put it into perspective, gone on with her life, while he has not. Luísa has, in short, been successful in carving out a separate identity for herself, while Sérgio has not. Unable to accept their separation and her independence, he "defends himself aggressively from what he considers his own inferiority in relation to her, using the same kind of sarcasm, repeating ironically the same complaints" (Cunha de Vincenzo 1992, 217). Luísa is a woman in full command of her life, her search for identity productively realized. In an ironic twist on traditional patriarchal discourse, it is Sérgio who flounders in his quest for identity. Severino Albuquerque touches on the social dimension of this quest: *De braços abertos* deals with

> a liberated woman, as she searches for a mature lover in contemporary São Paulo. Although educated and successful, the . . . men with whom she becomes involved are insecure and destructive, woefully unprepared to accept a new reality in which Brazilian women, emotionally and intellectually fortified by a better understanding of their social and political situation, demand to be treated as equals. (Albuquerque 1989, "*Abertura,*" 92)

Is this, then, a feminist play? Cunha de Vincenzo responds that in spite of the author's and the critics' comments to the contrary, "if one eliminated the negative connotations attached to feminism, the systematic connotations of aggressive activism and underlying hostility against men, we see no reason not to classify as feminist a play . . . in which men are enraged by the independence and professional success of their mates" (Cunha de Vincenzo 1992, 215). According to Cunha de Vincenzo, then, the play fits in precisely with a feminist agenda: woman's recognition in nondomestic work, her professional identity, division of labor in the home. The play is also an indication that an increasing number of middle-class women in Brazil are facing this problem and that there is an increasing feminine, and feminist, awareness of this issue. In our interview, Amaral made this ambiguous statement about the matter: "I have no commitment to feminism. I have a commitment to my gender, to women, to myself. Basically, I have a commitment to human beings."

Other critics view the play in the context of recent historical events, but however one defines the play in social terms, there is no question that it has been the most influential and successful play written by a woman in Brazil to the time of this writing. Sábato Magaldi accords it such status, irrespective of the author's gender: *De braços abertos* "is artistically the most praise-worthy play of the Brazilian repertory in recent seasons" (Magaldi 1989, "Texto," 1082). The piece performed stunningly at the box office, received universal acclaim from the critics, and won the São Paulo Association of Theater Critics award (for the play) and the Mambembe Prize (for the playwright). In terms of its impact on audience members, according to the author, *Braços* "persuaded many people to make important decisions in their lives: to separate, to reconcile, to break up a long-term affair, to go back to an old affair. The play moved people. Which is what I'm looking for. To affect people's lives, to help them think and make better decisions for themselves, to make their lives happier." To conclude the discussion of *De braços abertos,* Amaral describes the final product as,

> one of the most fortunate gatherings I've ever seen on the stage, and one of the most important moments in the career of all those involved. It was a climax, a moment of integration, of perfection, where everything fit together harmoniously: actors, text, music, direction, lighting, set design, everything. It was the greatest moment of my professional life. After living through that experience I understood why so many authors say that it's difficult to survive your own success. The expectations about your work are absurd. And you also demand too much of yourself. Everything becomes extremely difficult. (Amaral, personal interview)

The next ten years would, indeed, be difficult for the author. Her meteoric rise as a playwright seemed to come suddenly and inexplicably to a halt. She published novels, wrote for television, and continued composing plays, few of which were staged and none of which were able to repeat the successes of the fruitful 1978–1984 period.[18] Although her playwriting career would reignite in 1994, at the time of our 1993 interview she was pessimistic about her own prospects and those of Brazilian dramaturgy in general.

The years 1994–1995, however, would bring a reversal of fortune when two of her plays would be staged. One of those works, *Intensa magia* (*Potent Magic*), opened in Rio in 1994 and later played in São Paulo in 1996. The author describes the play in the program notes:

> *Intensa magia* is this: a family reunion, similar to those held at my parents' house, with equal doses of comedy and tragedy, misunderstandings

> and comprehension, resentment and gratitude, generosity and bitterness. After the first reading of the play . . . several people were crying. People who identified the father or the mother in the play with their own, who identified with one of the children. Which would lead one to affirm, with apologies to Tolstoy, that all unhappy families are alike. So in the end, my father wasn't much different from so many others whose dreams went unfulfilled and who took out their bitterness on those they considered responsible for their unhappiness.

Although *Intensa magia* was reasonably successful in terms of box office and critical reception, Maria Adelaide Amaral re-energized her theatrical reputation fully with *Querida mamãe,* which opened in Rio in 1994 and ran in São Paulo in 1995–1996. The piece won all the major playwriting awards, such as the Molière and Mambembe. The title means literally "Dear Mom"[19] but the author prefers to translate it as "More Than You Know." That choice reveals a great deal about the author's views on the play itself, on Brazilian drama, and on the way foreigners view that drama. In our 1993 interview, Amaral told the story of a German publisher who came to Brazil looking for plays. After seeing *De braços abertos* the publisher expressed disinterest; the work was not exotic enough, she complained, it was too "urban," its setting could be anyplace in world. According to the author, "they don't want us to have an international flavor" (personal interview). This incident illustrates a phenomenon that Brazilian artists and intellectuals have been protesting at least since the 1930s; to wit, foreigners see Brazil through an exotic lens and tend to ignore those phenomena that might be classified as cosmopolitan. That is why, for example, the international reading public devours the novels of Jorge Amado, with their backhands bandits and voodoo gods, while the Brazilian intelligentsia snubs his work. Although Brazil's more cosmopolitan fiction writers such as Clarice Lispector are translated and have a foreign readership, few playwrights are so fortunate. Even Nelson Rodrigues, with his intense *carioca* (Rio) flavors, is virtually unknown in the United States. A corollary to the taste for exoticism is the U.S. and European cult of *terceiromundismo,* or "thirdworldism." This has led to the continuing U.S. and European fascination with Augusto Boal and 1960s populism, even though they are long absent from the Brazilian stage. Dramatists concerned with their own time and place, with neither folklore nor a populist axe to grind, have little chance in the so-called "first world." Amaral, who like many contemporary Brazilian writers consciously avoids any hint of exoticism, was understandably affronted by the German publisher's remarks.[20] There is another issue at stake here. According to Judith Ismael Bisset, "Brazilian women authors work within a linguistic tradition which limits the possibilities of universal communication" (Bisset 1991, "Feminina"). What this suggests is that the international path is open to Brazilian men but not to women. For all these reasons, when Amaral asked me to translate *Querida mamãe* for a possible New York production, she insisted on internationalizing it as much as possible. Flying in the face of conventional wisdom, she even requested that references to Brazil be excised (e.g., allusions to popular music), making the setting unidentifiable, forcing the spectators to focus on the characters and their conflicts. Musical choices are especially important; the playwright felt that the original selections would fail to elicit the emotional responses she desired. Therefore, we had lengthy discussions and conducted research on choices (e.g., Gershwin, Cole Porter) that would establish the proper mood for a New York audience. Having said all of this, I want to focus attention to the Brazilian context, for that is where the play was written and staged. I will, where appropriate, bring up the changes that would internationalize the play.

*Querida mamãe* is closely linked to the author's previous work:

> Maria Adelaide Amaral's playwriting deals essentially with relationships from a psychological perspective. Whether she considers this subject in the workplace (*A resistência*), in marriage (*Bodas de papel*) or in amorous conflicts (*De braços abertos*), the author always observes closely emotional strife which reveals carefully delineated psychological behavior. [In *Querida mamãe* she] maintains the same characteristics that she has displayed in her other texts: the perspective which exposes individuals in conflict and captures them in excruciating situations. (Luiz 1994, "Psicologia" 6)

*Querida mamãe* is a recipe for overcoming the impediments to staging Brazilian plays, at least at home. There are two characters and a simple (and therefore inexpensive) set. Furthermore, the role of the mother was played by Eva Wilma, a legendary stage actress who has become immensely popular through her TV work and who provided instant box-office recognition and a sure audience draw.[21] The stage directions indicate that the set is a living room in a fifties-style apartment. A few props include dresses, hats, records, and other objects depicting the 1930s, 1940s, and 1950s. Furniture is limited to an armchair, a sofa, a TV set, a record player, and a large mirror. Although the time frame is present-day, the set lends an air of timelessness and nostalgia, a longing for an age which memory and imagination make more graceful. The records serve as a device justifying extensive use of music, which establishes mood and ironic counterpoint. The music in the original script includes Brazilian popular singers and composers (Tom Jobim, Maria Bethânia), Latino composers (Gregorio Barrios), international classics ("Nutcracker Suite," "Le Lac de Côme," "Emperor's Waltz"), Neapolitan sentimental favorites ("Mamma"), as well as American standards (Glenn Miller's "Pennsylvania 6500," Fred Astaire singing "Let's Face the Music and Dance").[22]

*Querida mamãe* tells the story of Helô, a doctor, and her mother, Ruth, a widowed housewife, in whose living room the play is set. These two characters, according to critic Carmelinda Guimarães in her review of the play, "have an archetypal density which suggests the text's universal quality" (Guimarães 1995, D-2). The work is an intricate psychological pas de deux in which the two women approach and retreat from each other, alternating mutual recriminations and attempts at reconciliation. At the center of the play is the daughter's quest for identity, as well as an enigma surrounding the mother's character. The latter, in the view of Carmelinda Guimarães, "can already be included in the list of great characters in Brazilian theater and promises an international career. This is a perfect character for a middle-aged actress" (Guimarães 1995, D-3). The daughter, Helô, is unlucky in love, with a failed marriage, an alienated teenage daughter, and an unhappy professional career.

As the play begins, Helô is searching through an old trunk looking for an outfit (dress, hat) to wear to a wedding. Each article of clothing she tries on represents a piece of family history which Ruth recounts to her daughter. This is a useful device which allows the playwright to provide background information on the characters, plot exposition, and foreshadowing. The stories of unrequited love, familial disapprobation of relationships, and fleeting moments of happiness presage dimensions of Helô's life. Related to the clothing is another of the play's central metaphors, the plot as a stitching together of pieces of fabric whose final form is not revealed until the end of the play. The related metaphors of clothing and fabric reveal to the spectator/reader the play's principal conflict, the inability of mother and daughter to come to terms, when this exchange takes place:

HELÔ: Let's not talk about grandma anymore. I've had it up to here with this nostalgic yammering. I just came over to pick out a hat. You don't need to bombard me with your family history.

RUTH: (Disappointed) I thought you were enjoying this.
HELÔ: I was at first, but enough is enough. (Amaral 1995, *Querida,* 19)

Trying on old clothes locked away in a trunk symbolizes both trying on identities and airing out old problems, which mother and daughter have never dealt with properly. Helô's resentful sarcasm, which hurts her mother, is ultimately aimed at herself. The daughter has been asked by a friend at the hospital to be her bridesmaid, an idea she finds preposterous. When her mother asks why she's going ahead with it, Helô responds that the friend thinks highly of her: "I want her to keep thinking I'm fabulous . . . There had to be somebody somewhere sometime who thought I was fabulous!" (Amaral 1995, *Querida,* 10). This statement revealing Helô's lack of self-esteem opens the door to one of the basic conflicts between mother and daughter. When mother protests that she has always held a high opinion of her daughter, Helô counters that her mother has only had eyes for her sister Beth, a biologist living in New York, successful in her career and her family life. Mother is unable to persuade daughter that not only does she admire her but that Helô's situation will improve. The mother's words ring hollow as the daughter's woes accumulate.

Another stitch is added to the fabric of sibling rivalry in a later scene when Ruth wants to know why Helô persists in a career that doesn't satisfy her. Nothing satisfies her, that's the problem, is her response. She blames her mother for her choosing the medical profession. Ruth pushed her into it, she avows, when Beth failed the entrance exams. The mother pulls the yarn in another direction: Helô, she insists, was trying to prove she was better than Beth. In a later scene, Helô berates her mother for favoritism towards Beth. While she belittles one daughter, Helô asserts, Ruth idealizes the other, even after the latter's fifteen-year absence. Helô refers to another clothing-related metaphor: "Beth is this perfect coat hanger where you can hang everything you wished you had: unconditional love, dedication, care and concern, all that cheap sentimental b.s. Doesn't matter; you'll never have the chance to find out if she's really all that great because it's obvious Beth is never coming back" (Amaral 1995, *Querida,* 50–52). Helô's fragile psyche will suffer yet another shock when her prophecy is proved erroneous.

That piece of the plot fabric first takes shape when Ruth discusses a medical checkup—a premonition of her own destiny–and in the same breath a trip abroad. She has never visited her daughter Beth abroad and she is terrified of flying, so Helô finds her sudden trip odd. The spectator/

reader will discern in the climactic moments of the play the design of Ruth's travel plans.

The conversation quickly returns to the subject of the wedding and to Helô's tribulations. She reveals another pattern in the conflict with her mother, who disapproves of her lifestyle. Helô is going to the wedding with a married man, which is only a prelude to proscribed behavior which will further distance mother and daughter. Ruth has always objected to Helô's life choices, her early desire to become a dancer, her marriage to the irresponsible but charming Sérgio, her childrearing methods.

The conversation turns to the past again. The two women discuss Ruth's marriage with her late husband, another thread that will be sewn later into the play's revelatory fabric. The latter idea is represented by another piece of stage business, Ruth's knitting of a sweater for an undisclosed purpose. The fabric and the plot are patterned in parallel fashion. Like a piece of knitting, which takes shape slowly, in a circular rather than linear fashion, the plot loops back upon itself and withholds its final design nearly until completion.

A key piece of this knitted fabric is Helô's unrelenting hopelessness. Ruth makes a brief speech in which she responds to her daughter's despair and attempts reconciliation by emphasizing the positive aspects of their relationship, subtle ways Helô made her happy: the birth of her granddaughter, "small gestures . . . a smile, a sign of affection you cut off when you suddenly remembered we're supposed to be hostile" (Amaral 1995, *Querida,* 25–26). The mother's insights, born of long experience, which Helô becomes aware of only later in the play, contrast with Ruth's oft-times naive or closed-minded perceptions of her daughter.

The fabric of the plot begins to display a more discernible pattern in a scene after the wedding. Helô has broken off the affair with the married man and she discusses the antique dress she wore to the wedding, a dress admired by another woman, a theater costume designer (a further extension of the fabric metaphor). The dress, which had been the focal point for family history, now foreshadows the future. Ruth is suspicious about this encounter, and some audience members will have speculated at this point that Helô and the costume designer, Leda, will have an affair. This presages a new path for the daughter in her quest for identity.

Mother and daughter, as they circle around each other warily, like loops in knitted fabric, touch on increasingly intimate subjects. Ruth overcomes her reluctance to discuss sexual matters and admits she felt no pleasure in bed with her husband. She also reprimands her daughter for bringing home men to sleep with, men who reportedly walk around the apartment nude in the presence of Helô's daughter Priscila. Helô is outraged: "You mean I don't have the right to do what I want in my own home? . . . Do you think Sérgio doesn't make it with his girlfriends when Priscila stays over at his house? Why hasn't she discussed her father with you? Why isn't she ashamed about daddy's playmates?" (Amaral 1995, *Querida,* 35). When Ruth defends her granddaughter, Helô explodes in resentment: "Stop defending Priscila! She's a lying, deceitful, hypocritical bitch! She's trying to find a way to move in with her father and she'll lie through her teeth to get what she wants!" (Amaral 1995, *Querida,* 35). This shocking attack on her own daughter annuls her role, her identity, as a mother. And in her bitter recriminations over her mother's preferential treatment of her sister Beth and perceived neglect and humiliation of Helô herself, she negates her identity as a daughter. Her options for identity collapse around her as the play progresses.

In a subsequent scene, Ruth returns to another thread in the dramatic fabric the author weaves: Ruth's purported trip to visit Beth. Maria Adelaide adds to this element of the design the mother's sudden consideration of her own death and the making of a will; the objects in the apartment take on further significance when Ruth discusses the issue of inheritance. That is, props in the play have shifting symbolic value and at various points they define Ruth's disparate attitudes toward her daughters. Helô misses the meaning of the conversation because she is about to drop a bombshell on her mother: she is having an affair with Leda. Ruth at first refuses to accept the idea of an "immoral" liaison. She insists that her daughter, having experienced intercourse with men, cannot be homosexual. When Helô contends that her happiness is the only important thing, Ruth rebuts that it is unseemly to carry on such a relationship in front of Priscila. She also dismisses out of hand the idea of allowing Helô to bring Leda into her own home. Helô, before she storms out, has a final defiant word on the issue: "Why can't I have an affair simply because it gives me pleasure and happiness? . . . I'll fight for it, against you, against Priscila, against anyone who tries to stop it" (Amaral 1995, *Querida,* 42).

The two women question each other's motivations relentlessly. Helô refuses to give her mother credit and turns every positive gesture into a negative through relentless irony. Paradoxically, Helô also desperately wants Ruth's approval, but the mother always withdraws it. Ruth, for all her maternal "concern," for all the time and attention she devotes to Helô, doesn't really believe in her daughter. Further, a cruel thread in their relationship is revealed when Ruth chooses to not confide her serious medical problems in her doctor daughter. The latter, in turn, though she has more than sufficient clues to detect her mother's looming health crisis, is so distracted by the turmoil in her personal life that she fails to notice.

The turmoil increases exponentially: Helô reveals she slapped her daughter, who treated Leda disrespectfully by calling her a "lesbo" (*fanchona*). Ruth does not offer solace; rather, to her daughter's consternation, she wants to know why Helô thought that such behavior—her "perverted" affair—would remain "unpunished." She claims she doesn't know the meaning of the word *fanchona,* but then adds insult to injury by referring to Leda as a "dyke" (*sapatão*). It is worth repeating Cunha de Vincenzo's comments here, referring to Leilah Assunção's *Fala baixo senão eu grito,* about "the problem of language forbidden to woman . . . forcing her to hide from outside eyes her doubts and anxieties, especially those that pertain to her sex life—in which bourgeois morality has placed all of its 'honor'" (Cunha de Vincenzo 1992, 95). Ruth's exposure to forbidden language, then, peels away her "pure" exterior, her "honor."

In a later scene Helô reveals another violent encounter that ensued when Priscila gave her an ultimatum: choose between her and Leda. After the subsequent melee, Priscila has moved in with her father. Leda, having witnessed the knock-down-drag-out, was horrified because she felt responsible for the rift between Helô and Priscila. As a consequence, she has turned away from her lover. Helô is shattered: "Leda's a wonderful person. She's the most sensitive person I've ever met! I'm desperate, Mamma! . . . It's not just that I'm in love! It's the realization I might lose her, because being with someone like Leda things'll work out for me!" (Amaral 1995, *Querida,* 53). It is at this point that Ruth allows compassion and maternal concern over her daughter's chronic unhappiness to overcome her reservations about Helô and her bias against lesbianism: she suggests inviting Leda to her home for dinner.

In the "guess who's coming to dinner" scene, props once again are featured on center stage. Their symbolic value shifts here to Leda's world of theatrical design: "The set has been transformed into a second-hand store displaying in a more creative manner all the objects which in the first scene Helô had taken out of the trunk. Helô is wearing the taffeta dress, evening gloves, and shoes with very high heels" (Amaral 1995, *Querida,* 55–56). In this metatheatrical scene Ruth's apartment ironically becomes the symbolic sanctuary of Leda, who, to compound the irony, never shows up. The antique objects become apparitions of the past projected on a phantom relationship in the present, and all paths become spectral paths toward the future on a barren quest. With the end of her affair with Leda, Helô seems locked in her melancholy, describing herself as "suspended in thin air," alone, with "just me and my grief."

Helô, at this vulnerable moment, briefly drops her guard and seeks reconciliation with her mother: "I know sometimes I'm more than you can take . . . I'm not unaware of the effort you make" (Amaral 1995, *Querida,* 65). The emotional chess game lures Ruth into making a startling disclosure: she herself once experienced illicit passion, a lengthy affair with a man not her husband. Her daughter's reaction is anger: how could her mother, having violated society's norms, have been so hard on her? She accuses Ruth of trying to place herself above good and evil merely because she slept with someone of the same sex. Ruth refuses to accept the comparison of her affair with Helô's and counters that in her affair no one was hurt and there was no scandal. Nevertheless, this secret thread in the fabric of her life has been exposed and she shares it fully with her daughter. She calls it a "great romance" and compares it to a movie. She finally admits to a parallel with her daughter's predicament: she is willing to uncover the clandestine strand because she wants Helô to understand that she, too, has been through the hell. She confesses that her greatest fear was that her lover would marry her and that one day he would look at her and say: " 'My god, I deserted my wife and children for you!' " (Amaral 1995, *Querida,* 69). Helô, however, does not empathize with her mother. She expresses regret on her father's behalf because she identifies with him as the unrequited lover. She sees a mirror image of herself in his blind devotion to his wife. And after her brief interlude of vulnerability, Helô returns to her irony and resentment. In the end, it is she who rejects the comparison of her affair with her mother's, jeering at Ruth's claim at insight into the human soul with the rejoinder, "as long as it's two heterosexual souls" (Amaral 1995, *Querida,* 70). This thread in the plot's fabric—gender identity—is completed at this point; then a surprising stitch is added.

Helô is shaken from her inattention to Ruth's illness when Beth arrives unexpectedly; Ruth has summoned her other daughter because she going to undergo surgery to remove a growth. Helô erupts in fury, accusing her mother of shutting her out of her life, discarding her. She is incredulous that she would summon Beth from New York instead of Helô, who is a doctor and close at hand. This is perhaps Ruth's greatest act of cruelty. Helô is further dismayed that during her visits to the doctor Ruth was accompanied by her niece and nephew. She expresses her anger in simple, crude terms: "I'm so pissed at you" (Amaral 1995, *Querida,* 75). Her mother, she alleges, "wanted to punish me! That's always been your way to punish me. Pushing me aside by using some noble excuse! It happened when Papa got sick! You left me out because I was splitting up with my husband!" (Amaral 1995, *Querida,* 76–77). Ruth's brutal rejoinder serves as the final humiliation: "to tell you the truth it's a relief to find out that Beth isn't that coat hanger where I hung all my maternal fantasies" (Amaral 1995, *Querida,* 77). This blow to the solar plexus does not stop Helô, who goads her mother into making this confession about her antipathy toward her daughter:

> You were sick all the time and you never stopped crying and throwing up! You were always a troublemaker. You hung out with a bad crowd, and I'm not just talking about that girl. Oh no, I'm talking about Sérgio. You just had to get pregnant with him so you could force us to put up with a marriage that obviously would never work out! But you didn't stop there: you dumped all your marital problems on me, not to mention your professional and personal problems. And to make matters worse you left it up to me to raise your daughter so you could study a subject you had no aptitude for! And during that whole time I never received a single thank you, a word of kindness, you never had the slightest consideration for me, all you did was blame me, blame, blame, blame. So there you have it. It's true there are times I regret it's Beth and not you who lives far away from me! It's also true there are times I hate you. But no matter how crude and warped you may be, you're still my daughter. And I love you. (Amaral 1995, *Querida,* 81)

The play's familial climax passes, and mother and daughter reach a degree of accommodation in the denouement. Ruth's speech ends Helô's complaints. Her mother has finally told her what she's always wanted to hear: the simple, unadorned truth. She takes a degree of masochistic pleasure in having her suspicions confirmed. She turns her attention to her mother's illness. As the play ends, mother and daughter offer each other what tenuous support they can, and the caretaking function of the mother subtly shifts to the daughter:

> Helô impulsively embraces Ruth. Ruth's hands caress Helô's face and hair. Suddenly, surprised by her own gesture, Helô pulls away. It is a gesture expressing mostly fear. But Ruth does not feel hurt; rather, she feels pity for her daughter's impossible situation. The two women look at each other.
>
> RUTH: I'm not going to die . . . I'm not going to die . . .
>
> HELÔ (AVERTING HER GAZE): No . . . (Amaral 1995, *Querida,* 86–87)

As the lights dim, Helô holds the yarn so her mother can wind it around the skein. In the closing words of last stage direction, the author herself brings the curtain down by knitting the final piece in the play's metaphorical fabric: "It is the means by which she is able to establish a bond with her mother. With a woolen thread. Symbolically" (Amaral 1995, *Querida,* 87). In the end, then, the thread used in knitting represents the tenuous strands that tie mother and daughter together in their tormented relationship.

The search for identity in the play, particularly Helô's, places *Querida mamãe* within the category I have established of women's quest literature. Carol Christ discusses the "problem of women in the modern world: they do not have images and models of self with which to shape their identities, chart their experiences" (Christ 1980, 56). Ruth is unable to serve as a role model for Helô in the latter's quest for professional and affective identities. And when the mother finally reveals the transgressive dimension of her life—her affair with another man—it is too late for Helô.

The latter's quest for identity in a homosexual relationship represents a new path in women's writing in Brazil. Although the theme of feminine homosexuality will not seem novel to American audiences, in Brazil it has remained a taboo subject. One of the few writers to deal with it is Edla van Steen, discussed later. If male homosexuality has had positive representation in Brazilian artistic production, Helô is one of the few protagonists in Brazilian theater to represent lesbianism as a positive experience.[23]

One can also view Ruth's identity quest as a failed ritual passage. Her life seems to be a circular ritual leading nowhere; it ends where it began, with Ruth suspended. Carol Christ's triad—life, death, regeneration—is incomplete. Ruth lacks ritual patterns by which to live; her rite of initiation in the impersonal urban space of São Paulo is bereft of the sacred. *Querida mamãe* casts doubt on the possibility of fulfilling utopian, spiritual, and identity quests.

Concomitant to the issue of the characters' identity in the play, is that of the writer herself. Maria Adelaide has chosen to fuse two apparently outmoded, not to mention incompatible, genres: psychological realism and melodrama. We observe the psychological realism in the way the author peels away, with psychotherapeutic skill, layers covering "open wounds in the context of a dysfunctional family . . . When the spectators realize that the author is taking them into deep waters, to an emotional intensity that will leave no one unscathed, it's too late" (Guzik 1995, "Emoções," 1). I return here to the metaphor of knitting: what the author constructs, or deconstructs, is the characters' deepest psychological fabric. In terms of this genre the play does not lie squarely within Brazilian traditions: "When it grapples with the abstract substance of the conflict between mother and daughter, the play explores the region of psychological realism, a genre more common to American playwriting than to Brazilian" (Guzik 1995, "Emoções," 1). What is more traditionally Brazilian is the playwright's use of melodrama, long the stuff of Brazilian stage. Even foreign plays one would not usually think of as melodramatic are performed as such by Brazilian actors. The soap opera (*novela*), which in Brazil runs in prime time and which is an updated form of melodrama, manipulates events without concern for the logic of plot or character development. Maria Adelaide herself writes TV scripts and is well-versed in the *novela* genre. And there is much in *Querida mamãe* that is redolent of melodrama, especially the strong tug at the audience's emotions and plot twists in the form of revelations (e.g., Ruth's affair, Beth's sudden appearance). A common *novela* theme is the poor-girl-meets-rich-boy war horse, a subset of the search for the perfect mate, and because the playwright's aesthetic choices parallel ideological choices, she is as artistically as she is politically incorrect in bringing this theme into the precinct of "serious" drama. But, like her *Cemitério sem cruzes,* this play skirts the edge of melodrama without succumbing to it. Because the revelation does not lead to resolution, because thick doses of emotion are always offset by irony, and because the search for the perfect mate leads to a gay affair, there is something of the postmodern in *Querida mamãe*'s deconstruction of the melodramatic genre and of traditional gender categories.

To conclude, the revelations and twists and turns in *Querida mamãe* are part melodrama and part acerbic commentary on family relationships. Some might claim that this play is a step backward because the protagonist is not strong like Luísa, from *De braços abertos,* or Chiquinha Gonzaga. Maria Adelaide, however, is not interested in promoting ideological agendas but in exploring the dynamics of relationships and families, in seeing where those dynamics lead, where they break down, and how the stresses and fracture points are homologous to the larger society. That Helô's generation of women can have professional careers is a given; her failure is not merely a function of her feminine condition. The author, indeed, takes a step beyond the quest for identity in the professional arena to examine a case in which professional difficulties emanate from familial and psychological difficulties, from the inability to establish bonds of love and trust, to overcome isolation.

The author asks major social questions regarding the institution of marriage: "Why isn't it possible to have in the same bed your friend, companion, and lover, along with the father of your children?" Further, she implicitly questions, "How can an honest woman have a lover? This role is reserved for people lacking character, and it is only forgiven in the case of men, never women" (Guimarães 1995). Alberto Guzik, in his preface to *Querida mamãe,* writes:

> This is Maria Adelaide Amaral's hunting ground. She captures in her texts disquieting and revealing snapshots of a troubled humanity, which always discovers, when it's too late, that we spend our lives searching for answers, when the game is apparently about nothing more than raising questions. Adelaide is a fearless writer who braves the phantoms of loneliness, maturity, old age, and death. With dignity and lyricism. And toughness. (Guzik 1995, "Difícil," 11)

*Querida mamãe* highlights a universal human quest that spares no one. As the two women awkwardly touch at the play's close, both facing crushing loss, the path seems to lead not to tearful reunion but—because the play always approaches melodrama and then wryly retreats—to a kind of *danse macabre* in which Helô and Ruth have become equal partners. In spite of the torrent of words unleashed by the two characters, the only communication they achieve is nonverbal, as in the final scene in which mother and daughter together take up the knitting, symbolic of the fabric of their lives.

To finalize this discussion about Maria Adelaide Amaral, let us listen a final time to her own words. Her views are shared by many Brazilian artists in the postdictatorship period, a time when ideologies have gone out of focus and out of fashion. First, the author defines her social intentions this way: "I want to speak to people. Right now I want to touch people deeply, to talk about feelings, human relationships. I want to be able to change people's lives, which is what happened with *De braços abertos*" (Amaral, personal interview). Second, when asked about her ideological stance, she sums up succinctly the quandary in which artists find themselves in the postdictatorship period:

> Ideologically speaking, I just don't know anymore. Because it's obvious there was a time when the good guys were on one side and the bad guys on the other and it was easier to take a stance. Today everything's become very complicated. And I detest the leftist party line of the PT

> [Partido Trabalhista/Workers' Party] and the PC do B [Partido Comunista do Brasil/Communist Party of Brazil]. They've suddenly become living fossils, people talking about things that no longer exist anywhere. Yet I do think Brazil needs to go through the experience of the PT in power so people can truly realize, oh, so that's not it either. In the meanwhile there remains this illusion that the working class will bring paradise. But at the same time I'm against social injustice, against low salaries, against exploitation, against corruption. Today I don't know any more what's right-wing and what's left-wing. What I do know is I'm against any circumstance in which human beings are oppressed. (Amaral, personal interview)

The final writer I examine in this chapter is Edla van Steen, another member of the group of distinguished women playwrights in Brazil who have become major voices and whose themes have been privileged with the democratization process: gender role and identity, stories of exemplary women, family ties, and ethnic roots. van Steen exemplifies that circle of writers who established themselves in fiction before trying their hand at drama.

Edla van Steen was born into a German-Belgian family in Santa Catarina in the south of Brazil. Her earliest professional experiences were in radio, journalism, and cinema. She starred in director Hugo Khoury's film *Garganta do diabo* (*The Devil's Throat*), receiving praise from critics and winning best-actress awards in Brazil and Italy. She soon gave up her budding film career, however, to become a full-time writer.

She published a book of short stories, *Cio* (*In Heat*), in 1965, garnering overwhelmingly favorable reviews. Her novel *Memórias do medo* (*Memories of Fear*), published in 1974, was written during Brazil's bleakest period of repression under the military dictatorship. Its veiled language and symbolic plot devices served to elude the censors, because the narrative implicitly denounced the generals' reign of terror. In 1981, *Memórias de medo* was adapted for public television by playwright Jorge Andrade.[24]

Edla van Steen published *Antes do amanhecer* (*Before the Dawn*) in 1977, a collection of short stories which merited an award from the São Paulo Association of Art critics, and in 1983 a second novel, *Corações mordidos* (literally "Bitten Hearts" but published in translation under the title *Village of the Ghost Bells*). Once again the author received lavish praise from the critics for her prose. The year 1985 saw two new publications: a short novel for young readers, *Manto de nuvem* (*Cloud Blanket*), as well as a new collection of short stories, *Até sempre* (*Forever After*).

Her next novel, *Madrugada,* published in 1992, received the Coelho Neto prize for the novel by the Academia Brasileira de Letras and, in 1993, the Pen Club of Brazil best-book award. Her most recent work of fiction, published in 1996, under the title *Cheiro de amor* (*Fragrance of Love*), won the coveted Nestlé Prize for best collection of short stories in 1997. The year 1996 also marked the publication of *Por acaso* (*By Chance*), her second novelette for young people.

The author has published many other stories in anthologies, in Brazil and abroad. Her work has been translated into English, Italian, German, French, Polish, and Spanish. Translations of her stories have appeared in such American journals as *The Literary Review* and *The Latin American Literary Review,* as well as in book-length anthologies (e.g., *One Hundred Years after Tomorrow*). Edla van Steen and I have collaborated on three translations of her fiction: an anthology of her stories, under the title *A Bag of Stories, Village of the Ghost Bells* (*Corações mordidos*), and *Early Mourning* (*Madrugada*).

And what of her theatrical production? Writing for the stage was a logical turn on Edla van Steen's path as a writer. She is a former actress, translates regularly for the stage, and her prose narrative is filled with theatrical elements. van Steen's first play, *O último encontro* (*The Last Encounter*), was staged in São Paulo in 1989 and published in 1991. The play won Brazil's most prestigious theatrical award, the Molière Prize for Best Playwright, as well as the Mambembe Award in the same category. She has written several other plays, among them her most recent, *À mão armada* (*Armed Robbery*), which she and I co-adapted from her novel *Madrugada* and which was published in 1996. Edla van Steen has also rendered numerous translations/adaptations for the theater.[25]

In order to examine the ways in which Edla van Steen's playwriting flows from her fiction, as well as the ways in which both genres exemplify the quest/identity paradigm, I first examine her 1984 *Corações mordidos* (*Village of the Ghost Bells*). The quest motif figures prominently in the novel and assumes spiritual modalities, taking the form of a rite of initiation in which place becomes a ritualized backdrop, a kind of sacred space, or the external projection of an inner world. The work also provides a clear example of the quest in terms of transformation of experience into art. The novel constitutes a play on the essential mechanisms of fiction: construction of character, plot structure, and narrative point of view. There are endless and highly suggestive variations on narrative focus by which the reader is invited to immerse herself/himself in the process of creation. The novel offers a complex mixture of selective omniscience, false third person, interior monologue, and dialogue, the latter often imagined by the characters as they project their mindscapes outward in the form of fictional social exchanges. The narrative voice is fragmented, kaleidoscopic, beckoning the reader to follow its echoes through a labyrinthine universe. On this level *Village* deals with a woman's quest for identity, and the narrative maze leads to many startling discoveries, including the fact that the protagonist, Greta, is the novel's undeclared narrator, who "writes" both in the third person and in the first, in the voice of her *alter ego,* Tina. Van Steen's novel plays with the reader's expectations in presenting a series of options, then removing them, at times surprising her/him with their reintroduction.

The twisting narrative turns of the labyrinth shape the plot in the form of a collage, the visual representation of which are the collages created by Tina: the novel is woven from bits and pieces, which are tested, accepted or rejected, until the narrative takes shape and becomes an autonomous structure. It is the story of the protagonist/narrator Greta's spiritual quest—again I quote Carol Christ—"a probing to the bedrock of a woman's experience of self and world that can support her quest to change the values of her society" (Christ 1980, 11).

Like the quest of Doris Lessing's Martha in *The Four-Gated City,* Greta's is essentially interior. Her inner exploration takes the form of a splitting off of the personality into several others, the first of whom is Tina. From this "garden of forking paths" arises the fictional cosmos described in Greta's internal code, through which the act of writing becomes an obsession, a projection of her inner phantoms and demons. This suggests a kind of creative exorcism or perhaps madness: "A friend of mine stopped writing to avoid turning into a schizophrenic. He lived with ghosts all around him. Maybe that's what's going to happen to me" (van Steen 1991, *Village,* 124). Doris Lessing's protagonist fights the same dragon on her quest: "The significance of Martha's battle with the myth of psychology is symbolized by Lynda, who was destroyed by a psychologist who called her powers madness" (Christ 1980, 64). It is a truism that all authors project personal demons and the unconscious in their writings, but in the case of Edla van Steen's novel the process is entirely deliberate, exposed, and questioned. The narrative structure is patterned after that of the unconscious mind. Greta's creation—a suburban would-be utopia known as the Village of the Bells (hence the title for the English translation)—almost always appears when she is looking through the window of her home; that is, one could say the narrator "sees" through the window of her soul.

Greta's rite of passage is the very act of writing, and she examines her own *psyche* by projecting the other characters: Tina, Greta, Alice, Luis, Sônia, Elisa, and Miriam. By researching their possibilities and trying to discover the paths they will follow, Greta allows the reader to accompany the creative process. As the narrator searches for solutions to her own life, she discards or "kills" creations that fail to work out. Characters arise from varied suggestions, ideas, and images. Greta tries to give them verisimilitude, to make them exist "in fact" rather than "in fiction." A question—"What could have become of Sônia?"—may lead to the transformation of an idea into concrete action. The narrator casts doubt on some characters, pokes fun at others, but when she finds their potential she persists in their cultivation. She first observes them, speculates about what will happen to them, and then frames them in close-up shots. In certain cases she even discusses with them their fictional possibilities. And one character, the old man Camilo, mischievously asks the narrator, "Who says I'm alive?" (van Steen 1991, *Village,* 196).

Greta searches for identity through her characters because they represent possible options for a woman's life. Her alter ego Tina's childhood diary is entitled "Intimate portrait in search of identity." The narrator, however, soon displays impatience with the quest for identity through the prism of childhood: "A short time ago I considered dumping these pages in the wastebasket and to hell with this search for identity" (van Steen 1991, *Village,* 21). But she finally gives up on it: "Does the idea of weeding the past, as if childhood were a kind of garden, really have anything to do with my present identity? I doubt it" (van Steen 1991, *Village,* 23). Greta also searches for identity at the other end of the chronological spectrum: her mother Elisa's generation. She rejects out of hand the traditional option, based as it is on the patriarchal imposition of female identity limited to the sphere of the family. In speaking of the mother, she writes: "Why not look into Elisa more carefully, who so far has played only a walk-on role? Because Elisa lost her identity when she was widowed" (van Steen 1991, *Village,* 43).

While the Greta/Tina relationship could be analyzed from various archetypal angles, in Jungian terms—the image of the woman-anima, the woman possessed by the animus, the perilous separation of conscious and unconscious—their relationship also refers to two sides of artistic creation: the intuitive and the rational. Tina creates the collages; Greta frames them and decides where to hang them. Tina represents a dimension of Greta's personality the narrator tries unsuccessfully either to repress or reconcile: "There's someone else hidden inside me . . . My other self is violent, obsessive, capable of uncontrolled, wild passion" (van Steen 1991, *Village,* 80). There is a continual struggle between the rational Greta and this "someone," an attempt throughout the novel to accept the duality. In Greta's *psychic* prism, Tina is the romantic refraction: she is all instinct, spirit, anima. The struggle with the Tina side also corresponds to the difficulties of constructing the narrative. Greta repeatedly seeks to discover her double in the act of writing. There are constant interruptions and deflections. Tina flees—the narrator commits her to a mental hospital—but Greta returns always to her in a search for equilibrium. Greta must listen to Tina's inner voice coaxing her to accept and express emotions she has denied. At the same time, Greta must impose her conscious and mature self on her infantile and romantic self. With Tina and indeed all Greta's female projections, the romantic solution is cast into darkness and doubt. Because it is associated with the animus-father, it is portrayed as an immature solution which obfuscates genuine transcendence: the relinking of the conscious and unconscious mind, maturity, and the integrity of the human person. In the solitude of her home, Greta takes a first step toward reconciliation and reintegration of her personality: "I have a name, whether I like it or not. I am somebody. 'Happy New Year, Greta Cris*tina* de Almeida'" (van Steen 1991, *Village,* 173). Two of Doris Lessing's characters engage in a similar quest for reconciliation: "Each is a guide and teacher for the other. Lynda shares with Martha her knowledge of the nonordinary regions . . . Martha shares with Lynda the strength to cope with ordinary life. It is as if two separated parts of women's experience, mother and witch or madwoman, are joined. From the integration of the separated comes a new power" (Christ 1980, 67). Integration, reconciliation of Greta/Tina, however, is a precarious and in the end ambiguous quest.

The narrator's quest, nevertheless, is a search for her own identity: "While she approached others in this return to childhood, with this skewed outlook, she was really groping for her own identity" (van Steen 1991, *Village,* 109). The narrator thus creates a self-encounter which she focuses through the Greta-prism. "Greta . . . felt an urge to take stock of her life. As if looking back would erase the scars from her memory. But they cannot be erased. No one is reborn. The simple act of recognizing the wounds alters nothing. . . . Might this question be in fact the motive for her neurotic search for identity?" (van Steen 1991, *Village,* 182). The *corações mordidos,* "bitten hearts" or "heart-bites," are fragments of her identity, as well as a quest for utopia: "She would never be an autonomous, complete being; only a part of the whole" (van Steen 1991, *Village,* 182).

Her search leads her to the Village of the Bells, a traditional utopian quest, a search for the promised land, which ends not in rebirth but in cataclysm. Her quest completes a full circle from the "urban hell" to the transformation of her promised land into another hell: the poverty of the slum-dwellers who live behind the Village of the Bells, the increase in prostitution resulting from the nation's deepening economic crisis, and the urban violence which more and more encroaches on the lives of the residents. "The Village is stuck with the limitations of its geographical location" (van Steen 1991, *Village,* 176). The Village of the Bells degenerates from utopia to microcosm of the Brazilian socioeconomic system, symbolized by Fortuna, the ironic name of the real-estate firm that controls the Village: after exploiting the residents' dreams for a better life and failing to keep a single promise, the company tries to force the homeowners out when it sees its hoped-for profits slipping away. To this end, the firm goes to extreme lengths: it causes flooding in the Village, allows prostitutes to frequent the streets, and generally carries on a campaign of intimidation and corruption. *Corações mordidos* calls into question the colonial paradigm, the notion of stepping out of history: "I repeat, you can't escape reality and hope to avoid implausibility. Imagine if the Village had really developed and become a model. In Brazil? . . . . No. You have to follow the rules. I'm going to drink a toast to those with the talent to change the course of History" (van Steen 1991, *Village,* 197). And so at the very end of the novel the narrator destroys her fictional utopia: "Greta stared into the flames crackling in the fireplace. A spark fell on the sawdust next to the books scattered about the floor. She knew what was going to happen, but she did not get up to extinguish the flame" (van Steen 1991, *Village,* 197).

*Village of the Ghost Bells* sets the stage for Edla van Steen's playwriting activities. For example, the novel includes an elaborate play imagined by one of the characters. The vigorous colloquial dialogue suggests, as does the best of theatrical dialogue, psychological depth and complexity. The richness of visual imagery and lighting effects in *Village* is reminiscent of the mythical-archetypal climate characteristic of much of modern Brazilian theater, particularly Nelson Rodrigues. Van Steen's play *O último encontro* externalizes and dramatizes both the fundamental themes of *Village* and its presentation of the intricate connections between artistic creation and the mythical-archetypal environment.

There are many other examples from Edla van Steen's fiction that illustrate her aptitude for playwriting. Her stories have often been filled with scenarios reminiscent of playscripts and stageworthy monologues and dialogues. Her story "A Beleza do Leão," from her 1977 collection *Antes do amanhecer* and included in *A Bag of Stories* with the title "The Beauty of the Lion," is told from the point of view of a protagonist trying to overcome an obsession with acting, only to meet a melodramatic fate in an empty theater. That same character's gender is ambiguous, which will also become a leitmotif in van Steen's play *O último encontro*. Another of her stories, "Aluga-se apartamento," also from *Amanhecer* and included in *Bag* as "Apartment for Rent," is a monologue, spoken by a pedophile, which could be staged nearly without revision. Finally, her long short story "Para sempre," from her 1985 collection of the same title and rendered in *Bag* as "Forever After," includes a section about a man who unveils the secret of his grandmother's illicit love affair, which was the seed from which *O último encontro* sprang.

As I wrote above, *Encontro* was successfully staged in 1989. It garnered prestigious awards and overwhelming support from critics and audiences, due to the quality of the play itself and of the cast and director. The latter was Silnei Siqueira, who in the 1960s had directed one of the most well-known productions in Brazilian theatrical history, *Morte e vida severina* (loosely translated, *Life and Death of a Stone*), based on a narrative poem by poet João Cabral de Mello Neto, with music by Chico Buarque de Hollanda. The author says this about her piece:

> My play *O último encontro* is not autobiographical but it is full of memories. Mine and other people's. Theater has been part of my everyday life for decades. And it has opened up new possibilities: some tales fit into the short story form, others need more extensive development and they turn into novels, and yet others are born for the stage. The memory of a house, with its characters in the present and the past. A love affair. That is The Last Encounter. A final and revealing encounter between the remaining members of a German family from southern Brazil. (van Steen 1997, "Woman")

The play deals with two characters on a quest for sexual and ethnic identity. The voyage to their German immigrant past reveals the ambiguity of a family history suspended between northern Europe and South America. The work, while portraying elements of international postmodernism—e.g., gender deconstruction—also features aspects of Latin

American magic realism. "Edla van Steen has brought to the stage the same intimate atmosphere she has explored in her prose. Faithful to her own concerns as a writer, *O último encontro* deals with family ties, in a world containing several levels of reality . . . Edla's dialogue flows naturally. The action unfolds in intricate rhythms, in a complex structure, which superimposes scenes from past and present" (Guzik 1989, "Intimista," 1). And, as Sábato Magaldi writes in the preface to the play: "The literary quality is to be found in the smooth flow of the action from present to past, in the spontaneous appearance of flashbacks, in the surfacing of another fictional element—the memory of the house, which is not that of the protagonists but is intimated in a magical atmosphere" (Magaldi 1991, "Contramão," 5).

The play is based on a series of fictions: different versions of past events, dreams, fantasies, and ghosts. The plot consists of two temporal planes, present and past. The present time frame focuses on the encounter—the *encontro* of the title—after twenty years, of the last survivors of the Buckhausen family, the protagonists Mira and Marcelo. The action unfolds in the ancestral German family home in the southern Brazilian state Santa Catarina, in the city of Florianópolis. The set is the interior of the old house, with multiple levels, which allows simultaneous and sequential actions to take place in different time frames. The upper level is a mezzanine, which includes doors leading to bedrooms. The lower level is not the main room of the house but a small parlor, a space off-center like the characters themselves. Faded furniture of leather and wood suggests the passage of time. Pictures and other objects in varying styles (e.g., art-nouveau chandelier, impressionist painting) also suggest different time periods in the history of the Buckhausen home. A glass wall—a translucid scrim on the set—adds a ghostly dimension to the time–space factor.

As the play begins, Marcelo is sitting in the small parlor. A young girl and boy appear on the mezzanine, complaining about Dona Berta—who, we later discover, is the Buckhausen governess—spying on them; the boy declares undying love to the girl. The boy and girl are figures from the house's past, which thus bursts into the present at the very beginning of—and, indeed, throughout—the play. Another character arrives, Mira, described in the stage directions as a "communicative, understanding personality, with a certain air of sadness" (van Steen 1991, *Encontro,* 9). Marcelo has been waiting for an hour; this is some sort of homecoming. We discover early on that they haven't seen the house in two decades. The house has an odor of mildew, which Mira describes as "the musty smell of the family" (van Steen 1991, *Encontro,* 10). Marcelo discovers the water is turned off, the house is dry, like the Buckhausen family cycle, as the reader/spectator will discover. Or will Mira and Marcelo, the last members of the family, resurrect the cycle?

The two characters soon enter a zone of conflict, the subtext of which is only revealed at the end of the play. Marcelo is extremely irascible, constantly criticizing her sentimentality and betrayal, but of what sort we do not know in the play's opening scenes. His aggressive and unpleasant attitude is also inexplicable. We find out that Marcelo and Mira have come to sell the furniture and other objects in the house to an antique dealer. Marcelo suggests a sidewalk sale to "show everyone the old folk's private stuff" (van Steen 1991, *Encontro,* 11). His statement is a foreshadowing of intimate family secrets which will be exposed over the course of the play. Mira finds a box of medals that once belonged to their uncle. She had remembered them as gold but ascertains they are made of tin. This incident reveals what has become of the family's gilded past, as well as Mira's sense of innocence lost. She recalls nostalgically that the medals were once their uncle's and the family's pride but Marcelo cuts her off scornfully: "There've always been butt-kissers. As long as they've got something to gain they give medals . . . Do you know how many people went to your dear and important uncle's burial? Three" (van Steen 1991, *Encontro,* 13).

At this point strange figures begin to appear, who, we eventually learn, are the family ghosts, as well as the main characters' memories, such as the boy and girl at the beginning of the play. Thus, memory precedes present-time action. The blocking, the phantom choreography, along with the lighting effects and music that frame the appearance of the ghosts, are among the piece's strengths, which was clear in the 1989 staging and in reading the play:

> Mira lays her head back against the headrest of the sofa. A lighting change focuses on a girl entering the room, sulking, carrying a music book. She sits at the piano and plays an exercise. The grandmother, Fernanda, wearing a red dress, appears on the mezzanine. She holds a mirror in her hands. She watches the girl practicing, puts on lipstick, and goes back into her bedroom. The girl looks up, slams down the piano lid, and exits the stage at the very moment Marcelo appears. (van Steen 1991, *Encontro,* 14)

The girl and the grandmother are wearing old-fashioned clothing, the only clue the audience has so far that they may be from another time. At least one critic, Marco Veloso, never understood what or who the phantoms were, other than something he termed an "organic climate," and he reacted angrily: "This business of creating an organic climate is worthless for theater" (Veloso 1989, "Guerra").

Mira and Marcelo's conflict deepens, particularly as regards family history. While she displays compassion, he has nothing but contempt:

"MIRA: I feel sorry for Uncle Artur, even if I didn't like him. Marcelo—
The renowned Artur Buckhausen squandered everything, and you feel sorry for him?" (van Steen 1991, *Encontro,* 15).

The irony is that later in the play it will be revealed that Marcelo himself is a kind of reincarnation of their uncle. While Marcelo attacks the family with "masculine" aggression, Mira defends their forebears with "feminine" delicacy. While Mira wants to keep up appearances—good manners, nice tableware—Marcelo wants to flout social conventions—drink fancy wine in plastic cups, put his feet on the table. Such gender identification, too, will prove ironic in the end.

Past family failures are not the only things on their minds. They also reveal their own predicaments: Mira's husband has left her and Marcelo is a failed writer. They are both at the end of their rope, and the question arises whether they will rescue not only the Buckhausen lineage but themselves as well. Marcelo subverts this rescue mission, not only by sullying the family name but by assailing Mira, accusing her of unnamed sins and betrayal, using shocking language: "You're the most horrendous person I've even met in my life. And you know I'm including the worst kind of people, crooks, bums, prostitutes" (van Steen 1991, *Encontro,* 20). This explosion of unconscious impulses follows the tradition set down by Nelson Rodrigues, whose characters speak from the deepest subliminal recesses. Mira insists that they weren't to bring up the past, that they had agreed there would be no "*acerto de contas,*" or "coming to terms," which, one might add, was the original title Edla van Steen chose for the play. This coming to terms ultimately relates to their search for identity, especially vis-à-vis each other. Mira then seems to contradict herself by alluding mysteriously to their past: "Your sick head almost drove us to insanity" (van Steen 1991, *Encontro,* 20). His response hints at an intimacy—and a tenderness—we had not guessed before, because we still do not understand the nature of their relationship: "I could describe your clothes, your obsessions, the way you walk. I know you by heart" (van Steen 1991, *Encontro,* 20).

Mira names objects in the house (e.g., art-nouveau lamp) that link her structurally to the past. Marcelo sneers at that sort of "feminine" sensibility—"Woman are usually superficial" (van Steen 1991, *Encontro,* 21)—and immediately oscillates to the opposite end of his repulsion—attraction response toward her—"You've never looked so attractive. I swear" (van Steen 1991, *Encontro,* 21). The attraction–repulsion is also expressed in the actors' body language. In many scenes, for example, Mira moves toward Marcelo into a comfortable social distance, he attempts to reduce that distance to an intimate, even seductive closeness, which she rebuffs by getting up or crossing the room.

As the play progresses, the ghosts take on more and more life and interact subtly with the present. Mira is seated at the piano. Fernanda enters. The phone rings. Fernanda answers on the mezzanine at precisely the same time that Mira answers in the parlor. Mira: "Odd. There was no one on the line" (van Steen 1991, *Encontro,* 22). This ghostly scene, in which characters in different time plays perform simultaneous movements, is reminiscent of Nelson Rodrigues's works, particularly *Vestido de noiva*. The young boy and girl from the opening of the play reappear as Mira and Marcelo sit in the parlor. The boy searches for the girl as she hides. He speaks, the first time we hear the ghostly voices: "I want a real kiss . . . a French kiss" (van Steen 1991, *Encontro,* 22–23). He attempts to kiss her; she screams for her grandmother. The reader/spectator's curiosity is piqued. Do these figures who seem to have no organic link to the main characters represent memories? Whose? Mira's? Marcelo's? The house's? Are they part of its history? The protagonists' subsequent dialogue leads one to suspect that the answer to all those questions is affirmative. Mira speaks of the house as her last refuge, her grave—will there be rebirth? Marcelo states that he views the house as that which he never had (although some will realize at this point he is talking about Mira, this only becomes explicit later in the play). He declares the only thing that matters is that they are alone together for the first time in their lives, the as yet unrevealed subtext of which is that as children they were always watched very closely. Why? Mira begins discussing her parents: their estrangement, the failure of the "factory" which robbed her father of the will to live, her mother not shedding a tear at his funeral. Marcelo's dismissal of her comments—just a "daughter's interpretation" (van Steen 1991, *Encontro,* 23)—does not clarify their relationship. They are clearly Buckhausens but how, specifically, are they related?

Mira begins feeling the presence of the ghosts: "Oh, I'm getting goose bumps . . . I get the feeling any minute grandma's going to show up and greet me" (van Steen 1991, *Encontro,* 24–25). As usual, Marcelo derides her feelings, calling her reaction "sentimental memory." Mira then begins to discuss her grandmother (who died when Mira was seventeen): she was a painter in a stuffy provincial environment, forced to play the housewife role, her husband a conventional patriarch. When Mira states that some of the grandmother's paintings are on the walls, we realize they are part of the set (the paintings used in the 1989 production actually came from Edla van Steen's private collection). Mira discloses that she has always identified with her grandmother in the sense of favoring her "Brazilian"—as opposed to German—side. This search for ethnic identity is a subject I explore later.

Night falls, indicated in the production by the fading light behind the translucid scrim upstage. Marcelo has persuaded Mira to stay in the house rather than go to a hotel, with the proviso that he "behave." With night the ghosts will appear with increasing frequency and intensity. The boy and girl make another entrance; the boy reads a passage from the Portuguese poet Fernando Pessoa; when the lights come up on the protagonists again Marcelo is also reading Fernando Pessoa. Other phantom characters appear who serve the function of flashback regarding the Buckhausen family history to which the protagonists' have alluded. Fernanda, the grandmother, as a young woman, is seen in the company of her brother-in-law João, suggesting an illicit affair. When her husband, João's brother Rafael, enters he seems oblivious to the possibility of a tryst, his concern being problems with the family factory, which, we have learned earlier, were passed on to the next generation, that of Mira's parents. Rafael is also indifferent to Fernanda's paintings and by extension to her inner life. When the lights come up in the present time frame, Mira is wearing one of Fernanda's dresses. Marcelo finds her stunning but wants to know why the "*fantasia*" (which means both "costume" and "fantasy" in Portuguese). Even in his admiration Marcelo manages to be negative. Mira is astonished to have found Fernanda's wardrobe intact and ordered. They look through a family album, which establishes another parallel with Nelson Rodrigues; one thinks here of his play *Álbum de família,* which deals with many of the same themes as *Encontro*. Several photos are missing; Marcelo surmises that the grandfather, Rafael, removed them because the "lover"—Fernanda's—may have been featured in them. Mira reacts angrily because Marcelo has broken his promise not to delve into "dangerous" affairs. The audience is intrigued as to the nature of the "danger." Although both characters are intent on unraveling the past, Marcelo is searching for literary solutions and identity. The family album—in the literal and metaphorical senses—is grist for his narrative mill, for the novel he is trying to write. Both characters have motives for distorting past reality; Mira, apparently, for the sake of delicacy, and Marcelo for the sake of fiction. Their motives, however, are more complex because family history impinges directly on them. When Marcelo announces that the family "curse" is being repeated he brings the audience closer to the crux of the protagonist's story. They argue about family history, about Fernanda's death—murder? accident?—at the hands of her husband.

Mira suggests that the grandmother was involved in a lesbian affair and she gives a kind of capsule gender history of patriarchal Brazil: "At that time, being a homosexual wasn't for just anyone. Grandma had to have strength of character . . . Besides, men only felt cuckolded by other men. Another woman could only be a female friend. The machos never imagined a homosexual relationship" (van Steen 1991, *Encontro,* 21). On the heels of this conversation, the ghost children return: the boy announces he will be the "marquise" and she will then be the "marquis"; they exchange clothing. This suggestion of total gender reversal will come to be one of the play's—and the protagonists'—dominant themes. There is a flashback to Fernanda and another woman, the latter dressed in "masculine"—or dominatrix?—fashion: riding clothes and whip. Fernanda is painting her portrait. The two are having an affair, a taboo beyond the patriarchal imagining of the period, as Mira herself has informed us. Nevertheless, Mira subsequently concludes that she considers a lesbian affair improbable in the social environment of the time, thus ironically contradicting the author's exploration of social and gender interstices and her implicit view, according to which there have always been those who would transgress against taboos. Mira further declares that if Fernanda had been capable of a lesbian affair she would have been a "real" painter, suggesting that the artist is the transgressor and the transgressor is the artist. According to this logic, it would be the role of the artist to contravene prohibitions, to shatter the surface of social convention. Yet another version of Fernanda's story is "told" by the ghosts, when Rafael confronts Fernanda about her betrayal with his brother João; she confesses and defiantly rejoins that he has no justification to preach morals because he has consorted with prostitutes since the first year of their marriage. He shouts that he will not be a *corno manso* (cuckold) and shoots her. This is Marcelo's version of events; the patriarchal order is thus reestablished. Mira responds to his account by asserting that the Buckhausen story is cheap melodrama, unworthy of attention in a country beset by poverty, hunger, and violence. The character, in this way, is criticizing not only Marcelo but the author, Edla van Steen herself, and by extension the many women writers who have been accused of turning their attention away from the social issues which have for so long been the stuff of "serious" and "committed" literature and drama. Van Steen thus airs publicly the criticism of which she, Maria Adelaide Amaral, and other "alienated," "psychological" writers have been the targets.[26] The author has also cleverly put the ideologically correct argument in the mouth of Mira while Marcelo espouses the "individual in society" viewpoint, turning gender identity on its head. This is no coincidence, because as the play ends Mira and Marcelo have switched identities, as I elucidate later.

The family name, Buckhausen, or "book house," contains multiple symbolic vectors. Mira dreams of opening a bookstore with her share of the inheritance—which will never materialize—while Marcelo fantasizes opening a publishing house specializing in the works of marginalized writers like himself. His characters, of course, are the ghosts of the Buckhausen past, key events of whose lives also pass before the spectators' eyes. But these past events represent not only history; they are projected in large part in variegated fictional viewpoints provided by Marcelo in his guise as writer, whose only theme is family history. Marcelo's function as implicit narrator is similar to that of Greta's in *Corações mordidos,* in that he creates a narrative maze leading to stunning revelations and he surprises the spectators/readers in presenting, removing, and sometimes reintroducing a series of options. The structure of the novel *Corações* is focused on a narrator-protagonist who invents a universe inhabited by other characters that are real in the metacontext of the fictional world but are imaginary as projections of the conscious and unconscious of the narrator. It is a world in the present haunted by ghosts from the past, from the memories of the house and the imagination of the protagonists. A fictional world unfolding, a labyrinth, a fun house of mirrors and *trompe d'oeil* effects. In the same way, *O último encontro* projects, from Marcelo's viewpoint, a hall of mirrors reflecting living beings and phantoms, alternative versions of past incidents, ambiguity in relation to the present, and unconscious desires made conscious. In the ancestral Buckhausen home, characters from the present invent and recreate those from family history, resurrect them, project themselves on them, and in the end become their reincarnations. Past and present, therefore, are mixed together in fictional variations, within which the overarching fictional form is the play itself, which thus becomes a kind of metafiction.

MARCELO: "Funny, I've invented [Fernanda's] death in so many ways and the idea of her falling in love with someone from her own family never occurred to me. That would explain some unclear features" (van Steen 1991, *Encontro,* 29).

But it is an odd kind of metafiction, not the traditional play within a play but the play within the novel—Marcelo's—within the play. Like Greta in *Corações mordidos,* Marcelo builds his story through projection of both inner phantoms and those of his ancestral past. These are the actors in the drama of the death of Fernanda and of the versions of the past presented not only in Marcelo's fiction but in the newspapers of the period that reported her death, as well as the story recounted by Dona Berta, the Buckhausen's old governess. Was Fernanda murdered by her jealous husband or did she suffer an accident? Did she betray her husband? With her brother-in-law? With a woman? These versions of the past determine the course of the story lived in the present by Mira and Marcelo. And what the past unleashes are their respective life crises.

According to Jungian psychoanalysts, the doors to the unconscious are open during significant life crises, dreams, and artistic creation. There are several indications in *Encontro* that its structure corresponds to the unconscious. The play begins late in the day, with the fading light from the outside penetrating the parlor: "The ambient light seems to come from the glass wall" (van Steen 1991, *Encontro,* 7). The external light slowly dims and the parlor is illuminated by the light of a fireplace. One could posit that the external light corresponds to the conscious level. When it fades the night is awakened, and with it the magical world of the unconsciousness, suggested by the ghostly light of the fireplace. What Jung calls the collective unconscious has an archaic character, because it contains the history of families, clans, and tribes, by extension of all of humankind. That archaic aspect is manifested in the play by means of the antique furniture and props, the musty odor of the house itself, in short, the setting for the story. The family name Buckhausen, "book house," is the labyrinth which parallels simultaneously the unconscious and myth.

It is in that environment where Mira and Marcelo project their ancestral phantoms in their quest to resolve their crises, anxieties, and problems of sexual identity. According to Jung, youth is spent disengaging from the unconscious and strengthening ties with the outside world. In maturity, however, one returns to and reconciles with the unconscious. In their maturity, Mira and Marcelo come back to their ancestral roots, to the unconscious, and endeavor to reconcile with their inner selves and with each other. Mira's initial reason for the return to Florianópolis seems a banal quest: to satisfy nostalgic longings. Yet she reveals much more complex motives when she says, "I once considered returning to Santa Catarina to hide from everyone" (van Steen 1991, *Encontro,* 10). She describes the ancestral home as her refuge, as a kind of tomb. Feeling that her life is a failure, her husband having left her, she flees from external tribulations to submerge herself in the origins of her life and therefore of her crisis. She plunges into the world of the unconscious in order to establish her lost inner balance. Marcelo, for much longer than Mira, has been delving into his roots through his writing, in a search for identity. The quest leads him to the ancestral house of books. Together, they try to lay bare their failures and decipher the decline of the Buckhausen family, whose ghosts eddy through the house. They are not only the ghosts of the dead but of the living, and they reveal ancestral secrets, the most significant of which relates to the question of sexual identity. And that identity is also the key to the protagonists' relationship.

Applying the idea of the collective unconscious to *Encontro* may create the impression the play presents the question of sexual identity in Jungian terms, that is, according to the archetypal definition of masculine and feminine. Jung's theories hold that the archetypes residing in the collective unconscious, universal symbols of human traits, include two that define and determine sexual identity: the anima, representing the supposedly "feminine" side of the male, and the animus, the hypothetical "masculine" side of the female. These archetypes, linked in childhood to mother and father figures, may serve as internal guides, aiding the man and the woman to maintain a balance between conscious and unconscious. At the same time, the animus and the anima frequently manifest themselves in negative ways, even to the extreme of becoming a sort of death demon. In the play, those archetypes would have variegated forms and representations. The negative animus would be projected in the form of *Encontro*'s father figures: the grandfather Rafael and the father. If the latter is a weak failure, the former is a repressive, macho patriarch, a death demon, because Rafael, in some versions of the family chronicle, kills his wife Fernanda. Marcelo himself embodies certain qualities of the animus in his excessively "masculine" behavior toward Mira; he is aggressive, acid-tongued, sardonic, and coldly objective.

> Marcelo, in his aggression stemming from his frustration, provokes Mira constantly yet neither does he spare himself from self-irony, in an effort to unmask his own illusions and to prevent either of them from

> becoming maudlin. In his zeal to discover the most intimate truths, he even pries into the details of Mira's sex life with her ex-husband. The function of these fictional devices is to break down barriers and to expose utterly the protagonists. (Magaldi 1991, "Contramão," 5-6)

In a sense they are mirror images of one another. Mira, in Jungian terms, would be projecting the animus on Marcelo and he the anima on her. At first glance Mira reveals supposedly "feminine" characteristics: she is sweet, delicate, passive, intuitive. The entire Jungian apparatus, however, is a mere illusion in the play. After the initial impressions, the spectator/reader begins to realize that the whole question of sexual identity is mitigated, and the author consciously deconstructs the masculine and feminine archetypes. The grandmother Fernanda, the paradigm for anima projection, is the mother—or grandmother—figure par excellence. But Mira proposes the hypothesis that grandma Fernanda carried on an lesbian relationship, an unambiguous transgression of social norms and the traditionally accepted image of the grandmother. Another male archetype, uncle Artur—addicted to gambling, he squanders the family's inheritance—is a transvestite. And one slowly discovers that Fernanda and Artur are mythical models repeated by Mira and Marcelo, who at the end of the play reveal that they are brother and sister—this is the play's melodramatic surprise—reverse sexual roles, and resume an incestuous relationship from their childhood, which had been interrupted in their adolescence. They recommence the game of "marquis" and "marquise," they are the adult incarnations of boy and girl who have appeared ghost-like throughout the play, as well as the heirs of their uncle and grandmother. On the one hand, their behavior could be analyzed in archetypal terms. Fernanda would be identifying excessively with the animus and Artur with the anima, in both cases leading to a loss of gender balance. On the other hand, the role exchange and the incest suggest that the siblings represent two poles of a single personality in search of equilibrium between masculine and feminine. They would thus symbolize reconciliation and integration of the personality. Here, too, there are parallels with *Corações mordidos*.

The characters in the novel are unable to fulfill their identity quests through conventional heterosexual love: the narrator presents the options of homosexual love, and in the case of two secondary characters, incest. It is no coincidence that these two characters are from Santa Catarina, because their incestuous affair is another of the antecedents—besides the story "Forever After," mentioned earlier—for *O último encontro*. A character in the novel, Miriam, leaves São Paulo to live incestuously with her brother. As do Mira and Marcelo, they go back to Santa Catarina, their place of origin.

How is the tortuous sexual path taken by Edla van Steen's characters to be understood? It is clear that the decadence of the Buckhausen family coincides with the dissolution of sexual identity. There is deterioration of the patriarchal system, in which sociosexual roles had been rigidly defined. The family fortune is dissipated, the house has been sold, and only two survivors remain. Yet there is another way to focus the characters' unconventional sexual choices: in a world characterized by personal and collective failure, where dreams and ideals have been crushed, isn't any type of love—two souls merging—valid? Would it not be legitimate to say that the ultimate quest of Mira and Marcelo is a return to the beginning, a search for mythical recreation and therefore identity?

*O último encontro* might be characterized, then, as a mythical-magical work which recounts the history of the tragic and incestuous circle of the Buckhausens, where time is cyclical and the protagonists embark on a quest to return to the beginning in search of regeneration. But what they encounter is the family's destiny. Marcelo and Mira meet in the old house ostensibly to wrap up the last of the family's affairs. They soon reveal, however, that their *encontro* has other meanings: for Mira the ancestral home is at the same time refuge and tomb, where she hopes to rediscover some part of herself that has been lost. For Marcelo it signifies finding something he never had. It is a quest for origins in which the siblings confront their family's fate, the repetition of collective failure, of which they are the last manifestation. Mira, abandoned by her husband, is resigned to that fate. Marcelo, the unsuccessful author, writes obsessively about betrayal and decadence in the house of books. Is his writing a way to overcome fate, a catharsis? Nothing seems to work because he remains unwaveringly bitter: "Grandfather was betrayed by his wife, his cousin Paulo, his brother João, by his son Artur . . . What the hell. Betrayal is apparently the family's common denominator" (van Steen 1991, *Encontro,* 16). Will the brother and sister repeat the family paradigm or do they represent a solution? Does their last encounter lead to the last phase in the Buckhausen's decline? The answer is ambiguous.

In many ways, they echo ancestral paradigms. They take on the identities of the ghosts that circulate through the house of books: Mira dresses up like a man (the intimation of Fernanda's lesbianism) and Marcelo like a woman (like uncle Artur). The governess, Dona Berta, who appears in a single scene, announces that the house and the furniture will be sold the next day; there will be no inheritance. Thus, the siblings, on the last night of the Buckhausens, in the final repetition of the ancestral paradigm, will complete the family destiny: "The link between family history and present fate reinforces the idea of inevitability, similar to the cycles in Greek tragedy" (Magaldi 1991, "Contramão," 5). Is incestuous love an antidote? The "tragedy" ends dialectically. There is a kind of happy ending in the finalization of the Buckhausen destiny. At the same time, Mira and Marcelo break with that aspect of this destiny that has denied fulfillment of and through love. On the last night they discover and express the plenitude of love. Like Fernanda and Artur, mythical archetypes they reincarnate, they try to escape destiny. Mira and Marcelo drink a toast to their forebears and at least for one night they defy fate and gain a fragile hold on identity. The curse becomes happiness and the quest for identity is fulfilled, however fleeting the former and tenuous the latter.

The archetypal elements in the play, the ghosts, bring it, to some degree, into the field of magic realism, which often features a house as mythical center where laws of cause and effect are suspended. One is reminded of such examples by woman writers as Isabel Allende's *The House of the Spirits* and the ranch house in Laura Esquivel's *Like Water for Chocolate*. One could also mention the Buendía family home in Gabriel García Márquez's *One Hundred Years of Solitude*. Edla van Steen's play also shares with these works the notion of family chronicle.

The mythical dimension lends the play tone and thematic structure. The past emerges in the play not only in the form of flashbacks to clarify plot points; it is a real presence that mingles with the present. The ghosts wandering through the house and their stories are echoed in the present. Submersion in the past, in the family roots, gives meaning to the present. Mira states that the return has given her for the first time a sense of belonging, pleasure in sensing her roots. After Marcelo and Mira come back to the house of books, time is suspended and there is a progressive dilution of the separation between past and present; the past, in fact, begins to intrude directly in the present. As the ghosts increasingly make their appearance, the protagonists come to resemble them more and more and they regress to their childhood, to the origin of their incestuous relationship. As in myths, time and events are cyclical; Mira and Marcelo come full circle in their own lives. At the conclusion of mythical cycles chaos is unleashed in the form of orgies, phantoms, demons, exorcisms. Similarly, as the Buckhausen cycle nears its end and the play comes to a close, Marcelo and Mira cross dress. The brother puts on one of his uncle

Artur's wigs as the latter's ghost observes him, smiling. For the first time in the play, one of the ghosts becomes aware of the present and the mythical interpenetration of past and present is total. Afterwards, as sister and brother kiss, the entire cast of family ghosts appears, murmuring "unintelligible words in an incoherent chorus" (van Steen 1991, *Encontro,* 47). It is the chaos that brings to an end the Buckhausen cycle, the final exorcism. Will there be rebirth, the beginning of a new cycle founded by the union of Mira and Marcelo? In the play's closing scene, the ghosts who appear as "boy" and "girl" swear undying love, vow that one day they will meet again in the family home. Because the children are Mira and Marcelo themselves, the tale ends where the protagonists' story began, the origin of their part in the cycle and the dawn of their moment within the family's destiny.

Another piece of the family's destiny is inserted within a larger social question, the decline of German culture in southern Brazil. Between the last decades of the nineteenth century and the early part of the twentieth, several Latin American countries experienced export booms which drew waves of immigrants from abroad, whose main destinations were Brazil and Argentina. Among the groups that settled in Brazil were Japanese, Lebanese, Jews, Italians, and Germans. The latter flourished in the south and became prominent in such cities as Florianópolis. Edla van Steen tells us in her own words how this footnote to Brazilian history has impacted her life and writing:

> Every moment in fiction has its own form, its internal logic. As well as its prior logic. My earliest memory of myself is of a skinny girl hiding beneath the furniture in my maternal grandmother's house. It was the time of the blackout. The Second World War. Santa Catarina, a state in southern Brazil. The Wendhausen family was anti-Nazi in Florianópolis, a city populated mainly by German immigrants. The German language was spoken in the home, in the street, in the schools. One night, my sister and I heard someone stamping up to our door. Who could it be and what did they want? We ran and hid under the table. My grandma Lucy stood firmly in the doorway: You cannot search my house now, gentlemen. My granddaughters are asleep. The only way you'll get in is over my dead body. A gallant gesture, to be sure, which would leave a deep impression on me. I learned from her how to be strong, how to fight tooth and nail to get what I wanted, in spite of a vulnerable side which makes it difficult to control emotions. The Wendhausens were wealthy merchants known all over the state of

> Santa Catarina. They founded schools and hospitals, they were involved in state politics. Like other famous German families in the south, they owned large properties all over the region. They worked hard for the common good of the larger society. But today there is very little left of the once vast German influence in the architecture and the customs of southern Brazil. Getúlio Vargas, Brazil's version of Juan Perón, promoted nationalist policies detrimental to the German business community in Brazil. Their fate was sealed by the Second World War, which halted imports of raw materials and machinery. Unscrupulous lawyers and Brazilian relatives took advantage of the situation to cheat the German community out of its wealth and property. The immigrants living in Brazil went to their graves heartsick over the twists and turns of history. (van Steen 1997, "Woman")

In the play, she puts this concern in the Marcelo's mouth: "I find the decline of German culture in Brazil moving. The effects of miscegenation, war, loss of identity . . ." (van Steen 1991, *Encontro,* 19). This story is worthwhile in its own right: it is a little known chapter in Brazil's history and it flies in the face of the stereotype of Germans in Brazil, who are usually depicted as Nazi war criminals, as in the film *The Boys from Brazil.*

A related issue is also brought up by Marcelo. Mira asks him if he uses the Buckhausen name in his fiction; he replies that using foreign names in fiction is in bad taste and pretentious. This relates to a significant issue in Brazil, that of cultural nationalism versus cultural "imperialism." Marcelo's view is in some senses a relic of the ideology of the 1960s which led many on the left to shun all things foreign. Another reason for Marcelo's attitude is that foreign names are quite popular in the Brazilian commercial sphere, leading the artistic community to a kind of backwards snobbery against them.[27] Edla van Steen and other women writers of the postdictatorship period, however, are turning their backs on the canon and ideological strictures that came to dominate the Brazilian stage in previous decades and that have obfuscated many of the issues—such as gender and ethnicity—important to these writers. The author clearly violates the canon and contradicts Marcelo by using the Buckhausen name in the play. And let us not forget that the author flaunts her own Belgian name, van Steen, which also may sound to some "foreign" and "pretentious."

To finalize the discussion of *O último encontro,* there are in the play neither solutions nor judgment. There are only possibilities. As in the works of Nelson Rodrigues, where unconscious sexual desires and identities explode society's norms, the most intimate reality of the characters in Edla van Steen's drama break through the confinement of the social and family prison. But if that inexorably generates tragedy in the work of Nelson Rodrigues, *O último encontro* presents a more optimistic view. Tragedy clearly constitutes one possibility (the case of Fernanda, for example). But van Steen proposes to us the following question: Could the transgression of sexual norms—and by extension of all norms—not also bring happiness? In the words of Sábato Magaldi, "In Greek tragedy, awareness of the forbidden leads the heroes to punish themselves. Order is reestablished with the loss of the transgressor. The fate created by Edla van Steen works in obverse fashion: all of the dialogue prepares for this long-delayed encounter, inexorable since childhood. It is happiness lived in transgression, even though none of it may matter later on" (Magaldi 1991, "Contramão," 6). Whether the characters complete Judith Christ's triad—life, death, regeneration—is an open question. What is interesting is that the triad applies to both protagonists, Mira and Marcelo, because what Edla van Steen has done in her play is to subvert, to abolish, gender categories.

To conclude this chapter, women's contributions to Brazilian fiction have been duly registered through scholarly studies and translations which have appeared all over the world. Women's role in shaping Brazilian drama, however, is little known. It is my hope that the history and analysis I have presented here will help to bring that role into the light of day and that further and more exhaustive studies will follow. That is a quest truly worth pursuing.

## NOTES

[1] Any list would have to include such great living actresses as Tônia Carreiro, Maria Della Costa, Vera Fischer, Marília Pera, Tereza Raquel, Irene Ravache, Marieta Severo, Eva Wilma, as well as ninety-year-old Dercy Gonçalves, still working as of this writing. In Chapter 1 I discussed Fernanda Montenegro. And the Brazilian pantheon includes late great actresses such as Cacilda Becker, Lilian Lemmertz, Glauce Rocha, and Dina Sfat.

[2] This and all other translations from Portuguese to English in Chapter 2 are mine.

[3] The author quotes here from Novak 1970, 115.

[4] José Vicente and Antonio Bivar are the two important male figures in the Nova Dramaturgia.

[5] In my article "Teatro de Arena and Theatre of Oppressed" (1995), I critique Augusto Boal's legacy: "There is no question that the name Augusto Boal deserves conspicuous standing in the ranks of contributors to the Brazilian stage. He collaborated on two vital projects carried out by São Paulo's Teatro de Arena during its heyday from the late 1950s to the mid-1960s: the *Seminário de Dramaturgia,* which earned the company the sobriquet of 'home of the Brazilian playwright,' and the production entitled *Arena conta Zumbi,* one of the first theatrical responses to the 1964 coup. Boal's name would subsequently be associated with the theoretical writings he published in the 1970s, after the demise of Arena and his exile, in particular *Teatro do oprimido e outras poéticas políticas* and *Técnicas latinoamericanas de teatro popular*. These books have engendered in the first world a staid critical tradition, as well as a network of social activists and psychotherapists who claim to practice 'TO' or theater of the oppressed. For two decades non-Brazilian scholars have taken these speculative—and sometimes practical—tracts entirely out of context and accepted them uncritically, never asking whether such systems as *coringa* can do what they claim and never examining their concrete results. The simple truth is that much of this theoretical legacy, particularly as it pertains to Brazil, is a western academic fantasy that has spawned a glut of articles, book chapters, theses, and conference addresses; in short, a critical industry that puts out assembly-line repetition of clichés about 'liberating' and 'original' techniques, as well as the virtual canonization of Augusto Boal himself. This practice of taking hypothetical claims at face value and never subjecting them to careful scrutiny has inflated the significance of theater of the oppressed and blinded scholars to blatant contradictions. Whereas Brazilian critics and theater artists have long questioned these claims, their promotion elsewhere has shrouded the history of the Brazilian stage in myth. Furthermore, although these techniques may constitute useful tools for the 'TO' network, they are essentially middle-class, first-world tools with dubious third-world connections and perpetuated via self-congratulatory accounts" (40).

[6] Teatro Oficina set the tone for theater of aggression in Brazil. In its 1967 staging of Oswald de Andrade's *O rei da vela,* the company managed to offend nearly everyone with its mocking of Brazilian superpatriotism—considered a tool of the generals running the country—its derision aimed at middle-class subservience to foreign "imperialists," and its flouting of sexual taboos.

[7] Sábato Magaldi, writing in the literary supplement of the *Estado de São Paulo,* 1969, quoted in Cunha de Vincenzo 1992, 87.

[8] The set featured a gigantic staircase covering the entire stage, which made movement, especially dancing, nearly impossible.

[9] *Bodas de papel,* though staged in 1978, was written in 1976.

[10] A similar character more familiar to some readers would be from the Argentine film *Official Story*. I refer here to the protagonist Alicia's husband

Roberto, who benefits financially and otherwise through his complicity with the military dictatorship, only to see his schemes fall apart. in the end.

[11] Quoted by Magyar. Cited in Cunha de Vincenzo 1992, 190.

[12] *Rasga coração* (*Heart Rending*) was written by Oduvaldo Vianna Filho (1936–1974), a playwright and actor who in 1956 joined Teatro de Arena, which produced his early plays. In 1964 he co-founded the Rio de Janeiro Teatro Opiniao, which along with Arena and Oficina was on the cutting edge of engagé theater in the 1960s. Vianninha, as he affectionately came to be known, spent the last ten years of his life working as an actor and writing for television, cinema, and the theater. His plays, however, were almost always censored and so they were staged only after his death from cancer in 1974. Several of his posthumous plays have been highly successful. The most important of these was *Rasga coração* (1974), staged in 1979—it ran until 1981—by Arena founder José Renato, with former Teatro Oficina member Raúl Cortez, one of Brazil's most acclaimed actors, in the lead role. Vianninha's dramaturgical production was immense, in spite of his short life. Along with Gianfrancesco Guarnieri, he established a legacy of well-crafted plays that communicated engagé social consciousness through a unique Brazilian fusion of Brechtian technique and high-powered emotion. He is one of the few authors of the 1960s engagé generation whose plays have survived into the postdictatorship period.

[13] "Organized by [Augusto] Boal, the [São Paulo] fair was based on the idea of soliciting opinions, especially political ones, in the form of sketches, skits, vignettes, and playlets. The *Feira* included contributions from several playwrights: Guarnieri, Jorge Andrade, Plínio Marcos, and Boal himself. Among the pieces were a parody of the military mentality and censorship, an examination of the pre- and postcoup conditions for workers' organizations, problems of rural poverty, and a paean to Che Guevara . . . The fair was equal parts wildly comic absurdism, melodrama, and didacticism; staged in the large space of the Teatro Ruth Escobar, it gained enthusiastic audience support [but] was closed by the censors following the military government's declaration of state of siege in December 1968" (George 1992, *Modern*. 52–53).

[14] These include playwrights Dias Gomes, Gianfrancesco Guarnieri, João das Neves, Jorge Andrade, Lauro César Muniz, Leilah Assunção, Carlos Queiroz Telles, as well as novelist Márcio Souza and critic Décio de Almeida Prado.

[15] The statement about the author's social milieu needs qualification. Born in Portugal, Maria Adelaide Amaral grew up in a poor, working-class section of São Paulo. Her social ascent, rare in Brazil, and her success are the result of her intelligence and tenacity.

[16] There was actually another exception. I saw, in 1983, a one-man show which unfortunately received very little attention and for which I have been unable to unearth any further information, other than my own notes. The show was

called *Maracatu misterioso* (*Mysterious Carnival Band*). Although it was a one-man show, it was such a brilliantly executed, varied, and high-voltage performance that one had the sensation of seeing a staging with full cast, chorus, and orchestra, a complete carnival band. The author-performer—alas! my notes do not include his name—based his piece on the music and dance of the Brazilian Northeast but went far beyond a mere presentation of folklore. He created a complex tapestry with such elements as the northern capital Recife's carnival costumes and its *frevo,* danced acrobatically with a parasol in one hand. Other northeastern forms in the performance included the *desafio* or "challenge," an improvisational duel between two singers (our performer played both parts). He also executed a *bumba-meu-boi,* the archetypal ox-dance processional. The author-performer played a variety of instruments, manipulated puppets, did standup comedy routines, and simply delighted the audience, awestruck by his virtuosity.

[17] The decade of the 1960s saw a number of musicals staged by Teatro de Arena and Teatro Oficina. Arena's musicals were called *Bossarenas* because they celebrated the jazz–samba fusion knows as bossa nova. The *Bossarenas* paved the way for one of Teatro de Arena's most memorable production, the 1965 *Arena conta Zumbi,* a historical musical play about Palmares, a *quilombo* or colony of escaped slaves in northern Brazil during the colonial period. The play protested, through allegory, the 1964 military coup. Teatro Oficina followed Arena's lead with its *Show musical Oficina* and *Roda viva* (*Spinning Wheel*), whose aggressive protest and sexual explicitness led to an attack by paramilitary goons and its eventual ban by the censors. During the 1970s, popular composer and novelist Chico Buarque de Hollanda experimented extensively with the musical. His productions included *Gota d'água,* based on *Medea,* and the successful *A ópera do malandro,* based on Brecht's *Three Penny Opera*. It was made into a movie in 1985, the first filming of a Brazilian musical.

[18] An exception of sorts was her 1988 play *Will,* a monologue with Shakespeare as the narrator, speaking about his life and times. The work opened the 1992 international festival of Iberian language theater in Portugal; the play represented that nation because Maria Adelaide was born there.

[19] An inadvertent translator might render the title as "Mommy Dearest," but Maria Adelaide assures us that she was not thinking about Joan Crawford when she wrote the play.

[20] Although Maria Adelaide's work is unknown to the U.S. theater-going public, her work is performed in Portugal and Argentina.

[21] Stage actors in Brazil survive by performing in *novelas* or soap operas, which play in prime-time TV. In the process, many of them attain a public recognition they would never achieve if they remained exclusively in the theater. At the

same time, several actors, including Eva Wilma, use the *novela* as a way to support their theatrical careers. And the theater uses their television marquee value as a marketing tool to draw audiences. Television, in this way, subsidizes the stage.

[22] In the translation for a possible New York staging, changes include mostly American standards from the swing era: "More Than You Know" (the theme song and title), "Begin the Beguine," "Love Is Here to Stay," "I Could Write a Book", as well as such standard French Impressionist pieces as Debussy's "Girl With the Flaxen Hair." The Brazilian music has been expunged. Nevertheless, I have kept the original music in my translation—as yet unpublished—indicating the choices for the altered version, providing potential directors the option of Americanizing the play, which, as any director knows, they are likely to do anyway. In the end, what Amaral has done is gain some control over the inevitable. Directors, myself included, are notorious for failing to respect stage directions indicated by authors. In this case, the author at least sends directors on a tack which, although it deviates from the original text, still respects her aesthetic choices.

[23] Although no one has written about gay themes in Brazilian theater, David William Foster has published an excellent study of the subject in Brazilian fiction (see Works Cited).

[24] See Chapter 3 for a discussion of one of Jorge Andrade's plays, staged by Grupo Macunaíma in 1993.

[25] Ms. van Steen's translations/adaptations include, among others: *O encontro de Descartes com Pascal* (*L'entretien de M. Descartes avec M. Pascal le jeune*), by Jean Claude Brisville, staged in Rio de Janeiro and São Paulo, by celebrated director Ítalo Rossi, 1987/88; *Três anos* (*Annie Wobler*), by Arnold Wesker, 1987; Henrik Ibsen's *Solness, O construtor* (*The Masterbuilder*), staged by Grupo Tapa, 1988/89; *Max* (*Jacke wie Hose*), by Manfred Karge, staged in 1990 by Walderez de Barros; *As parceiras* (*Annabela et Zina*), by Claude Rullier, 1990; Strindberg's *Senhorita Júlia* (*Miss Julie*), staged by William Pereira, an acclaimed member of Gerald Thomas's *encenador* generation, in 1991; Georg Kaiser's *Da manhã à meia noite* (*From Morn to Midnight*), 1993; *Cala a boca e solte os dentes* (*Lips Together and Teeth Apart*), by Terence McNally, 1994; *A última carta* (*The Last Letter*), by Nicolas Martin, directed by Gianni Rato in 1994; Molière's *O doente imaginário* (*Le malade imaginaire*), staged by Moacyr Góes, another prominent member of the new generation of directors, with Ítalo Rossi in the lead role; Ibsen's *A dama do mar* (*The Lady from the Sea*), directed by Antunes Filho disciple Ulysses Cruz in 1996; David Mamet's *Vida no teatro* (*A Life in the Theater*), directed by Francisco Medeiros in 1996.

[26] Marco Veloso, in his review cited earlier, rails against the play's lack of "violence" (i.e., seriousness), terming it a banal take on the "war of the sexes."

[27] This snobbery is not only a nationalist rejection of imposed foreign cultural models, but a desire to avoid the ridiculous. A good example are some of the commercial names one can observe on any São Paulo street: Slide Dog Dog (a hot dog and hamburger joint), Dink House (a children's clothing store), Hotel Pink, and so forth.

CHAPTER 3

# General Considerations on Scholarship, Playwriting, and Theater Companies

In this chapter I set forth some general considerations on the state of the Brazilian stage and consider important trends in its journey from repression during the 1964–1984 military dictatorship to theater's resurgence in the 1980s and 1990s. My examination of Brazil's journey away from repression includes the following topics: an overview of the career of Brazil's foremost theater critic, Sábato Magaldi; a report on the Curitiba theater festival, which in itself sums up the trends of the postdictatorship period; discussions of playwriting and the return of comedy; and an appraisal of theater companies in the postdictatorship period, with a special focus on Grupo Macunaíma.

## I. SÁBATO MAGALDI: LIFE AND WORKS

Theater scholar Sábato Magaldi was inducted into the Academia Brasileira de Letras on 25 July 1995, at the Academy's headquarters in Rio de Janeiro. Professor Magaldi is the first theater critic in Brazil ever to receive such an honor. The two previous occupants of the chair he holds were novelist Cyro dos Anjos and poet Manuel Bandeira. Current members of the Academia include fiction writers Jorge Amado, Antonio Callado, João Ubaldo Ribeiro, Rachel de Queiroz, Lygia Fagundes Telles, and Nélida Piñon, as well as poets João Cabral de Mello Neto and Lêdo Ivo. The latter, in his presentation speech on the occasion of Sábato Magaldi's induction into the Academia, attempted to explain why a theater critic had been chosen, stating that in his writings, one observes "the splendid fusion of the evening reviewer and the historian laboring in daylight and striving to remain in mankind's memory—as well as the journalist and reporter attuned to vital details" (Ivo 1995, 77).[1] That is, Sábato Magaldi has followed two related but usually disparate paths, that of the scholar-historian and that of the journalistic reviewer. Ivo gives further evidence of Dr. Magaldi's distinction when he asserts that he has not only laid the scholarly foundation for the study of the works of Nelson Rodrigues, but that he has "invented" the myth of that playwright. Lêdo Ivo's words only scratch the surface of this remarkable man's career, whose influence on the Brazilian stage has persisted now for nearly fifty years, and whose contributions include the first complete history of Brazilian theater, the conceptualization of a uniquely Brazilian dramaturgy, the creation of the scholarly field of Brazilian theatrical history, the training of a whole generation of theater critics and scholars, as well as the influence, direct or indirect, on three distinct generations of theater artists, those who came before the 1964 military coup, those who struggled during the dark night of the generals, and those who labored to reconstruct the theatrical edifice in the postdictatorship period.

Sábato Magaldi formerly occupied the chair of Brazilian Theater at the University of São Paulo's Escola de Comunicações e Artes. He has taught as a visiting professor at such foreign universities as the Sorbonne and the Université de Provence. A former theater critic—Rio's *Diário carioca* and São Paulo's *Jornal da tarde* and *Estado de S. Paulo*—Dr. Magaldi has published over 3,000 reviews of Brazilian and foreign plays. In addition to numerous scholarly articles, he has written eight books, including *O texto no teatro, Nelson Rodrigues: dramaturgia e encenações, Um palco brasileiro: O Arena de São Paulo,* and *Panorama do teatro brasileiro*. His definitive editions of the works of Nelson Rodrigues, in particular, deserve mention: (1) a four-volume edition with critical commentary, published between 1981 and 1989; and (2) his 1993 edition of Rodrigues's *Teatro completo,* which includes Dr. Magaldi's own critical introduction, the complete plays, and a selection of some of the finest scholarly analyses of the playwright's work.

His list of honors, culminating in his election to the Academia Brasileira de Letras, is too lengthy to enumerate. An abbreviated list, nevertheless, is in order. From 1975 to 1979, he served as the city of São Paulo's first Minister of Culture. He established, together with stage designer Aldo Calvo, the Biennial of Theater Arts, in conjunction with São Paulo's Biennial of the Arts. He has held myriad influential positions in state and local arts organizations and received countless awards and prizes from Brazilian and foreign organizations.

Let us go, now, back to the beginning: Sábato Antônio Magaldi was born on 9 May 1927 in Belo Horizonte, the capital of Minas Gerais state. His father was an Italian immigrant and his mother a first-generation Italian-Brazilian. At age 17 he joined the Communist Party, partly in defiance of Brazil's fascist dictator Getúlio Vargas.[2] Within a few months, Sábato Magaldi broke with the Party, chaffing under the Party's ideological rigidity, realizing that as a party functionary his creative freedom as a writer would be compromised. His sociopolitical concerns, coupled with his distaste for dogmatism, have characterized his work throughout his career.

By late adolescence he had become the youngest member of a brilliant *mineira* (Minas Gerais) generation of writers and intellectuals who published a journal called *Edifício*. "It so happened at that time I was interested in theater. For example, I believe I published the first article on Sartre, on his play *La putain respecteuse,* in 1945 or 46" (Magaldi, personal interview, 1995). Such was his interest in theater, even at that early age, that he tried his hand at playwriting.

Sábato Magaldi left Minas Gerais in 1948—he would receive his law degree in 1949—and moved to Rio, where he began his career as drama critic for the newspaper *Diário carioca*. He began working as a reviewer at the precise moment when Brazilian theater was coming into its own. The Rio company Os Comediantes had brought the national stage into the modern era with its revolutionary staging of Nelson Rodrigues's *Vestido de noiva* (*Bridal Gown*) in 1943. That epochal event was followed by other innovative productions by Os Comediantes and other groups, in Rio and in São Paulo, so that by 1950 it was possible to say that Brazilian theater had become as au courant as the other arts. From that point on, the national stage would establish a shining legacy, of which Sábato Magaldi would become an integral part: supporter, interpreter, chronicler, and, in some ways, arbiter.

In 1952–1953 Dr. Magaldi studied aesthetics at the Sorbonne, with a fellowship awarded by the French Embassy. In addition to his studies in Paris, he saw many of the pivotal plays of the Modernist canon: Büchner's *Death of Anton;* one of the very first performances of *Waiting for Godot,* in a nearly empty theater; performances of works by Montherlant, Pirandello, Merimée, Ionesco, Giradoux, Genet, and Anouilh. He also attended productions of the classics in the Comédie Française: Molière, Racine, Marivaux, and Corneille. He observed the work of Jean Vilar's National Popular French Theater. He wrote four reviews a week on French theater for the *Diário carioca* during this period.

In 1953 he transferred to São Paulo, at the invitation of Alfredo Mesquita, who invited him to teach History of Theater at the EAD, or Escola de Arte Dramática (School of Dramatic Arts). Mesquita founded the EAD, at that time Brazil's foremost school of the performing arts, in 1948. Along with its sister institution, the School of Communications and Arts—they are now housed in the same building at the University of São Paulo—it has trained, and continues to train, some of Brazil's most important playwrights, directors, designers, and actors. In 1962 Professor Magaldi introduced a new discipline to the curriculum: History of Brazilian Theater, a vital contribution to an area that was in the early stages of self-discovery. In 1967 he was invited to become Professor of History of Universal Theater in the newly created School of Communications and Arts. There he taught, until 1991, a wide array of undergraduate and graduate courses on such topics as theater criticism, theatrical legislation and ethics, and Brazilian dramaturgy and theatrical companies. He became Brazil's first full professor in the discipline of Brazilian theater. From 1985 to 1987 he was visiting professor at the University of Paris III (Sorbonne Nouvelle), and from 1989–1991 at the University of Provence in Aix-en-Provence. His academic career also included mentoring and/or directing dissertations with some of Brazil's most distinguished new generation of critics, scholars, playwrights, and directors; for example, playwright and professor Renata Pallotini, director Celso Nunes, and critic and novelist Alberto Guzik (who would eventually replace him, based on Dr. Magaldi's recommendation, as drama critic for the São Paulo newspaper *Jornal da tarde*). Sábato Magaldi has also given hundreds of talks and symposia on myriad aspects of Brazilian and world theater in Brazil and other parts of Latin America, Europe, and the United States (including a U.S. State Department–sponsored visit).

The year 1953 marks the continuation of another dimension of Professor Magaldi's multifaceted career. For a brief period he worked as drama critic for the magazine *Anhembi* and was editor-in-chief and critic for the journal *Teatro brasileiro*. He also became, in 1956, theater editor of the literary supplement of the newspaper *Estado de S. Paulo,* which published both reviews and extensive essays well beyond the scope of the play review format. The prime example of the latter is a seminal series entitled "*Cem anos de teatro em São Paulo*" ("100 Years of São Paulo Theater"), which Sábato Magaldi co-authored with Maria Thereza Vargas and which the *Estado de S. Paulo* ran in 1975–1976, in commemoration of the paper's centennial. The piece ran after he had left the supplement—in 1972—to become drama critic for the newly founded São Paulo daily *Jornal da tarde;* he retired from that position in 1988.

His work as a reviewer made him both witness to and participant in the most crucial developments in his nation's theater, both in terms of stagecraft and playwriting. In the first place, studies on Brazilian theater—produced in Brazil and abroad—characteristically cite Sábato Magaldi's reviews as the most authoritative sources, the ones that define the moment in question. He almost unfailingly spotted new trends; to repeat an observation from Chapter 2, it was he who recognized that the women playwrights in the "new dramaturgy" movement, which burst on the scene in 1969, provide "the most intense picture of the feminine condition in Brazilian playwriting, in a faithful portrait that goes beyond the middle class to mirror the condition of almost all women."[3]

He contributed in other ways as well; for example, he introduced Augusto Boal into São Paulo's Teatro de Arena, and he participated in Teatro de Arena's renowned playwriting workshop, or *Seminário de Dramaturgia,* the first systematic attempt in Brazil to develop the art of playwriting. The *Seminário* launched a whole new generation of Brazilian playwrights, including Oduvaldo Vianna Filho and Gianfrancesco Guarnieri. Sábato Magaldi was also a long-time supporter of Arena's principal engagé theater rival, Teatro Oficina, which revolutionized Brazilian stagecraft in the 1960s. He wrote the lead article in the program notes and the book that accompanied Oficina's defining moment, its 1967 production of a forgotten 1930s play, Oswald de Andrade's *O rei da vela* (*The Candle King*).[4] In fact, he championed the company through most of its existence.[5]

More recently, he has been one of the principal supporters of Grupo Macunaíma, which renewed the Brazilian stage in the wake of the dark days of the military dictatorship in the 1980s, (which I discuss later). His reviews and commentary are often included in the program notes of the productions of Grupo Macunaíma and other postdictatorship companies and playwrights. Further, Professor Magaldi was the first to recognize Maria Adelaide Amaral as one of Brazil's most important living dramatists.

Sábato Magaldi's countless publications include pioneering scholarly works which have made him a unique voice in national letters and for which he was honored with his election to the Brazilian Academy. I mentioned above his series "100 Years of São Paulo Theater." This work provided the first indepth examination of the development of the stage and drama of Brazil's largest city and cultural center. In 1962 he published the book *Panorama do teatro brasileiro* (3rd edition, 1997).[6] Through this work he defined and shaped for the first time the conception of a unique Brazilian dramaturgy. It is still the definitive "history"—

although Professor Magaldi prefers not to categorize it as such—of Brazilian theater. He has also published several books on international drama, which have conceptualized a unique Brazilian way of interpreting classical and modern works and schools.

Although his publications are too numerous to examine here (see Works Cited), perhaps his most significant legacy are his writings on Nelson Rodrigues, in particular his 1987 *Nelson Rodrigues: dramaturgia e encenações,* as well as his editions of the playwright's work, cited earlier. Many observers believe that Sábato Magaldi's seminal studies of Rodrigues's work, along with Grupo Macunaíma's stagings, rescued the playwright from oblivion and transformed him posthumously into an icon, the most widely staged playwright in Brazil today. That is, if Dr. Magaldi's "attention had not converged with a nearly fervent critical reflection, applied in such an imposing manner to Nelson Rodrigues's theatrical creation, the fate of the author of *Bridal Gown* would have been quite different." The critic, in short, transformed the "accursed author into a classic one" (Ivo 1995, 78). He thus saved for Rodrigues a "fulgurante" or resplendent posterity and opened the way for ambitious directors to throw the full weight of their imagination and creativity into widely divergent productions. Among the directors Ivo mentions are some of the brightest lights in the theater of the postdictatorship period, such as Antunes Filho, Ulysses Cruz, and Gabriel Villela. These are unusual claims to make about the influence of a critic, especially coming from the mouth of a poet. How could Sábato Magaldi have had such an impact on the historical position of the playwright, as well as the widespread staging and interpretation of his works? Ivo compares criticism to a kind of fiction, "a memorable or marvelous act of myth-making. The literary critic might be to the author what the director is to the playscript, seeing in the text the embryo of or pretext for his own creative reflection or his prophetic imagination" (Ivo 1995, 78).

It was Sábato Magaldi who first recognized that, although Oswald de Andrade was Brazil's first modern playwright, Nelson Rodrigues had a profound impact on stagecraft and introduced theatrical innovation to the broader public. "Nelson Rodrigues's plays constitute the broadest theatrical picture of urban Brazilian society. . . . Through a language that is crisp, concise, and vibrant, and by exposing his characters' most deeply hidden selves, he opened the way for all the dramatists of recent decades" (Magaldi 1963, *Dramaturgia,* 18). Nelson Rodrigues was singular, as the critic has shown, in that he introduced expressionism to Brazilian theater by laying bare on the stage the hidden zones of the subconscious and of social behavior. He examined taboo subjects such as incest and sexual abuse. He put forth the revolutionary idea that women are sexual beings. For all these bold innovations he was marginalized, even censored for his "immorality" and "perversion." He was also rejected by the ideological patrol as "reactionary." All of this in spite of such revolutionary notions of stagecraft—ferreted out by Sábato Magaldi—as extensive use of the flashback, break with linear plot and present time frame, removal of the fourth wall, psychoanalytic techniques applied to characters' unconscious motivations, and cinematic effects. Sábato Magaldi also created the definitive typology for Rodrigues's plays, which he places in three categories: psychological plays, mythic plays, and Carioca tragedies. He follows these categories in his four-volume edition of the playwright's works. In sum, the pioneering studies of Sábato Magaldi, along with the ingenious stagings of the playwright's works—especially those performed by Antunes Filho and his Grupo Macunaíma—not only brought Nelson Rodrigues into the mainstream, but made him the sacred—or to some, still, accursed—icon of the modern Brazilian stage.

In addition to Dr. Magaldi's scholarly contributions, his journalistic activity deserves scrutiny. But the journalist himself has told this story, not the account of his thousands of reviews but the tale of reviewing in Brazil, its rise and fall. In a 1987 article entitled "O teatro e a função da crítica" ("Theater and the Function of Criticism"), he discusses the role of journalistic play reviewing in Brazil, its history and present status.

In Brazil, the role of reviewing is a function of the nation's artistic and political history. Critics have often supported new trends before there was public support:

> The artistic renewal undertaken on the Brazilian stage, beginning in the 1940s, would have faced greater obstacles were it not for immediate support from critics. [In] both São Paulo and Rio de Janeiro the critics joined the struggle against the old star system which marginalized the rest of the cast. This struggle led to the establishment of ensemble theaters, under the guidance of directors; that is, a high quality repertory structure in which all elements, including stage and costume design, functioned in aesthetic harmony. (Magaldi 1987, "Função")

Professor Magaldi speaks to one of the principles that has grounded his life and work: avoidance of dogmatism. I mentioned above that his rejection of the dictates of the Communist Party in his youth would characterize his life-long refutation of rigid doctrine. He relates this to criticism, affirming that critics must not be aesthetically dogmatic or they will be operating in a vacuum, out of synch with artists. Rather, he believes, critics must be open and flexible. To explain this, Dr. Magaldi gives a capsule summary of recent trends in Brazilian theater:

> At one moment, [the critic] highlights the role of the director and ensemble theater. He then sees that this formula is unsatisfactory: the national playwright should be privileged over the dominant foreign repertoire. Once the Brazilian play has been transformed into the common currency of theater companies, it is time to apply more rigorous standards and be attentive to new concerns, to the widespread establishment of experimental collective groups and the testing of new spaces, some completely outside the traditional theater space. (Magaldi 1987, "Função")

In light of this constantly shifting tableau, the critic must detect and nurture new trends until they have matured. "This does not mean that the critic should be a weather vane, but that he must be aware that schools, movements, and aesthetic standards are cyclical, and they eventually run their course" (Magaldi 1987, "Função"). Speaking specifically of Brazil, he states that no critic today defends the "the concept of good taste, the legacy of certain European criteria; rather, he recognizes that bad taste is a component of our tropicalist style" (Magaldi 1987, "Função").

Corollaries to flexibility are that the critic be honest, write well, know the ins and outs of stagecraft, and have a broad cultural background. The latter quality will enable the critic to distinguish between the hackneyed and the original. The critic, therefore, must continually update his or her knowledge and viewpoints or be left behind. In regard to intimate knowledge of stagecraft, the critic must pay attention to all aspects of the play and not only the verbal text. Critics should emphasize those aspects of a particular spectacle that are most significant, whether the director's overall conception, acting, design, or the text itself.

Magaldi also compares the mission of the critic in Brazil and abroad:

> Newspaper reviewers in such centers as New York, Paris, or London are usually cautious because they more nearly reflect so-called public taste. In those cities commercial theater is preponderant and critics must yield to it without a hint of disdain. Perhaps because we are younger, freed from tradition, or because we see ourselves as commit-

> ted to experimentation, we tend to turn up our noses at theater labeled as simple entertainment. Anything outside the quest for renewal is branded as "show-biz," even if one admits it is well staged. Critics abroad either identify with the aesthetic and ideology of readers and of the media outlets they write for or risk becoming the odd man out in the communication process. (Magaldi 1987, "Função")

That reviewers in Brazil tend to be less conservative than the owners and editors, in Professor Magaldi's view, is a legacy of the dictatorship when the former had to struggle against censorship. Brazilian critics, as opposed to their counterparts in New York, Paris, and London, do not carry the burden of determining the success or failure of a play after opening night. Freed from the tyranny of the opening night review, they are more at liberty to express themselves. Dr. Magaldi gives a very simple reason for this: there are many more openings in Brazil and playgoers are inclined to make up their own minds and fashion their own choices.

In spite of a situation that is in some ways healthy, there is a crisis facing Brazilian theater criticism. Newspaper reviewing in Brazil, according to Professor Magaldi, has suffered because of changing economic circumstances. The space allotted to theater criticism has been reduced due to competition from video, TV, pop music, and so forth. "Dislodging theater from its absolute sovereignty has been a natural process" (Magaldi 1987, "Função"). Complicating this situation, the number of new plays has steadily increased and indepth analysis and full coverage have suffered. Dr. Magaldi also laments the severing of the dual role traditionally occupied by the critics of his generation, that of the essayist/reviewer: "the current philosophy of the press is to encourage brief, light, easy-to-read reviews . . . The more substantial essay is the province of other publications, which unfortunately are few in number or non-existent" (Magaldi 1987, "Função"). Likewise, fewer and fewer reviewers are employed full time with attendant salary and benefits. The trend, increasingly, is for newspapers to pay per article and to provide no benefits. This, Dr. Magaldi fears, has the potential of making theater reviewing in Brazil obsolete.

In concluding this section, I reproduce Sábato Magaldi's closing paragraph from "O teatro e a função da crítica" (1987), which sums up both his views on theater criticism and his own life's work:

> The serious critic participates in the theatrical process by acting to improve the art form. It is unnecessary to mention the numerous campaigns

> he has sponsored or supported to improve conditions for those who work on the stage. It has oft-times been alleged that there is a sadistic pleasure in destroying, when it is much more difficult to be constructive. I do not believe that critics are guilty of this. During my long career, it has always been extremely unpleasant for me to express reservations; I have always preferred to praise. After all, the critic, like any audience member, enjoys seeing a good show, and he feels he has wasted an evening if he gains nothing from what he has seen. It gives the critic great pleasure to view his role as partner of the artist, both joined together, always with the aim of creating theater.

## II. UP FROM THE ASHES: FESTIVAL DE CURITIBA

Whatever regressive tendencies may characterize outside scholarly interpretations of Brazilian theater, artists in Brazil have continued to move forward. To provide a sense of the sweep of Brazilian stage in the post-dictatorship period, I begin by reporting on a pivotal event which I attended in 1993, the second annual theater festival held in the southern city of Curitiba, Paraná, which has in its brief existence become Brazil's unofficial national theater showcase. Although I have revised some of its conclusions and have edited some sections, the report I wrote for *The Latin American Theater Review* provides useful perspectives on Brazilian theater's "flash."

The twenty-five productions featured over a ten-day period demonstrated with dazzling clarity that the stage is alive and well in Latin America's largest country, that it has overcome the trauma of twenty years of military dictatorship, the dismantling of arts funding agencies under the corrupt Collor administration, and the ideological patrol, epitomized by Augusto Boal's stifling dicta designated as "theater of the oppressed." A whole new generation has burst on the Brazilian stage with creative vigor. Much of what is best in this generation was represented at Curitiba: directors Bia Lessa, Moacyr Góes, Gerald Thomas, and Gabriel Villela, as well as such companies as Belo Horizonte's Grupo Galpão. The rehabilitation of Nelson Rodrigues begun by Antunes Filho and his Grupo Macunaíma with their 1981 production *Nelson Rodrigues o eterno retorno* was reaffirmed at the festival. Another recent tendency in Brazilian theater was also evident: the staging of both international and national classics. The most visually stunning example of the latter was director Enrique Dias's production of Oswald de Andrade's modernist text *A morta* (*The Dead Woman*). Less stunning was the stage adaptation of João de Minas's *A mulher carioca aos 22 anos* (*The Rio de Janeiro Woman at Age 22*), a novel from the same period but marginalized from the modernist canon. This tedious production was justified by the author's status as a supposed forerunner of Nelson Rodrigues. Examples of international classics—dramatic and nondramatic texts—were productions of *Romeo and Juliet, Othello, O paraíso perdido* (*Paradise Lost*), a Strindberg adaptation entitled *Epifanias,* as well as productions based on the writings of Artaud and Kafka. Nor was Brazil's engagé old guard unrepresented, with two productions of Plínio Marcos's works. There were, however, conspicuous absences. The distinguished post-*abertura* generation of playwrights was nowhere to be heard (e.g., Maria Adelaide Amaral, Naum Alves de Souza, Edla van Steen, and Mauro Rasi). And the two most important theater companies, Grupo Macunaíma and Teatro do Ornitorrinco, did not participate in the festival.

There were revelations and falls from grace in Curitiba. The most striking example of the former was Grupo Galpão's *mambembe*[7] production of *Romeo and Juliet,* presented both outdoors in true *mambembe* fashion and in the dazzling Ópera de Arame,[8] an architectural fantasy out of a thousand and one nights, a glass and wire auditorium featuring lagoons, illuminated waterfalls, and the sky visible through the ceiling (a handy visual escape for spectators bored or exasperated by the few tedious productions in the festival). Grupo Galpão's mixture of itinerant medieval theater (a panel truck replaces the old horse-drawn wagon), commedia dell'arte, circus techniques, and the *mineiro*[9] flavor of Guimarães Rosa resurrected Shakespeare's play from the dust of accumulated romantic clichés to the delight and fascination of audiences and critics alike. Grupo Galpão, which has been in existence for over a decade, collaborated on this production with director Gabriel Villela, whose previous resurrection of an international classic—Calderón's *La vida es sueño*—was one of the 1991–1992 theater season's most innovative productions.

The Ópera de Arame also housed the festival's biggest disappointment, *O império das Meias verdades,* directed and scripted by Gerald Thomas, with his Companhia da Ópera Seca. *Império* was a confused hodgepodge of theater of the absurd, biblical myths (Adam and Eve), and pretentious narration blasting from powerful loudspeakers. Examples of the latter: "*no Brasil não há poetas, não há encenadores*" ("in Brazil there are no poets, no directors") sprinkled with liberal doses of "fuck you" in English. Even Thomas's most ardent supporters were perplexed and concluded that either this was an *espetáculo de crise,* or as one eminent critic diplomatically put it, "*todo grande artista tem direito de errar de vez em quando*" ("all great artists have the right to err now and then"). The principal problem with the production may have been that as a work in progress it was simply not ready for an audience. During the month after the festival, Thomas completely revised *Império,* which opened in São Paulo on 30 April to critical acclaim.[10]

One of the most intriguing presentations was a piece entitled *25 homens* (*25 Men*), based on a Plínio Marcos short story about a group of men wallowing in filth and descending into madness in a tiny jail cell. If the subject matter sounds like the author's usual neo-naturalist depictions of the lumpen proletariat—his *Dois perdidos numa noite suja* (*Two Men Lost in a Bleak Night*) also played at the festival—it was in fact a production that emphasized mythical themes and the spiritual value of redemption. The production was based on Grotowskian poor-theater techniques to create the purest visual poetry. Marcos's story was narrated by a single actor—Cacá Carvalho, who played Macunaíma in Antunes Filho's acclaimed 1979 production—with a single stage light shining horizontally from downstage to up, a collapsible set of iron bars placed at certain moments in front of the light, a steel table and chair, shackles, matches, a cigarette, and oft-times barely perceptible movement. This most minimalist of stagings achieved a power that put more costly and elaborate productions to shame.

Another of the festival's most effective pieces, *A vida como ela é* (*Life as It Is*), achieved a dual purpose. It brought Nelson Rodrigues's journalistic endeavors—his newspaper *crônicas* of the same title—to the stage and clearly illustrated their inextricable links to his drama. Directed by Luis Arthur Nunes, the production consisted of eleven vignettes featuring the usual Rodriguean themes of incest, confused sexual identity, puritanical repression of the libido, madness, and suicide, presented in the also usual Rodriguean high comic fashion, proving once again that the author, among his many other accomplishments, lifted the rock of patriarchal society and uncovered the dark creatures lurking beneath it. *A vida como ela é* displayed illuminated expressionist panels that summed up the action of each *crônica,* and fused them all with the panels lit simultaneously while the ensemble of actors assembled for a kind of family album pose at play's end. In short, it was a tour de force.

Another tour de force was *encenadora* Bia Lessa's adaptation of a classic from Portuguese literature, the seventeenth-century *Cartas portuguesas*—also known as *Lettres portugaises*—based on the letters of a nun, Sister Mariana Alcoforado, written to an unattainable French lover.

The set represented not the confining atmosphere of a convent, but in poetic contrast a forest and stream, symbolizing the nun's interior world. Lessa, a bright light in the *encenador* generation led by Gerald Thomas, attempting to redefine Brazilian theater in visual terms, utilized actual water, earth, greenery, even live earthworms, to create the forest.

The festival was a model of efficient organization led by Yacoff Sarkovas, representing one of the two independent cultural promotion agencies that co-produced the event, which was almost entirely self-supporting through ticket sales and corporate sponsorship. The latter characteristic may be an anathema to some, but it is the only way such a festival could be held in these days of scant government support for the arts.

The festival clarified a number of things. First, the Brazilian stage is dominated at the present time by the *encenador* generation. Second, theater's doors are now wide open to any and all themes and styles; there are no checks on artists' creative imaginations (except, of course, finances). Third, for good or for ill, the bias against foreign drama has all but disappeared. Fourth, despite its signs of vitality in the 1980s, Brazilian playwriting is not in the best of health at this moment. What does all this bode for the future? In this writer's opinion, the vitality of the theater as an institution, its diversity and unflagging energy, put to rest any notion that it is an art form on the wane. And if "serious" Brazilian playwrights are quiet these days, they are waiting in the wings and they will soon be heard from again.

## III. PLAYWRITING

Playwriting in the postdictatorship period has been overshadowed by directors, but, as I pointed out at the beginning of Chapter 1, that is not a new phenomenon. I devoted Chapter 2 to women's voices, the most significant playwriting phenomenon to come out of the period in question. Nelson Rodrigues, as I discussed earlier in the context of the Curitiba festival and as I reiterate later in the section on the Macunaíma group, has been rediscovered and is now the most highly regarded and frequently staged of all Brazil's playwrights, though he died in 1980.

In spite of playwriting's, shall we say, secondary position, it must be affirmed that it has been a vital force in the postdictatorship period. Brazilian dramatists have struggled to overcome myriad hurdles—mostly of the economic variety in recent years—to make themselves heard. The struggle has achieved a measure of success; all one has to do is look at the play offerings on any given weekend in Brazil's major capitals to discover that over half the works being staged are by Brazilian authors. Maria Adelaide Amaral states categorically that the "public likes national authors. That's been demonstrated over and over. Because it's about a reality they can identity with, things that touch audience members" (Amaral, personal interview). This is a new departure. In the 1940s the Brazilian stage was in part revolutionized by quality plays, but with the exception of one pivotal work by Nelson Rodrigues, *Vestido de noiva,* play selection was based on the best of the international repertoire. It was only in the late 1950s and through the 1960s that Brazilian playwrights were squarely in the ranks of the theatrical vanguard, though even then this vanguard was still led by directors and theater companies. These were the engagé playwrights, Gianfrancesco Guarnieri, Augusto Boal, Oduvaldo Vianna Filho, and Plínio Marcos, voices raised in protest against dictatorship and social injustice. But only two of those voices—Marcos's and Filho's—have survived the end of the dictatorship, and marginally at best.

So what happened to the *abertura* of the late seventies and early eighties when censorship was relaxed, even before the military turned over the reins of power? In Chapter 2, I discussed this issue in the context of women playwrights. Here I examine the question in regard to playwriting in general. Alberto Guzik, in his essay "Um exercício de memória: dramaturgia brasileira anos 80," provides some provocative answers to this question. "By the late 1970s, Brazilian theater was in the last gasp of its courageous and glorious oposition to the military dictatorship" (Guzik 1992, 10). With the advent of the *abertura,* "everyone in theater was waiting for the magnificent eighties, when censorship's files would be opened and out would pour original, creative, intelligent, banned works . . . But from the locked drawers in Brasília out peeped a mouse, not a lion. The censored plays were almost always bad. And the decent texts were dated" (Guzik 1992, 10). Theater, in short, was left speechless. Of course, once the dictatorship was out of the way, "the discourse of protest against the dictatorship would be obsolete [and] everyone searched deep into memory or into immediate experience, looking for ways to communicate with the audience. Infinite new possibilities appeared, from inner conflict to comedic nonsense. [However], playwriting taken as a whole had not yet discovered a way to give voice to current concerns" (Guzik 1992, 11). So Brazilian theater, after decades of struggle to transform reality, "exploded and reassembled into hundreds of experiments in the 1980s" (Guzik 1992, 15).

There have been in post-*abertura* theater a few anomalies, in a sense engagé, "Death of the Maiden"–type plays which attempt to keep alive the national memory of the horrors of the dictatorship. This became possible, of course, only when censorship was relaxed. Low-level censorship, particularly on the local level, has always been a fact of life in Brazil, even during periods of democratically elected governments. During the first few years of the dictatorship installed in 1964, censorship was not rigorous. In time, however, the generals declared war on artists and writers, and with the December 1968 state of siege an increasingly repressive military attempted to impose total thought control. The government banned certain works that it deemed subversive or "immoral," and right-wing paramilitary organizations like the Communist Hunting Command (*Comando de Caça aos Comunistas*) carried out physical attacks, bombings, and assassinations. Whatever misery befell Brazilian literature and theater before the December 1968 state of siege was nothing compared to what would follow. By 1971 the situation had become intolerable. The police began to arrest and torture some of the nation's most important artists, many of whom went into exile, and anything and everything was subject to censorship.

What was it that the generals and the police were so afraid of or incensed at that they would go to such extreme lengths to stop it? The obvious targets of their wrath were so-called "subversive" plays, books, and movies. Subversive could mean anything from outright condemnation of the dictatorship to declarations of human rights. A newspaper, for example, was banned from printing articles from the U.S. Constitution. But just as frightening to the military, police, and political hacks who collaborated with them was so-called "pornography," which could mean anything from romantic eroticism to hard-core pornography. This is because one of the essential characteristics of the politically repressive mind-set is puritanism. The generals called themselves Brazil's "redeemers," who would bring their version of "morality" back into national life. Anyone deemed immoral or subversive, one and the same in their eyes, could be subject to indignities, arrest, torture, execution, and in the case of women, rape. Why would these moralists commit rape? Because women under arrest, with or without cause, were automatically subversives, and subversives were whores, and whores got what was coming to them.

But there was light at the end of the tunnel. When the *abertura* got underway in the late seventies and the dictatorship was nearing its end in the early eighties, it was possible to write books and perform plays about the dark days of repression, with a significantly lessened threat of censorship. Governments, local and national, began to allow previously banned artistic expression, including eroticism. Perhaps the best example of the kind of work that had been banned for two decades was the 1982 publication of *Feliz ano velho* (*Happy Old Year*), one of the truly extraordinary literary happenings of the *abertura*. An autobiography by author Marcelo Paiva, it has achieved a nearly unprecedented degree of success in Brazil: it has been a continuing best-seller since its publication, and it has been translated into six languages, with editions in Germany, Italy, Spain, Argentina, Denmark, and the United States. Its 1983 theatrical adaptation by the São Paulo group Pessoal do Víctor ran for five years in Brazil, where it was seen by over a million spectators. It toured to several other countries, playing at the Joseph Papp Festival Latino in New York (1985) and at the Havana International Theater Festival (1987). *Feliz ano velho* was also made into an award-winning film in 1988.

The book, which would have been banned even a year or two before its publication, was one of the pioneering works expressing all the previously taboo subjects. The author, Marcelo Paiva, is the son of Rubens Paiva, a deputy in the Brazilian congress who was "disappeared" and presumably murdered by the Brazilian military in 1971, a case which became an international *cause célèbre*. For example, there were several articles on the case in such venues as the *New York Times* and *Newsweek*. In 1974, Fernando Henrique Cardoso, then in exile and teaching at Stanford University, appealed to Senator Edward Kennedy to look into Paiva's disappearance.[11] Kennedy later announced to the U.S. Congress that Rubens Paiva had been killed. In 1979, when his son Marcelo was a 20-year-old engineering student and budding musician, he suffered an accident that left him a paraplegic. As part of his recovery process he wrote his autobiography, *Feliz ano velho,* which functions on three simultaneous narrative levels: his childhood in Rio before and after the disappearance of his father, his life immediately prior to the accident, and his subsequent struggles to create a new life as a disabled person. On a broader level, *Happy Old Year* is the story of a nation's suffering under military dictatorship and of the social and cultural values of the young people who grew up under repression. Told simply, directly, and with great humor, Marcelo Paiva's story has come to symbolize the new generation's attempts to overcome political and spiritual paralysis.

Eroticism is one of *Feliz ano velho*'s essential motifs. Interwoven with recollections of a happy childhood in Rio before the disappearance of his father, his family's subsequent feelings of shock and desolation, and the young adult's simultaneous discovery of music and politics, are the fond and confused memories of hormonal awakening and adolescent sexcapades. Eroticism becomes a metaphor of loss: Paiva's permanently missing father and his country's devastation at the hands of the military. It is the focal point for the sudden and inexorable destruction of his young body and of all his life had been: his agricultural studies and interest in ecology, his career as a musician, his mobility and independence. Erotic memories and fantasies in the book thus become a search for paradise lost. Moreover, the act of writing and reconstruction constitutes a path, if not to acceptance, at least to a beginning of understanding and reconciliation. The author matures through his erotic recollections, in ways that he may not have, at least not so quickly, had he remained sound in body. Filtered through the vision of a disabled person, eroticism is a poignant reminder of the fragility of existence and an ironic symbol of the absurd shell in which humankind skitters through life.

After Paiva dives into shallow water and is unable to move, his friends rescue him and rush him to the hospital. While convalescing, the process of reconstruction of his past begins. In a series of flashbacks Paiva reveals his painful response to the loss of his father and bitterness toward the military officers responsible, who not only denied the crime but offered up the absurd explanation that the father had never been arrested at all, alleging that he was in hiding with a band of terrorists. The author also describes how life goes on, painting in the process a mocking self-portrait. Marcelo Paiva recounts his clumsy adolescent search for sexual experience with good-natured self-deprecation. His ironic view of his own sexuality continues after his accident, a view of his disabled condition that colors all areas of involuntary physiological response. The paraplegic's hope to regain use of his body is poignant when Paiva imagines the return of sexual function. The young man finally must confront the reality of his new sex life as a disabled person, and he describes initial awkward attempts. The very possibility of some form of sexual participation only accentuates his helplessness, which he demonstrates with his characteristic irony. Auto-eroticism provides the author the clearest path to rediscovery of his body. The book ends with many questions unanswered, and the opening passage is repeated, now in the third person, as he returns to the description of the accident that left him a paraplegic.[12]

An ironic footnote to the story of *Feliz ano velho* involves my 1991 English translation of it (see Works Cited). The publisher had originally considered including it in a series sponsored by the National Endowment for the Arts (NEA) but recanted as a consequence of fears about a possible controversy over the book's explicit eroticism. Eventually, the book was published outside the auspices of the NEA. It is to me no small irony that as I scrutinize Brazil's deep breath of freedom after twenty years of military dictatorship, I see authoritarianism on the rise in the United States.

In spite of *Feliz ano velho* and a few other "national memory" plays, for the most part *abertura* and the end of the dictatorship have led to a depoliticized theater, which wants to disentangle itself from the political crises and ideologies of the 1960s and 1970s. An early example of at least partial disengagement, or at least a calling into question of political activism, was the staging in Brazil, in the early 1980s, of *Kiss of the Spider Woman* (*Beijo da mulher aranha*), based on Argentine Manuel Puig's 1976 novel entitled *Beso de la mujer araña. Kiss of the Spider Woman* deals with persecution of both opponents to military dictatorship and homosexuals in Argentina, spotlighting the evolving relationship, in a jail cell, of an apolitical gay man and a political activist, ending in a stunning role reversal. The "macho" political prisoner Valentín seduces the gay window-dresser Molina, who, after leaving prison is killed while fulfilling a mission for Valentín's cause. *Kiss of the Spider Woman* has been exposed to audiences around the world in variegated forms. The novel has been translated into several languages; it has seen myriad international stage adaptations (the first, by Puig himself, opened in Spain in 1981); it was adapted to the cinema in 1984 by Argentine-Brazilian director Hector Babenco, with William Hurt and Raúl Julia in the lead roles; it transmogrified into a 1993 American musical (book by Terence McNally, directed by Harold Prince); the musical spawned a CD containing songs from the production; there is now a profusion of Web sites dealing particularly with the musical and film version.[13] *Beijo da mulher aranha* introduced Brazilian audiences to dimensions of international postmodernism, with its blurring of genres—narrative based almost entirely on dialogue, film script and other cinematic modes, official documents—and mixing of high art and low. Indeed, when the work was first published it was classified as a *novela pop*. When *Kiss of the Spider Woman* was staged in Brazil for the first time, it produced "a shockwave among critics and audiences. That staging placed head to head as antagonists art and politics and ultimately suggested that life lived aesthetically is more transforming than political praxis. . . . That stage production may well have been the first sign that, as had been occurring for some years in European and North American theater, theater was preparing to rid itself of its activist burden." When it is guided by aesthetic principles, "theater's sources of inspiration multiply . . . The result is a fragmentation that is almost impossible to be grasped by critical appraisal" (Alves de Lima 1992, "Tendências," 16–17).

There are abundant signs that the new generation of theater artists has rejected prior ideological models. This includes not only the women playwrights discussed in the previous chapter but men as well, who share many concerns with their female counterparts, such as gender identity. A good example of this phenomenon are the works of Naum Alves de Souza from the 1980s: *A aurora da minha vida* (*The Dawn of My Life*), *No natal a gente vem te buscar* (*Next Christmas We'll Come by for You*), and *Um beijo, um abraço, um aperto de mão* (*A Kiss, a Hug, a Handshake*). This cycle of personal memory plays is related to the childhood ghosts—one is reminded here of Edla van Steen's *O último encontro*—of a man who was raised by a Protestant family in the interior of São Paulo state. Utilizing the themes of mysticism and loss, presented with both tenderness and irony, Nuam Alves de Souza became a unique voice in the post-*abertura* 1980s. His more recent works, less successful than his memory cycle plays, include *Nijinsky* and *Suburbano coração* (loosely translated, *Low-Class Heart*), the latter with music by popular composer Chico Buarque de Hollanda.[14] Among the dramatists of the postdictatorship period who followed Naum Alves de Souza, one could mention Alcides Nogueira, whose *Lua de cetim* (*Satin Moon*) paints poignant family portraits; Zeno Wilde, who deals with the theme of marginalized adolescents, victims of urban life, in *Blue jeans* and *Uma lição longe demais* (*A Lesson Too Far*). One of the most significant trends in this depoliticized climate has been the resurgence of comedy, once a staple of the Brazilian stage but eclipsed by the engagé generation's bitter struggles against dictatorial repression.

## IV. THE RETURN OF COMEDY

When scholars focus our aesthetic and ideological lasers on playtexts, we easily lose sight of the complexity of theater. We forget that it is an institution with many parts which, however disparate they may appear when examined in isolation, are interconnected and interdependent. In the case of the Brazilian stage, comedy is one of its staples, the glue holding the boards together. It has been there from the start, providing work for actors and directors, keeping playwrights busy in a collective honing of their craft, and most important, bringing in audiences, preparing them to take bolder steps toward the unusual, the experimental, the tragic, the sober, and the ponderous.

Scholars, this writer included, have paid Brazil's comic theatrical tradition little heed. We have focused our attention on innovation (Grupo Macunaíma, Nelson Rodrigues) and protest (Oduvaldo Vianna Filho, Augusto Boal). We are biased in favor of works that give voice to marginalized groups and address the race-class-gender triad. We have been preoccupied about the development of national dramaturgy or lack thereof, ignoring the fact that comic writers have been churning out plays in a steady stream in the best of times and the worst of times, plays at times demonstrating mastery of form and technique and illustrating a wide diversity of comic genres, which include such unique modes as the comedy of manners, *revista,* and *besteirol,* as well as the full range of comedy and farce found around the world.

The comedy of manners, a form of light farce which dates back to the nineteenth century when Martins Pena shaped it into a unique form, has a number of characteristics: the setting is typically confined to a drawing or living room, the time frame is limited to the present, the subject matter usually deals with the family as a microcosm of the larger society that is being satirized, and stock characters or types are featured. The form had degenerated into a worn-out formula by the 1930s but has been resurrected with the infusion of modern—and postmodern—theatrical innovations. *Besteirol* is based on the word *besteira,* silliness, foolishness, nonsense. It is a style of zany farce noted for its utter lack of serious intent, a kind of extended *revista* or vaudeville sketch. *Besteirol* exploded on the scene during the 1980s as a reaction to the deadly serious engagé theater of protest that had arisen in response to the military dictatorship, but whose precepts, when continued into the postdictatorship period, became often a formulaic ideological exercise (e.g., the theories of Augusto Boal). *Besteirol*'s apolitical impertinence helped Brazilian theater artists and audiences to break old ideological habits, defy the ideological patrol, and adapt to new circumstances. Furthermore, the authors of these irresponsible farces, including three of the playwrights discussed below, used *besteirol* as a springboard to more ambitious forms of comedy, to plays with more depth and artistry.

In personal interviews with Mauro Rasi and Naum Alves de Souza, both discussed *besteirol*'s importance as a transitional tool and reaction to the asphyxiating prescriptions of the ideological patrol. I include here some of their comments. Naum Alves de Souza, though not an author of *besteirol* farce, defended it vehemently, as a member of a new generation of theatre artists: "Mauro Rasi's *besteirol* challenged the ideological patrol and the Boals of the world. That dreary leftist establishment. All of us were maligned by the ideological patrol after it turned vindictive and spiteful. They said I was alienated because my theater wasn't overtly political. But I started out favoring political theater. After all, I was part of a historical moment and fought against repression. But when history changes, art changes" (Alves de Souza, personal interview).

Mauro Rasi, long after he left *besteirol* behind, continued to justify it.

> That thing called *besteirol* was created by intelligent, critical people, orphans of the dictatorship. People in their thirties, outside rancid party politics, looking for a fast and efficient way to produce theater. At first, the critics lambasted us because it was a time when political theater still held sway. We were considered a bunch of alienated nuts. The Marxists hated us because where was [Boal's] *coringa*? But we were reacting against that very ideological rigidity that likes to make up rules. It was an iconoclastic defiance of their position. We talked about things like sex, which that kind of political theater kept at arm's length. The ideological patrol was puritanical and stuffy. (Rasi, personal interview)

Mauro Rasi and Miguel Falabella were once Brazil's best known purveyors of *besteirol,* but that form represents only one side of their work and they have moved beyond it. This is evidenced by Rasi's *A cerimônia do adeus* (*The Goodbye Ceremony*), first staged in 1987. *Cerimônia* opened a series of autobiographical plays about growing up in a small town, the latest installment of which is the 1995 *A pérola* (*The Pearl*).

*Cerimônia* is on the surface a *comédia de costumes:* the setting is limited to two rooms in a house and the usual family conflicts and stock characters are portrayed. Aspázia, mother of the protagonist Juliano, is driven to distraction by her son's strange behavior, yet while she complains about the "pornography" in his room she and her sister Brunilde read aloud steamy passages from Harold Robbins. Brunilde, a stereotypical housewife, is an indefatigable devotee of seances. Juliano's other parent is never seen—the audience only hears him coughing in his room—a parody of the absent, uninvolved Brazilian father.

*Cerimônia,* however, transcends the comedy-of-manners formula in many ways, especially by utilizing an ingenious comic device. Juliano attempts to escape from the stifling conventions of middle-class provincial life through literature. His retreat takes the extreme form of bringing authors and their worlds to life through his imagination. Thus, his bedroom balcony serves as the entrance to another world where Juliano—

along with the audience—views scenes from his books (e.g., the arrondissements of Paris at different times and seasons). Even more arresting is the use of the device vis-à-vis the authors themselves, trapped in Juliano's room through the power of his imagination. Two of the characters in the play are Jean-Paul Sartre and Simone de Beauvoir, whom the other members of Juliano's family see as books in the protagonist's room but whom he and the audience see as flesh-and-blood. This running joke advances through the comic scales. It takes the form of slapstick: Juliano's mother Aspázia picks up and throws a book by "that French hussy," whose name she pronounces Simone de Suvuá. What Juliano—and the audience—sees is Aspázia knocking down Simone de Beauvoir herself. The device, if limited to slapstick, would soon exhaust its comic potential. Fortunately, the playwright does not waste the myriad possibilities of his conception. Juliano develops an ever-deepening relationship with Beauvoir and Sartre—the latter played in 1987 by the late great Sérgio Britto—leading to a myriad of humorous situations and misunderstandings. But Juliano's association with the two French writers also moves in the more complex human direction of affection and pathos. There is a subplot in the play, the union of Beauvoir and Sartre, who discuss with Juliano their love lives. Their time passes before his eyes, Sartre declines, and as the play ends they depart for France where Sartre will die. They also review with Juliano their writings and their links to the events—many key historical moments appear visually beyond Juliano's balcony—and the changing ideologies of the period from the 1930s to the 1960s: feminism, the rise of fascism, the Spanish Civil War, World War Two, the changing fortunes of socialism, the Cuban Revolution, as well as dictatorship in Latin America and its left-wing corollary, guerrilla warfare. The latter circumstance provides the most immediate link with Juliano's reality, as the play takes place in the wake of the 1964 military coup.

Sartre's historical link with Brazil is his 1960 visit at the time of Teatro Oficina's staging of his *L'engrenage* (in the 1950s the Teatro Brasileiro de Comédia had staged such works by Sartre as *Huis clos,* and in 1959 Teatro Oficina had staged his *Les mouches*). Sartre stated in 1960 that the imaginary country in which *L'engrenage* took place could actually be Brazil. A further Sartre–Brazil connection are his statements in support of the kind of guerrilla movements that sprang up in Brazil and elsewhere in opposition to military dictatorship. Juliano's two friends in the play, Francisco and Lourenço, represent the opposite poles of the ideological schism that tore Brazil apart during the 1960s and culminated in the repressive 1964–1984 military dictatorship. While Francisco dreams of joining a guerrilla movement, it appears that Lourenço belongs to a right-wing paramilitary organization active particularly in the late 1960s (an example of such an organization would be the Communist Hunting Command). Lourenço also embodies a brutal form of machismo as he throws a naked woman—he has impregnated her—from his moving car, a story he tells his friends proudly. Juliano himself is trying to come to terms with his own sexual identity, a painful process in a provincial environment in which homosexuality is an anathema.

*A cerimônia do adeus* treats all these issues without dogma. Although Rasi's sympathies clearly fall to the left, he treats revolutionary struggle not in a heroic but in an amused manner, a clear indication that the new generation of playwrights which has sprung up in the postdictatorship period has abandoned the political solemnity of the 1960s generation. In that sense, the play represents a coming to terms with the events of the 1960s.

The second comic playwright under consideration in this section is Miguel Falabella, currently one of Brazilian theater's most active and peripatetic members: playwright, director, and stage and TV actor. Although *besteirol* has been his trademark, he has written more ambitious comedies, the most successful of which is *A partilha* (*The Division*). The play has its zany *besteirol* moments, while its farcical look at family conflicts, its setting—a living room—its time frame in the present, and its characters—four sisters representing four types—place it in the comedy of manners tradition. The play goes beyond formula, however, by providing a moving look at the generation that came of age in the 1960s. While *Cerimônia* treats the same generation in its youth, *A partilha* focuses on its middle age. Furthermore, all the characters are women. Both Rasi and Falabella, therefore, break with comic tradition in that the former treats homosexuality sympathetically while the latter offers a feminine, if not feminist, perspective. That is, routinely in the past and in some cases even today these perspectives would have been the objects of comedy, not the subjects.

*A partilha* deals with four middle-aged sisters who are thrown together when their mother dies. The first scene, which the authors entitles "prologue," is set in a funeral chapel. The setting for all subsequent scenes in the play is the living room in the late mother's apartment. The four sisters have followed divergent paths: divorced devotee of the occult, Paris resident, gay journalist-academic, traditional housewife. Much of the humor in the play is derived from their dissimilar world views and lifestyles. They begin in conflict, recriminations over old wounds fly, and they move slowly toward resolution. No male characters appear onstage, and when the sisters discuss the men in their lives they put them in an unfavorable light. Falabella's play lacks the ingenious plot devices, bizarre situations, and distance-creating irony of Rasi's *Cerimônia*. Nevertheless, its simple resolution—the sisters, reconciled, tearfully embrace at the end—has a very strong appeal for audiences, who identify with the characters, their experiences, and their immediate situation. The play portrays with great accuracy Brazilian mores and family foibles. The interaction of siblings who have lost a parent captures perfectly a slice of Brazilian life, which the playwright distorts just enough to provide comic incongruity.

Another significant comic writer is Flávio de Souza, a disciple of Naum Alves de Souza. His plays include *Parentes entre parênteses* (*Parents in Parentheses*), *Sexo dos anjos* (*Angels' Sex*), and *Fica comigo esta noite* (*Stay with Me Tonight*), the final comic piece I discuss in this section. Flávio de Souza has been one of Brazil's most successful—in terms of box office—and prolific comic playwrights. *Fica comigo* displays attributes of the comedy of manners, *besteirol,* and—superficially at least—Theater of the Absurd. This play will remind many readers of Chilean playwright Jorge Díaz's *Cepillo de dientes* (*Toothbrush*). There are two characters, Ela and Ele (She and He), a childless couple who interact with a large cast of unseen and unheard characters. As the play begins Ele has died—he's lying on a bed—and Ela is dealing with the invisible family members who have come to view the body and to pay their condolences to the widow. As the play progresses the husband speaks from beyond the grave—like Machado de Assis's Bras Cubas—and eventually returns from the dead to settle accounts, seek reconciliation, and—like Vadinho in Jorge Amado's *Dona Flor*—make love with his wife. The play also includes flashbacks to their life before the husband's untimely death of a heart attack.

*Fica comigo esta noite* includes elements of the comedy of manners: the setting is simple—the bedroom where the husband's body has been laid out—the Brazilian family and social mores are lightly satirized—gossip, lack of respect for privacy, meddlesome family members—and such stock characters as the *penetra* (uninvited guest) who without knowing anyone joins the wake in order to devour the food. In spite of the flashbacks mentioned above, the time frame is limited mostly to the present. At times Souza's work plays like *besteirol.* At one point the husband induces the wife to repeat word for word and hurl against the invisible guests a series of insults which descend into pure silliness.

The play, with its archetypal couple interacting with a cast of imaginary characters, is reminiscent of Theater of the Absurd, in particular Ionesco's *The Chairs*. A caveat: the comparison is more formal than substantial, because *Fica comigo* lacks Theater of the Absurd's philosophical dimensions, its despair over the human condition, its tragedy masquerading as comedy.

A final consideration is the sponsorship making possible the publication—under the title *Cinco textos do teatro contemporâneo brasileiro*—of the comedies discussed in this section. Government support for the arts—local, state, and federal—declined precipitously under the administrations of José Sarney and Fernando de Collor Mello. Although some funding has been restored during the presidencies of Itamar Franco and Fernando Henrique Cardoso in the 1990s, the private sector has fequently filled the vacuum. Grupo Macunaíma, arguably the most important company in the last three decades and which I discuss next, receives private support from an organization known as SESC (Serviço Social do Comércio). Brazil's unofficial annual national theater festival in Curitiba is a private undertaking organized by arts promoters utilizing corporate sponsorship. *Cinco textos* was published with the support of Shell Oil. Few playtexts are published in Brazil because they are not commercially viable, and so this kind of undertaking is especially welcome. Moreover, whereas the few theatrical texts that do get published are poorly designed and printed on cheap paper, the finished product in the case of *Cinco textos* is a handsomely produced hardcover edition with excellent photographic documentation. I hope there will be more editions in the future, making hard to obtain theatrical texts available to researchers, students, and anyone else interested in reading Brazilian plays.

## V. ANTUNES FILHO AND GRUPO MACUNAÍMA

It could be argued that it was the theater companies, more than playwrights, which broke out of the postdictatorship slump and found a way to go beyond the engagé language of the 1960s. One of their paths was humor, farce, and parody. "Comedy was rediscovered . . . as spectacle. Circus techniques were revived, as aspects of burlesque were borrowed" (Guzik 1992, "Exercício," 12). An excellent example is São Paulo's Teatro do Ornitorrinco, founded and directed by Cacá Rosset, whose actors command circus techniques, singing, and dancing. Their productions have been characterized by "sensuality, bawdy humor, direct communication with the audience. . . . Recycling classics, always paying attention to the humor the real public wants, Ornitorrinco created a captive audience, even though it may not have gained unanimous critical support. Its international tours have always been marked by scandal . . ." (Labaki 1992, 27). American audiences will remember the group for its controversial 1991 staging of *A Midsummer Night's Dream* as part of two New York events sponsored by Joseph Papp: the Festival Latino and the Shakespeare in the Park Festival. The production generated controversy for its nudity and for its exclusive use of Portuguese. Much of the press was positive. The *New York Times* reviewer credited the troupe with a "forthright" appreciation for Shakespeare and praised the production for its amusement value, stating that the director "is interested in the comedy as a springboard for entertainment and performance art with a distinct Brazilian tang. . . . He is content to present a frolicsome Brazilian carnival, what could be called a Bottom's 'Dream,' and it is most welcome in its outdoor environment" (Gussow 1991, C3). The *Newsweek* reviewer, however, complained: "There's a case to be made for baring nearly every bottom but Bottom's in 'A Midsummer Night's Dream' . . . but there's a limit. [Putting] it into Portuguese, the first language of .137 percent of the New York City population—and you wind up with a patchwork mess, part bad sitcom and part street fight in a strange neighborhood. The only thing missing is Shakespeare" (Jones 1991, 63). Grupo do Ornitorrinco also staged Shakespeare's *The Comedy of Errors* in the 1992 Shakespeare in the Park Festival.

Rio's Grupo Tapa, directed by Eduardo Tolentino, has been one of the most stable artistic projects of recent times. It has staged important dramas from the international canon and related thematically to Brazilian society. The company has produced works by J.B. Priestly, Nelson Rodrigues, Jean Tardieu, Machiavelli, Molière, Ibsen, and Shakespeare.

The most important company of the post-*abertura* period, in the view of most critics and the theater-going public, has been São Paulo's Grupo Macunaíma, directed since its founding by Antunes Filho. The company's stagings, beginning in 1978, have won numerous awards in Brazil and in the international arena. The work of Antunes Filho and his company has revolutionized the Brazilian stage by: (1) almost single-handedly awakening the stage after the nightmare of dictatorial repression and illuminating its path in the transition to democracy; (2) drawing two of Brazil's greatest playwrights, Nelson Rodrigues and Jorge Andrade, out of the shadows of oblivion; (3) bringing to life on the stage modern classic narrative works by Mário de Andrade and João Guimarães Rosa; (4) diving deep into Brazil's myths; (5) nationalizing universal dramatic literature and theater methods; and (6) redefining the role of the director and engendering a new generation of *encenadores,* of which Gerald Thomas is the most notable example.

Grupo Macunaíma was born from a course taught by veteran director Antunes Filho in 1977, under the sponsorship of the São Paulo State Ministry of Culture, a course based on the theme "Macunaíma," protagonist of the 1928 seminal Brazilian modernist fictional work of the same name. The author, Mário de Andrade, called the work a "rhapsody" rather than a novel. In addition to becoming a classic of Brazilian literature, the work has been the theme of a Rio Carnival Samba School and was adapted for the cinema in the 1960s. The course became a stage production, one of the most spectacularly successful in the history of Brazilian theater. During its long run, from 1978 to 1985, *Macunaíma* played throughout Brazil and, indeed, throughout the world, playing in such venues as the 1984 Los Angeles Olympic Arts Festival and numerous international theater festivals. The production was compared favorably to other Latin American artistic works which have gained international prestige such as García Márquez's *100 Years of Solitude*. Antunes Filho has been compared with other internationally known directors of stage and screen such as Robert Wilson, Peter Brook, Fellini, and Buñuel.

The work was based on—one might say it "Brazilianized"—Polish director-theorist Jerzy Grotowski's poor-theater techniques. For example, newspaper and strips of cloth were the "raw materials" of costume and set design. This "third-world" design conception led to great richness of imagination, spectacle, and ritual, presenting Brazil in all its regional and ethnic diversity. The production's submersion in Brazil's roots seemed to call forth appealingly archetypes wherever it played, from the United States to Europe to Japan. And from that first staging the company's name became, of course, Grupo Macunaíma.

If Antunes Filho's new experimental phase had been limited to *Macunaíma,* it surely would have gone down as a milestone in Brazilian theatrical history. But it was only the beginning. The next project, entitled *Nelson Rodrigues o eterno retorno* (1981), gave the playwright, whose name is celebrated in the title, his deserved place in the dramatic pantheon. Nelson Rodrigues, most—though not all—critics and theater directors now agree, is the most revolutionary and provocative figure in modern Brazilian drama, acclaimed for his thematic and stylistic innovations, as well as his ingenious ideas about stagecraft. His works excavate not only Brazilian social reality but its myths, as well as what Jung called the "collective unconscious." To find a comparable author one would have to consider narrative (Guimarães Rosa, Clarice Lispector) or poetry (Manuel Bandeira, Carlos Drummond de Andrade). The playwright attracted wide public attention in 1943, with the staging of his play *Vestido de noiva* by the innovative Rio de Janeiro group Os Comediantes, under the direction of Polish emigré Zbigniev Ziembinski. The event, which brought Brazilian theater into the modernist mainstream, seemed to portend a glorious theatrical career for the author, but such was not the case. Nelson Rodrigues, although many of his subsequent works were staged, became a marked man, at least as a playwright. The right condemned his work as obscene and immoral, and he spent decades muzzled by the censors. The left considered him a reactionary and so during the 1960s snubbed his work, and when censorship eased in the wake of the *abertura* the ideological patrol continued to marginalize him. Nevertheless, Nelson Rodrigues maintained a fruitful journalistic career, as author of a regular column of *crônicas* entitled "A vida como ela é" ("Life As It Is").[15] But it was Antunes Filho who revealed, shortly after Rodrigues's death in 1980, that his playwrighting had continued to grow and mature in the decades after the 1943 success of *Vestido de noiva*. That event had not been an accident after all. Antunes carefully researched mythical and archetypal suggestions in Rodrigues's work for his staging, bringing into play the theories of Mircea Eliade and Carl Jung. This archetypal perspective allowed Antunes Filho to alter the playwright's image from author of comedies of manners to that of a prodigious expressionist. While Nelson Rodrigues, in some plays, does portray the Brazilian bourgeoisie, both subject and object of the *comédias de costumes,* he at the same time tears off the veil concealing another universe which is atemporal and grotesque. Antunes invented another new stage language for this second production with Grupo Macunaíma, based on the processions that are an inextricable part of religious life in Brazil. Rituals were used in the spectacle to create dream-like archetypal images and also as anti-rituals to parody liturgical ceremonies of renovation, in reference to the sterility of the characters' everyday lives. *Nelson Rodrigues o eterno retorno,*[16] like *Macunaíma* before it, was a huge success, in terms of critical and audience reception and national and international tours and awards.

The company's next step was to plunge into international dramatic literature, with Antunes Filho's 1984 staging of *Romeo and Juliet*. The director based the production on a Roland Barthes idea, the discourse of love, an anti-dogmatic concept, the obverse of the authoritarian discourse of power (the discourse, in Antunes's view, of both the Brazilian military and the ideological patrol). The director filtered Shakespeare's play through the music of the Beatles, thus creating a song of youthful resistance, a visual and auditory poem of passion and nostalgia; that is, universal and timeless nostalgia (the tale of the young lovers of Verona), reflected through the nostalgia of Antunes's generation (Beatles songs). And drawing from those two British sources, the director succeeded in creating a deeply Brazilian spectacle, because if in Europe and the United States the excess of amorous emotion and melodrama belong to subliterature and kitsch, in Brazil they still command respect, at least in the hands of a consummate craftsman like Antunes Filho and his talented young cast.[17] The result was a one-act piece, as "poor" in its stagecraft as Grupo Macunaíma's previous offerings, which played triumphantly in Brazil and abroad.

In 1986, Antunes/Macunaíma turned for inspiration to another Brazilian narrative classic with his adaptation of the short story "A hora e vez de Augusto Matraga" (loosely translated, "Augusto Matraga's Time Has Come"), by João Guimarães Rosa. The purpose, as in the case of the company's debut, *Macunaíma,* was to explore the roots of national culture. The new production, titled simply *Augusto Matraga,* maintained the Grotowskian poor-theater techniques. The props and other objects in the stage design recreated visually the richness of the folk art and oral traditions of the Brazilian backlands, as does Guimarães Rosa's prose.[18]

*Xica da Silva,* staged in 1988, commemorated Grupo Macunaíma's first decade, as well as the centennial of the abolition of slavery in Brazil. It was a transitional production, because for the first time a Macunaíma/Antunes production featured an elaborate set design, by J.C. Serroni, who would from then on be an integral part of the company. Based on the historical character of the title, a famous slave woman from the colonial period, also the focus of Carlos Diegues's 1977 film *Xica,* the play examined the colonized–colonizer relationship. The production toured extensively; among the many venues it visited was the Olympic Arts Festival in Seoul.

In 1989, Antunes/Macunaíma returned in full aesthetic form with a new staging of Nelson Rodrigues's works. The production was entitled *Paraíso, zona norte* (literally, *Paradise, North Zone*), a reference to the working-class districts in North Rio. Two plays were included, both set in the *Zona Norte*: *A falecida* (*The Dead Woman*) and *Os sete gatinhos* (*The Seven Kittens*), defined by the author as *tragédias cariocas* (Rio tragedies). The allusion to "paradise" parodies Rio's nickname *cidade maravilhosa* ("marvellous city"), a title which has slowly faded in the face of the social crises—crime, street children, cocaine mafia, pollution—

the city now faces. Nelson Rodrigues, who wrote these "tragedies" in the 1950s and set them in the then tourist paradise, presciently demystified *carioca* boosterism. As a counterpoint to the *paraíso* of the production, the actors, when they exited the stage, descended down a stairway into a netherworld, which also represented the region of the human psyche Jung defined as the collective unconscious (Antunes Filho once again utilized Jungian theory as the backdrop for a Nelson Rodrigues staging). The staircase was but one detail in J.C. Serroni's set design, which included a plastic semitransparent structure which audiences associated variously with a working-class train station, an old sanatorium, and a crystal palace. Antunes Filho called it a "bubble," a point of eternal return, outside of time and space, where the daily tragedy of the "north zone" dwellers unfolds. The production featured a sound track with recorded music from biblical films and other epics, a reference that the director defined as the cloying mysticism served up by Hollywood. The lighting for the production was designed by Max Keller of the Munich Municipal Theater. *Paraíso zona norte* was yet another Antunes/Macunaíma success in terms of box-office and critical reception, receiving several national and international awards. Its 1990 tour included the Caracas International Theater Festival.[19]

In 1991, Antunes/Macunaíma made another radical departure, staging a version of the fairy tale "Little Red Riding Hood," giving it the title *Nova velha estória* (*New Old Story*), with an intriguing set design by J.C. Serroni. Here, the director dispensed with conventional spoken language. It was not that the actors did not speak, but that they communicated in a nonsense language invented in improvised rehearsals, simulating the preverbal speech of children. Emphasizing the mythical dimension of fables—rites of initiation and of passage, especially the sexual awakening of the protagonist—the actors utilized gestures evoking primitive states of aggression and lust, as well as childlike curiosity. A notable success in Brasil, *Nova velha estória* was also presented in the 1991 New York International Arts Festival. *New York Times* critic D.J.R. Bruckner (1991) wrote:

> The Macunaíma is an enormously intelligent troupe: every move, dance and pause is vividly imaginative; nothing, and everything, is innocent. Here Red Ridinghood's adventure is a passage to womanhood and the wolf is the eternal tempter who arrives with the new moon (glowing huge above the auditorium) to seduce, not devour. The grandmother meets her end dancing ecstatically with him, and his conquest

> of Red Ridinghood—all growls, yelps, and flailing feet—leaves him broken, howling. When he is caught, Red Ridinghood saves him from the hunter's gun and he floats off inside the moon, to return another year. . . . 'Nova Velha' is perfect fantasy perfectly realized.

In 1992, Antunes Filho abandoned preverbal fantasy to plunge into the verbal terror of *Macbeth.* The director, as an homage to Japanese director Kurosawa's film based on Shakespeare's tragedy, titled his new production *Trono de sangue* (*Throne of Blood*). The set design by J.C. Serroni and the costumes by Romero de Andrade Lima included strips of upholstery fabric and other inexpensive materials, reminiscent of the "poor theater" which distinguished Antunes/Macunaíma's early productions. Noh theater techniques were incorporated into the acting. The director, who is not afraid to entrust challenging roles to inexperienced actors, chose a nineteen-year-old actress to play Lady Macbeth, Samantha Monteiro—she also played Little Red Riding Hood in *Nova velha estória*—who was quite effective as the treacherous queen. Reviews were effusive in their praise of *Trono de sangue,* painting it in glowing colors. Jairo Arco e Flecha wrote in the magazine *Veja* that the production is "one of the best moments in the Brazilian theater of recent years [and] it sends chills up the spine of audience members as only the great horror films are capable of doing" (Arco e Flecha 1992, 96). According to Alberto Guzik, "Antunes Filho transformed his version of the tragedy into a scenic boom equivalent to the author's exquisite poetry" (Guzik 1992, "Eletrizante," 14).

In December 1993, Grupo Macunaíma opened Jorge Andrade's *Vereda da salvação* (*Path of Salvation*). One of Brazil's most significant modern playwrights, Jorge Andrade (1922–1984) focused much of his attention on the decline of the São Paulo rural aristocracy in such works as *A moratória* (*The Moratorium*). By 1993, Andrade was a dramatist relegated to oblivion, because like Nelson Rodrigues his works seemed incapable of addressing the concerns of the 1960s and 1970s generation of artists devoted to engagé theater.[20] Jorge Andrade, however, was returned to center stage with this new operation rescue performed by Antunes Filho/Macunaíma. The 1963 *Vereda da salvação* tells the story of the police massacre of an obscure messianic sect in the backlands of Minas Gerais state. The play, staged in 1964 by Antunes Filho himself, irritated both left and right, because, according to Sábato Magaldi, "Jorge was the victim of a very unfortunate misunderstanding: the left did not support his theater, which it considered nostalgic and aristocratic, while the right judged that in the light of the political events of 1964 it was an outrage to bring to the stage of issue of the poverty of the masses" (Magaldi 1980, "TBC," 54). By late 1993, however, the time was ripe for this rural tragedy. The ideological polarization of the 1960s no longer divided audiences. Massacres of rural workers in the Brazilian interior continue to be a fact of life, particularly in association with a movement known as *Sem Terra,* groups of landless farm workers whose level of organization and political support are significant, but whose clashes with police and military forces have been at times deadly for the workers. Religious fanaticism as a phenomenon apropos of the poorest sectors of society is a universal question. Islamic fundamentalists in the Middle East, evangelical fundamentalists in the United States, and religious strife in India are but a few examples. On the basis of its themes alone, then, the rediscovery of *Vereda da salvação* was a significant event. But Antunes and Grupo Macunaíma also revealed with this new production a great theatrical work, so much so that for the first time the company staged a work with virtually no changes in the text. And the staging was worthy of the text. J.C. Serroni's set design consisted of a forest of barren trees, which reminded spectators of a jail. The production included religious processions, another trademark of Antunes/Macunaíma. The lights came up on the actors standing in a row of coffins placed on end across the stage, an explicit reference to a recent massacre of farm workers. Reviewers were ecstatic. For example, Alberto Guzik wrote: "Until last Thursday, the most important event of the theater season had been the reopening of Teatro Oficina, with José Celso Martínez Correa's magnificent/exasperating *Hamlet*. But now, Oficina and Zé Celso will have to step aside for Antunes and Grupo Macunaíma. Because *Vereda da salvação* is an ambitious, bold, challenging, enormously important undertaking" (Guzik 1993, "Resgate," 14).

To conclude, Grupo Macunaíma revived the theatrical cycle interrupted by the military dictatorship. The company has been able to create a singular Brazilian theatrical style, without bowing to imported culture. If it utilizes foreign models—the theories of Jung, Eliade, Barthes, Grotowski—it nationalizes them to the point of transforming them into original theatrical concepts. Antunes Filho and Grupo Macunaíma have gone to the core of Brazil's myths, its roots, in ways unique to the nation's stage. They have opened up previously untapped levels in the drama of Nelson Rodrigues and made him the icon that he is today. The company has adapted for the stage the fiction of Mário de Andrade and João Guimarães Rosa. Its performances of Shakespeare have been highly innovative. The Antunes/Macunaíma alchemy, in short, has produced a theatrical legacy that is as much universal is it is Brazilian. Finally, the changes brought about by Antunes Filho have given rise to the new generation of *encenadores,* featuring the work of Gerald Thomas, which is the topic I began this book with in Chapter 1. Their theatrical revolution is as profound and wide-ranging as any in previous decades.

## NOTES

[1] All translations from Portuguese to English in this chapter are my own.

[2] The Great Depression of 1929 shattered the economies of Latin America, including Brazil's coffee economy, which in turn spelled doom for the Old Republic (1889–1930). Getúlio Vargas was swept into power via military revolt in 1930. Vargas assumed dictatorial powers, imposing censorship and quelling political dissent. The paradigm for his government was Mussolini's fascist regime; Vargas called his administration the *Estado Novo,* or New State. While many Brazilians remember Vargas for his repressive measures, others look to his economic policies in terms of nationalist sentiments. He gave a boost to industrialization and set up state-run industries. His populist policies, in short, can be compared with those of Perón's in Argentina. And like Perón, he remains a controversial figure. Finally, it is no small irony that Vargas himself was a member of the Brazilian Academia de Letras of which Sábato Magaldi would become a member a half century later.

[3] Sábato Magaldi, writing in the literary supplement of the *Estado de São Paulo,* 1969, quoted in Cunha de Vincenzo 1992, 87.

[4] An ironic footnote to this story is that Sábato Magaldi recommended the play to Augusto Boal in 1964, but the latter passed on it, not seeing the play's potential as political parody.

[5] The company would eventually turn against him when he published a less-than-enthusiastic review of its Living Theater–style, countercultural theater of aggression piece entitled *Gracias, señor*. "In response to a negative review from Sábato Magaldi, who heretofore had been one of Oficina's staunchest defenders, the group circulated a letter, which the following paragraph sums up: 'Sábato Magaldi is a *critic,* perhaps the most respected, because he is the most reactionary: his function is to stabilize, to keep theater just as it is, like a vampire sucking a little new blood here and there for his own survival. His ideological position is blind due to his inability to distinguish what he sees as long as its stagecraft is high-level and lends seriousness to the pap consumed by the dead clientele of the Theaters. Every year he tries to "save" the season by praising its diversity; he is a perky model selling a nice, clean product' " (George 1992, *Stage,* 71).

[6] The third edition saw a printing of 20,000 copies—an unheard-of number for a scholarly book in Brazil—and was distributed to schools and libraries, deemed an essential reference work by the Minister of Culture.

[7] The term *mambembe* refers to an itinerant theatrical troupe.

[8] Other venues included four local theaters, a park, a forest, and a church.

[9] *Mineiro* refers to the Brazilian state of Minas Gerais.

[10] As the reader will have noted, Chapter 1 demonstrates that I have subsequently made a thorough and more positive reassessment of Gerald Thomas's work.

[11] Fernando Henrique Cardoso was elected Brazil's president in 1994 and re-elected in 1998.

[12] Since the publication of *Feliz ano velho* Marcelo Paiva has gone on to a successful writing career, the civilian government has opened the archives which document Rubens Paiva's arrest and torture—though the location of his body remains a mystery—and Marcelo's mother, Eunice, has been appointed to head a human rights commission entrusted with investigating cases of the disappeared in Brazil.

[13] Several questions arise from all this, which I intend to address in a future project. For example, has the re-creation of *Kiss of the Spider Woman* as a Broadway musical led to a "watering down" of the novel and the play in formal and ideological terms? While the musical maintains setting and characters, does the substitution of the gay character Molina's B-movie fantasies with show-stopping song and dance numbers produce estrangement on the part of the audience? Another possibility: Does the musical adaptation foster cross-cultural fertilization, suggesting that *Kiss of the Spider Woman* may enrich the American musical comedy genre by opening its doors to such unlikely themes as police-state torture and persecution of homosexuals?

[14] It is worth noting that Naum Alves de Souza began his career as a visual artist and designer. For example, he conceptualized the design for the internationallly renowned production of *Macunaíma,* discussed later.

[15] As I discusses earlier, director Luis Arthur Nunes's transformation of Nelson Rodrigues's *crônicas* into a theatrical piece with his production entitled *A vida como ela é* at the 1993 Festival de Curitiba clearly illustrated the inextricable links between Rodrigues's journalism and his drama.

[16] Antunes/Macunaíma produced a shorter version in 1984, entitled *Nelson 2 Rodrigues.*

[17] In Chapter 2 I discussed Maria Adelaide's skillful handling of melodramatic material. Nelson Rodrigues was another Brazilian theater artist who bent melodrama to his own—corrosive—ends.

[18] I have written extensively about the stagings of *Macunaíma, Nelson 2 Rodrigues,* and *Augusto Matraga* in *The Modern Brazilian Stage* and *Grupo Macunaíma: carnvalização e mito.*

[19] Antunes Filho was not finished with Nelson Rodrigues: in 1992 he successfully staged two of the playwright's work in Spanish with the New York Teatro de Repertorio Español.

[20] This in spite of the fact that Andrade's last play, *Milagre na cela* (*Miracle in a Cell*), deals with the subject of torture during the dictatorship.

# Afterword

As I bring this project to a close in early 1999, it is difficult to resist the temptation to succumb to fin-de-siècle melancholy, not to mention millennium fever, the elevated temperatures of frenzied futurology and the slow, burning gaze on the past 100 or 1,000 years. I choose to resist. In the first place, I have misplaced my crystal ball—I think my son's dog ate it or he's using it for a soccer ball. In the second place, by the time the reader opens this book all the predictions will have been rendered ephemeral and anachronistic, the Y2K bug will or will have not spelled the end of "civilization as we know it." I take the path of discretion and limit my remarks to a summary of Brazilian theatrical events that have unfolded since completing the research and writing for the main body of this book and to a very brief conclusion.

Chapter 1: Gerald Thomas continues to work with his Dry Opera Company in Brazil. One of his most recent pieces, entitled *Nowhere Man,* continues his experiments in the postmodernist vein, presenting a central character embodying the self-referential artist. In 1997, working with the Minas Gerais dance company Primeiro Ato, he directed a piece entitled *A breve interrupção do fim* (*A Brief Interruption of the End*). His play entitled *Chief Butterknife,* performed at the Dr. Dante Theater and featuring Danish actors, opened the 1996 European Cultural Festival in Copenhagen. A postmodernist pop fantasy, *Butterknife* featured such characters as Lois Lane and Clark Kent. Thomas has also kept up his opera directing in Europe. In 1998, for example, he directed Arnold Schoenberg's *Moses und Aron* in Austria. A major book on his work, entitled *Um encenador de si mesmo,* has been published in Brazil.

One of the most fascinating aspects of Gerald Thomas's current activities has nothing to do with theater. For the past few years he has been writing a regular column for the newspaper *Folha de São Paulo*. His topics are wide ranging: action films, avant-garde art movements, the Royal Shakespeare Company, a Turkish community in Germany, the Academy Awards, talk shows, the O.J. Simpson trial, the explosion of tabloid journalism, Thomas's own Jewish family history in Nazi Germany. In one piece he discusses his work with Amnesty International in London during the 1970s, explaining that Augusto Pinochet was the chief villain for Amnesty workers, who are now celebrating the former dictator's arrest and possible extradition to Spain. In another he takes to task the Brazilian icon Xuxa, a children's program host and marketer of her own line of toys and clothing.

Also worth mentioning in the context of Chapter 1 is the work of the mother and daughter tandem of actresses who made *Flash & Crash Days* so memorable. The daughter, Fernanda Torres, has a lead role in the 1997 film *Que é isso companheiro* (*Four Days in September*). The film, based on former political prisoner Fernando Gabeira's memoir of the kidnapping of the American ambassador to Brazil, also features Alan Arkin. Fernanda Montenegro, the mother, is currently starring in the award-winning and highly praised 1998 film *Central do Brasil* (*Central Station*).

Last but not least, Professor Philip Simmons, who provided invaluable aid in conceptualizeing postmodernism, has published a book on the subject (see *Deep Surfaces* in Works Cited).

Chapter 2: Maria Adelaide Amaral's theatrical activities, since the staging of *Querida mamãe,* have continued apace. During the year 1997 the Brazilian theater-going public attended two more award-winning productions scripted by the author, *Inseparáveis* and *Para sempre*. The latter production, about the trials and tribulations of a gay couple, featured an acclaimed veteran of the Brazilian stage, Paulo Autran, in the lead role.

An event especially important to Brazilian theatrical scholars and historians was the publication of the script of Amaral's musical about Chiquinha Gonzaga. The piece was published as *Ó abre alas,* the title of one of her fabled compositions, still a staple of the Carnival samba repertoire. Reading the script for the first time reinforces the commentary included in Chapter 2 and provides new insights. We learn, for example, that Chiquinha Gonzaga is shunned by the family on her father's orders, a decision seconded by her mother. No one in her family is allowed to speak her name, such is the "dishonor" she has brought to the family. Her crime? She leaves her tyrannical husband and takes on a lover. She also has to give up her children because she has no means to support them; she is forbidden to see them, and they have been told their mother has died. Her father is intent on punishing her in other ways, such as attempting to thwart her musical career by hiring people to buy up and discard the sheet music of her compositions (her principal means of livelihood) and threatening those who would perform her music. And yet, in spite of relentless persecution, overwhelming deterrents, and acute suffering, she succeeds in her musical career against all odds. Reading the play also brings out satire relating to the period during which it was performed, 1983, the final year of the military dictatorship. In one scene, for example, a policeman watches like a hawk an operetta for which Chiquinha has composed the music. In his role as censor, the policeman forbids a tango—it is "indecent" for a man and woman to touch as they dance together on stage—but he then allows the tango as long as there is no encore. This burlesque treatment of censorship in Brazil betrays the absurdity and gratuity of its practice.

Another author whose work I analyzed extensively in Chapter 2, Edla van Steen, has continued her theatrical career with the 1998 publication of a play entitled *Bolo de nozes* (*Nutcake*), which deals with the disintegration of a family whose professor father has become a victim of political repression.

Chapter 3: Sábato Magaldi continues to win awards, publish original works, and see former publications in new editions. In 1998, he received the Juca Pato Prize, bestowed by the União Brasileira de Escritores on the individual the organization has chosen as "intellectual of the year." Also in 1998, Professor Magaldi published his definitive work on Brazilian playwrights, entitled *Moderna dramaturgia brasileira*. The work begins with Oswald de Andrade in the 1930s and concludes with today's playwrights. There are chapters on several authors considered in this book, including Nelson Rodrigues, Jorge Andrade, Plínio Marcos, Leilah Assunção, Maria Adelaide Amaral, and Edla van Steen.

Mauro Rasi—along with Maria Adelaide Amaral—is the most successful author writing for the stage today in Brazil (the late Nelson Rodrigues, however, remains the most frequently staged dramatist). Rasi has completed his rural trilogy which began with *A cerimônia do adeus,* continued with *A pérola*—both referred to in Chapter 3—and was completed with *A rainha do lar* (*The Queen of the Home*). The trilogy contains many autobiographical elements dealing with Rasi's growing up in the rural São Paulo city of Bauru. With these plays, Rasi left behind his career as a purveyor of the irreverent, lightweight farces known as *besteirol* and gained a reputation as one of contemporary Brazil's most important dramatists. At the time of this writing, he is about to return once again to his roots with a new play entitled *O crime do Dr. Alvarenga* (*Dr. Alvarenga's Crime*), which is actually based on a play written by his father, a small-town merchant and politician. His father penned the text in the 1950s for an amateur theater group founded by Italian immigrants. *O crime do Dr. Alvarenga* will star actor Paulo Autran.

Antunes Filho's work with his Grupo Macunaíma has continued unabated since the 1993 staging of *Vereda da salvação*. He staged an adaptation of the ancient epic *Gilgamesh,* as well as a version of *Dracula*. He is currently preparing a piece based on Greek tragedy, tentatively titled *Fragmentos troianos* (*Trojan Fragments*). This will be his first attempt to stage Greek theater, something he has avoided in the past because he saw it as leading inevitably to histrionics on the part of the actors, an anathema to his conception of theater. He will attempt to apply to the production a more modern, naturalistic acting method.

Antunes's work is receiving the kind of attention that speaks to its enduring contribution to the Brazilian stage. At the time of this writing, a documentary series is being prepared to commemorate his nearly fifty-year theatrical career, with a special focus on his methods of training and directing actors. The documentary has been scripted by Sebastião Milaré, who has been writing about the director for twenty years. In 1994, Milaré published *Antunes Filho e a dimensão utópica,* a critical biography that covers the period before the director's epochal staging of *Macunaíma*. He is currently readying a work entitled *Hierofania—O teatro segundo Antunes Filho,* which will codify what is now widely recognized as the "Antunes method."

Another footnote to the Antunes/Grupo Macunaíma/Nelson Rodrigues phenomenon is that *A falecida,* one of the plays featured in the production *Paraíso zona norte,* has recently been translated into English under the title *The Deceased Woman*. The translation has received a well-crafted review by B. Campbell Britton (see Works Cited for references to the play and the review).

To conclude this Afterword, my observations about tendencies in Brazilian theater in the postdictatorship period continue to hold true. The stage remains diverse in terms of form and content—or merely fragmented in the view of some—with no overarching trend to define its current state. The postmodernist *encenadores* remain in the vanguard, although the passions they aroused have cooled. Time may well be ripe for a new vanguard to lead the way. Dramatists continue to find it difficult to stage plays with more than two or three characters. Neoliberalism—the new market reform policies fomented by President Cardoso—is the new bogeyman scorned by most intellectuals and artists. This opposition, however, has not translated into specific forms of theatrical protest, because there is no specific repression associated with neoliberalism, not to mention the fact that many theater artists benefit from private sector support, particularly given the scarcity, unreliability, and unpredictability of government support.

Finally, I close with pertinent observations from the critic I have relied on most in this book, Sábato Magaldi:

> Whenever I am tempted to feel discouraged, disagreeing with paths taken by plays being staged, getting angry over state cultural policies, I read the offerings displayed in the newspapers' arts sections and I conclude that, in its provocative diversity, the mere existence of Brazilian theater is a miracle. Because, in other centers, to obtain similar artistic results, astronomical sums are provided by the government, or else by private foundations and donors. One must recognize that more than a professional activity, the Brazilian stage has become an irresistible vocation . . . To do theater in this environment is nothing short of heroic, something not generally recognized. And its creators are never satisfied with routine—they experiment with new languages, challenging established aesthetic patterns, questioning the basic precepts of their own art. From a scholarly perspective, we are most fortunate (Magaldi 1992, "Onde está o teatro," 6-7).

# Works Cited

## I. DRAMA, FICTION, AND BIOGRAPHY


Amaral, Maria Adelaide. *Cemitério sem cruzes. Feira brasileira de opinião*. Ed. Ruth Escobar. São Paulo: Editora Global, 1978: 213–230.

———. *De braços abertos*. Rio de Janeiro: Memórias Futuras Edições, 1985.

———. *Intensa magia*. São Paulo: Caliban Editorial, 1996.

———. *Luísa (quase uma história de amor)*. São Paulo: Nova Fronteira, 1986.

———. *Ó abre alas. Coleção teatro brasileiro*. Vol. 1. Belo Horizonte: Hamdan Editora, 1997: 7–61.

———. *Querida mamãe*. São Paulo: Editora Brasiliense, 1995.

Falabella, Miguel. *A partilha. Cinco textos do teatro contemporâneo brasileiro*. Rio de Janeiro: Xenon Editora and Shell Brasil, 1993: 142–175.

Lispector, Clarice. *A hora da estrela*. 9th ed. Rio de Janeiro: Nova Fronteira, 1984.

Paiva, Marcelo. *Feliz ano velho*. São Paulo: Editora Brasiliense, 1982.

Parente Cunha, Helena. *Woman between Mirrors*. Trans. Ellison and Lindstrom. Austin: University of Texas Press, 1989.

Puig, Manuel. *Beso de la mujer araña*. Barcelona: Editorial Seix Barral, 1976.

Rasi, Mauro. *A cerемônia do adeus. Cinco textos do teatro contemporâneo brasileiro*. Rio de Janeiro: Xenon Editora and Shell Brasil, 1993: 94–141.

Rodrigues, Nelson. *The Deceased Woman*. Trans. Joffre Rodrigues and Toby Coe. Rio de Janeiro: Fundação Nacional de Arte, 1998.

———. *Teatro completo*. Vols. I–IV. Ed. Sábato Magaldi. Rio de Janeiro: Nova Fronteira, 1981–1989.

———. *Teatro completo*. Ed. Sábato Magaldi. Rio de Janeiro: Nova Aguilar, 1993.

Sadlier, Darlene, ed. *One Hundred Years after Tomorrow*. Bloomington: Indiana University Press, 1992.

Souza, Flávio de. *Fica comigo esta noite. Cinco textos do teatro contemporâneo brasileiro*. Rio de Janeiro: Xenon Editora and Shell Brasil, 1993: 8–39.

van Steen, Edla. *A Bag of Stories*. Trans. David S. George. Pittsburgh: Latin American Literary Review Press, 1991.

———. *Bolo de nozes. Coleção teatro brasileiro*. Vol. 2. Belo Horizonte: Hamdan Editora, 1998: 47–87.

———. *Early Mourning*. Trans. David S. George. Pittsburgh: Latin American Literary Review Press, 1997. Trans. of *Madrugada*. São Paulo: Editora, 1992.

———. *O conto da mulher brasileira*. São Paulo: Vertente Editora, 1978.

———. *O último encontro*. São Paulo: Editora Scipione, 1991.

———. *Village of the Ghost Bells*. Trans. David S. George. Austin: University of Texas Press, 1991. Trans. of *Corações mordidos*. São Paulo: Global Editora, 1983.

van Steen, Edla, and David S. George. *À mão armada*. São Paulo: Caliban Editorial, 1996.

## II. CRITICAL BOOKS AND ARTICLES

Albuquerque, Severino João. "From *Abertura* to *Nova República*: Politics and the Brazilian Theater of the Late Seventies and Eighties." *Hispanófila* 96 (1989): 87–95.

———. "O teatro brasiliero na década de oitenta." *Latin American Theatre Review* (Spring 1992): 23–36.

———. *Violent Acts*. Detroit: Wayne State Press, 1991.

Almeida Prado, Décio de. *Apresentação do teatro brasileiro Moderno*. São Paulo: Martins Editora, 1956.

———. *O teatro brasileiro moderno*. São Paulo: Editora Perspectiva; Editora da Universidade de São Paulo, 1988.

Alves de Lima, Mariângela. "Tendências atuais do teatro." *Revista USP* (1992): 16–21.

Arco e Flecha, Jairo. "Triunfo na tragédia." *Veja,* 27 May 1992: 72–73.

Birringer, Johannes. *Theatre, Theory, Postmodernism*. Bloomington and Indianapolis: Indiana University Press, 1991.

Blau, Herbert. "The Oversight of Ceaseless Eyes." *Around the Absurd: Essays on Modern and Postmodern Drama*. Eds. Enoch Brater and Ruby Cohn. Ann Arbor: University of Michigan Press, 1990: 280–289.

Boal, Augusto. *Teatro do oprimido e outras poéticas políticas*. São Paulo: Civilização Brasileira, 1975.

———. *Técnicas latinoamericanas de teatro popular*. Buenos Aires: Corregidor, 1975.

Brandão, Tânia. "Visionários ou alienados?" *Revista USP* (1992): 28–33.

Britton, B. Campbell. Rev. of *The Deceased Woman*. Trans. Joffre Rodrigues and Toby Coe. *Luso-Brazilian Review* 35:2 (Winter 1998): 122–123.

Brooke, James. "Environmental Opera Leaves Rio Puzzled." *New York Times* 20 July 1989.

Brustein, Robert. *Dumbocracy in America: Studies in the Theatre of Guilt, 1987–1994*. Chicago: Ivan R. Dee, 1995.

Bruckner, D. J. R. "New Old Story." *New York Times,* 12 June 1991.

Camargo, José Carlos. " 'Mattogrosso' leva Thomas ao ápice de sua obra." *Folha de São Paulo,* 19 October 1989.

Campos, Haroldo de. "Gerald Thomas joga tragédia grega no urinol." *Folha de São Paulo* [1987?].

———. "Thomas liberta Carmen de seu mito de origem." *Folha de São Paulo,* 13 May 1990: E9.

Cândido Galvão, João. "Cenografia brasileira nos anos 80." *Revista USP* (1992): 58–61.

Christ, Carol P. *Deep Diving and Surfacing: Women Writers on Spiritual Quest*. Boston: Beacon, 1980.

Coelho, Marcelo. "Thomas encena a luta entre o velho e o novo." *Folha de São Paulo*, 13 November 1991: E12.

Cunha de Vincenzo, Elza. *Um teatro da mulher: dramaturgia feminina no palco brasileiro contemporâneo*. São Paulo: Editora Perspectiva; Editora da Universidade de São Paulo, 1992.

Dapieve, Arthur. "Introdução à obra do acaso total." *Jornal do Brasil,* 5 July 1989.

Escobar, Ruth. *Aprsentação* to *Feira brasileira de opinião* (1978): 7-8.

Fernandes, Sílvia. "O espectador emancipado: apontamentos sobre uma encenação contemporânea." *Revista USP* (1992): 70–73.

Fernandes, Sílvia, and J. Guinsburg, ed. *Um encenador de si mesmo: Gerald Thomas*. São Paulo: Editora Perspectiva, 1996.

Fonseca, Vera, and Thereza Jorge. "Amor, vertigem e decadênica em Mattogrosso." Interview with Gerald Thomas. *O Estado de S. Paulo,* 2 July 1989.

Foster, David William. "Duas modalidades de escrita sobre a homossexualidade na ficção brasiliera contemporânea." *Toward Socio-Criticism: "Luso-Brazilian Literature*." Ed. Roberto Reis. Tempe: Arizona State University Press, 1991: 55–65.

Frias Filho, Otavio. "O fim do teatro." *Revista USP* (1992): 50–57.

Garcia Lima, César. "Fernandas duelam no palco." *Folha da Tarde* [1992?].

"Gerald Thomas, eis a questão." TV Cultura Documentary. São Paulo, 1994.
George, David S. "A pós-modernidade de Gerald Thomas." *Um encenador de si mesmo* (1996): 244–269.

———. "Brazil's Festival de Teatro de Curitiba II—The Healthy State of the Art." *Latin American Theatre Review* (Spring 1994): 139–144.

———. "*Encenador* Gerald Thomas's *Flash and Crash Days*: Nelson Rodrigues without Words," in *Latin American Theatre Review* (Fall 1996): 75–88.

———. "Gerald Thomas's Postmodernist Theatre: A Wagnerian *Antropofagia*?" *Luso-Brazilian Review* 35:2 (Winter 1998): 99–106.

———. *Grupo macunaíma: carnavalização e mito*. São Paulo: Editora Perspectiva; Editora da Universidade de São Paulo, 1991.

———. *The Modern Brazilian Stage*. Austin: University of Texas Press, 1992.

———. "Sábato Magaldi: Interpreter, Chronicler, Arbiter." *Latin American Theatre Review* (Spring 1998): 163–172.

———. "Teatro de Arena and Theatre of Oppressed: In and Out of Context." *Latin American Theatre Review* (Spring 1995): 39–54.

———. *Teatro e antropofagia*. São Paulo: Editora Global, 1985.

"Ginástica em família." *Veja,* 20 November 1991: 105.

Gonçalves Filho, Antonio. "Caetano Veloso vai participar de 'Mattogrosso'". *Folha de São Paulo,* 6 July 1989: E3.

———. "'The Flash and Crash Days' satiriza Wagner." *Folha de São Paulo,* 11 January 1992: E5.

———. "Os nibelungos caem no samba em 'Mattogrosso', de Gerald Thomas." *Folha de São Paulo,* 21 October 1989: F1.

Griffiths, Paul. "Screening the Music." *The New Yorker,* 31 July 1995: 86–87.

Grotowski, Jerzy. *Towards a Poor Theatre*. New York: Simon and Schuster, 1968.

Guimarães, Carmelinda. "'Querida mamãe': grande peça e uma relação difícil." *A Tribuna,* September 1995: D2-3.

Gussow, Mel. "Shakespeare as Carnival in Amazonian 'Dream'." *The New York Times* 2 August 1991: C3.

Guzik, Alberto. "Essa difícil humanidade." Preface to *Querida mamãe*. By Maria Adelaide Amaral. São Paulo: Editora Brasiliense, 1995: 7–11.

———. "Fortes emoções no palco." *Jornal da Tarde,* 10 September 1995. Teatro/Crítica: 1.

———. "O resgate de uma obra prima." *Jornal da Tarde,* 4 December 1993: 2A.

———. "Um eletrizante Macbeth." *Jornal da Tarde,*. 23 May 1992: 14.

———. "Um encontro intimista com Edla van Steen. No palco." *Jornal da Tarde,* 13 June 1989. Teatro/Crítica: 1.

———. "Um exercício de memória: dramaturgia brasileira anos 80." *Revista USP* (1992): 10–15.

Holden, Stephen. "Not a Pair to Go Shopping Together or Out to Tea." *New York Times,* July 16 1992: C15.

Jabor, Arnaldo. " 'D. Juan' choca elite sexual paulista." *Folha de São Paulo,* 14 February 1995: E5.

Jacobson, Aileen. "Though Nearly Silent, 'Days' Is Disturbing." *New York Newsday,* 16 July 1992.

Jones Jr., Malcolm. "Shakespeare as a Second Language." *Newsweek,* 12 August 1991: 63.

Kristeva, Julia. "Modern Theatre Does not Take (A) Place." *Substance* 18/19 (1977). Quoted in McGlynn, "Postmodernism": 140.

Kroker, Arthur, and David Cook. *The Postmodern Scene: Excremental Culture and Hyper-Aesthetics.* 2nd ed. New York: St. Martin's Press, 1988.

Labaki, Aimar. "Os diretores e a direção do teatro." *Revista USP* (1992): 22–27.

Luiz, Macksen. "A psicologia do conflito em cena,." *Jornal do Brasil,* 9 April 1994: 6.

———. "Os estilhaços da modernidade." *Jornal do Brasil,* 21 November 1991: B1.

———. "O samba da ópera seca." *Jornal do Brasil,* 19 July 1989.

Magaldi, Sábato. *Aspectos da dramaturgia moderna.* São Paulo: Comissão de Literatura do Conselho Estudual de Cultura, 1963.

———. "Na contramão." Preface to *O último encontro.* By Edla van Steen. São Paulo: Editora Scipione, 1991.

———. *Iniciação ao teatro.* 6th ed. São Paulo: Ática, 1997.

———. *Moderna dramaturgia brasileira.* São Paulo: Editora Perspectiva, 1998.

———. *Nelson Rodrigues: dramaturgia e encenações.* São Paulo: Editora Perspectiva; Editora da Universidade de São Paulo, 1987.

———. *O cenário no avesso.* São Paulo: Editora Perspectiva, 1991.

———. "Onde está o teatro." *Revista USP* (1992): 6-9.

———. "O teatro e a função da crítica." *Jornal da Tarde,* 22 September 1987.

———. "O teatro social no Brasil contemporâneo," *Iberomania* 38 (1993): 41–60.

———. "O texto no moderno teatro brasileiro." *Arquivos do centro cultural português* XXIII. Lisbon-Paris: Fundação Calouste Gulbenkian, 1987: 1059–1082.

———. *O texto no teatro.* São Paulo: Editora Perspectiva; Editora da Universidade de São Paulo, 1989.

———. *Panorama do teatro brasileiro.* 3rd ed. Rio de Janeiro: Serviço Nacional de Teatro, 1997.

———. "Surge o TBC." *Dionysos* 25 (1980).

———. *Um palco brasileiro: o arena de São Paulo.* São Paulo: Editora Brasiliense, 1984.

Magaldi, Sábato, and Lêdo Ivo. *As luzes da ilusão*. São Paulo: Global Editora, 1995.

Magaldi, Sábato, and Maria Tereza Vargas. "Cem anos de teatro em São Paulo." Spec. supplement of *O estado de S. Paulo* (17 January 1976).

Magyar, Vera. "M. Adelaide Amaral. Autora, protagonista e espectadora de *Bodas de papel*." *Jornal da Tarde,* 24 January 1979.

Martins, Ana Maria. "Entrevista cum Ana Marin Martins" Interview. *Revista Numen* 5 (September 1990).

Martins, Marília. "Antropofágica vanguarda." *Isto É,* 15 April 1987: 41.

McGlynn, Fred. "Postmodernism and Theater." *Postmodernism—Philosophy and the Arts*. Ed. Hugh J. Silverman. New York: Routledge, Chapman and Hall, 1990: 137–154.

Mesguich, Daniel. "The Book to Come Is a Theater." Trans. Carl R. Lovitt. *Sub-Stance* 18/19 (1977).

Michalski, Yan. "Gerald Thomas, um inovador." *Tribuna do advogado,* July 1986.

Milaré, Sebastião. *Antunes Filho e a dimensão utópica*. São Paulo: Editora Perspectiva, 1994.

Milleret, Margo. "An Update on Theatre in Brazil." *The Latin American Theatre Review* (Spring 1995): 123–130.

Mitchell, Emily. "Postcards from the Edge." *Time,* 24 August 1992: 50.

Motta, Nelson. "Gerald marreta o bumbo." *O Globo,* 22 July 1989.

Myers, Robert. "A Brazilian Legend Comes to New York as a Monster Mom." The *New York Times,* 12 July 1992.

Novaes Coelho, Nelly. "A Mulher na Literatura Brasileira." *Proceedings from the Primeiro encontro com a literatura Brasileira*. Sao Paulo: Secretaria de Cultura and Câmara Brasileira do Livro, 25–30 September 1977: 31–39.

Novak, Michael. *The Experience of Nothingness*. New York: Harper & Row, 1970.

Pallottini, Renata. *Introdução à dramaturgia*. São Paulo: Editora Brasiliense, 1983.

Patai, Daphne. *Myth and Ideology in Contemporary Brazilian Literature*. Rutherford: Farleigh Dickinson University Press, 1983.

Peixoto, Marta. "Writing the Victim in the Fiction of Clarice Lispector." *Proceedings from the Transformation of Literary Language in Latin American Literature*. Ed. K. David Jackson. Austin: University of Texas Press, 1987: 84–97.

Riding, Alan. "In Brazil, It's Lonely in the Avant-Garde." *New York Times,* 2 October 1988.

Santarrita, Marcos. "A síndrome de Wagner." *Jornal do Brasil,* 2 April 1987: B1.

Shank, Theodore. "Framing Actuality: Thirty Years of Experimental Theater, 1959–89." *Around the Absurd: Essays on Modern and Postmodern Drama*. Ed. Enoch Brater and Ruby Cohn. Ann Arbor: University of Michigan Press, 1990: 240–271.

Simonsen, Mário Henrique. "Confusão a bordo." *Veja,* 8 April 1987: 113–114.

"Simonsen quer processar Thomas." *Folha de São Paulo,* 12 April 1987.

Simmons, Philip E. *Deep Surfaces: Mass Culture and History in Postmodern American Fiction*. Athens: University of Georgia Press, 1997.

Süssekind, Flora. "A imaginação monológica: Notas sobre o teatro de Gerald Thomas e Bia Lessa." *Revista USP* (1992): 43–49.

van Steen, Edla. *Viver e escrever*. Vol. 1. Porto Alegre: L&PM Editores, 1981.

Veloso, Marco. "Drama de van Steen cai na guerra dos sexos." *Folha de São Paulo,* 10 June 1989.

———. "'Mattogrosso' é a melhor crítica do teatro nacional'". *Folha de São Paulo,* 17 October 1995.

———. "'Mattogrosso' sintetiza o teatro de Gerald Thomas." *Folha de São Paulo,* 14 October 1989: 7.

Voltolini, Ricardo. "Três diretores em discussão." *Jornal da Tarde,* 13 May 1988: A-12.

## III. PROGRAM NOTES

Amaral, Maria Adelaide. Notes for *Intensa magia,* 1995.

Thomas, Gerald. Notes for *Mattogrosso,* July 1989.

## IV. PERSONAL INTERVIEWS

Alves de Souza, Naum. 23 June 1993.

Amaral, Maria Adelaide. 22 June 1993.

Magaldi, Sábato. 8 July 1994; 4 December 1995.

Rasi, Mauro. 20 June 1993.

Thomas, Gerald. 20 January 1996.

van Steen, Edla. 20 December 1995.

## V. TALKS

Bissett, Judith Ismael. "A Space in the Wilderness: Storytelling in *A República dos sonhos*. Address presented at the 35th annual conference of the MMLA, Minneapolis, 4–5 November 1993. Quoted with permission of the author.

———. "A voz feminina em *O grande amor de nossas vidas* de Consuelo de Castro." Address presented at the 33rd annual conference of the MMLA, Chicago, 14–16 November 1991. Quoted with permission of the author.

van Steen, Edla. "A Woman in the World of Literature and the Literature of the World." Lecture given at several American universities in the spring of 1997. Quoted with permission of the author.

# Index

# Permission Acknowledgments

Material from "Antunes Filho: mago do palco brasileiro," by David S. George, originally published in *Brasil/Brazil: Revista de Literatura Brasileira* (1996), reprinted by permission of *Brasil/Brazil,* Brown University/PUC-RS/Editora Mercado Aberto.

Material from "Sábato Magaldi: Interpreter, Chronicler, Arbiter" (1998); "Encenador Gerald Thomas's Flash and Crash Days: Nelson Rodrigues Without Words" (1996); "Festival de Teatro de Curitiba II—The Healthy State of the Art" (1994), by David S. George, originally appeared in *Latin American Theatre Review,* reprinted by permission of *Latin American Theatre Review,* Center of Latin American Studies, University of Kansas.

Material from "Mattogrosso: The Postmodernist Stage in Brazil," by David S. George, forthcoming in *Modern Drama,* reprinted by permission of *Modern Drama,* University of Toronto.